Go Green, Spend Less, Live Better

*The Ultimate Guide to Saving the Planet,
Saving Money, and Protecting Your Health*

Crissy Trask

Skyhorse Publishing

Also by Crissy Trask

It's Easy Being Green:
A Handbook for Earth-Friendly Living

Skyhorse Publishing books may be purchased in bulk at special discounts for sales promotion, corporate gifts, fund-raising, or educational purposes. Special editions can also be created to specifications. For details, contact the Special Sales Department, Skyhorse Publishing, 307 West 36th Street, 11th Floor, New York, NY 10018 or info@skyhorsepublishing.com.

Skyhorse® and Skyhorse Publishing® are registered trademarks of Skyhorse Publishing, Inc.®, a Delaware corporation.

Visit our website at www.skyhorsepublishing.com.

10 9 8 7 6 5 4 3 2 1

Library of Congress Cataloging-in-Publication Data is available on file.
ISBN: 978-1-62087-210-9

Printed in China on recycled paper

CONTENTS

List of Tables   iv

Introduction   vi

Disclaimer   viii

CHAPTER 1: Green Living Is . . . *Not* Exclusive   1

CHAPTER 2: Getting Off to a Good Start   21

CHAPTER 3: Energy Efficiency Pays   37

Part I: Walls, Windows, Doors, and Roof—
a.k.a. Your Home's "Envelope"   41

Part II: Major Appliances and Systems   52

PART III: Lighting and Electronics   99

CHAPTER 4: Getting from Here to There
Without Breaking the Bank   122

CHAPTER 5: Stop Flushing Money Down the Drain   149

CHAPTER 6: Healthy Food Can Be Affordable   178

CHAPTER 7: Anything You Can Buy New Is Cheaper Used   228

CHAPTER 8: Adding It All Up   245

Notes   253

Index   261

TABLES

CHAPTER 1

1: Small Home Guidelines

CHAPTER 3

2: Structure Thermal Performance with and without Insulation
3: Estimated Savings from Some Weatherizing Scenarios
4: Average Life Expectancy of Various Home Appliances and Equipment
5: Energy Ratings for Various Home Appliances and Equipment
6: Home Energy Consumption by End Use
7: Washing Machine Comparison
8: Refrigerator Comparison
9: Clothes Dryer Comparison
10: Typical Flow Rates for Various Household Devices
11: Water Heater Comparison
12: Natural Gas Boiler Comparison—Northern Climate
13: Natural Gas Furnace Comparison—Northern Climate
14: Electric Heating System Comparison—Mild Winter Climate
15: Estimated Savings from Various Energy Efficiency Upgrades Focused on Windows for a Home with Higher Than Average Cooling Bills
16: Estimated Savings from Various Energy Efficiency Upgrades Focused on the Attic for a Home with Higher Than Average Cooling Bills
17: Mechanical Cooling Systems Comparison
18: Estimated Savings from Automating Exterior Light Fixtures
19: Comparison of Exterior Security Light That Is Continuously On for an Average 12 Hours Per Day
20: Light Output Equivalency
21: Efficiency of Lighting From Least to Most
22: Estimated Savings Through Lighting Upgrades
23: Matching Viewing Distance and Screen Size
24: TV Set Comparison
25: Computer Comparison

CHAPTER 4

26: Estimated Savings When Reducing Miles Driven
27: Estimated Savings for a Light Driver Substituting a Car Sharing Arrangement for an Owned Vehicle
28: Vehicle and Fuel Cost Comparison

CHAPTER 5

29: Toilet Water Use Through The Years
30: Estimated Savings When Upgrading One Toilet in a Two-Person Bathroom
31: Washing Machine Capacity
32: Washing Machine Comparison
33: Dishwasher Comparison
34: Estimated Savings When Installing Aerators to Three Heavily Used Faucets
35: Showerhead Comparison
36: Estimated Savings When Replacing Turf Grass with Low- and No-Water Alternatives
37: Estimated Savings When Supplementing Outdoor Water Needs with Captured Water

CHAPTER 6

38: Pesticides in Produce
39: Average Retail Price of Food Per Pound
40: Meat Consumption Comparison (Household of Four)
41: Estimated Savings When Growing Some of Your Own Vegetables
42: Prepackaged Meal Versus Scratch Meal Comparison (Two Servings)
43: Three Mostly Organic Meals, All for Under $9 Per Person Per Day (Household of Four)
44: Estimated Annual Consumption of Disposable Kitchen Products and Their Cost (Household of Four)
45: Estimated Savings When Kicking the Paper Towel and Napkin Habit (Household of Four)

CHAPTER 7

46: Estimated Savings When Avoiding Ownership of Seldom Used Home and Garden Equipment
47: Alpine Ski Package (Skis, Poles, Boots) Comparison
48: Kitchen Cabinets Comparison
49: Portable DVD Player Comparison

CHAPTER 8

50: Savings Outlook Estimate from Chapter 2
51: Savings Outlook Estimate from Chapter 3
52: Savings Outlook Estimate from Chapter 4
53: Savings Outlook Estimate from Chapter 5
54: Savings Outlook Estimate from Chapter 6
55: Savings Outlook Estimate from Chapter 7
56: Savings Outlook Estimate, All Chapters

INTRODUCTION

For countless Americans, spending less and saving money are constant struggles. Even before the 2008–2009 recession, three out of four Americans surveyed by the Pew Research Center said they weren't saving enough money;[1] then the economic downturn shrank paychecks, shattered budgets, and drained accounts, making it even tougher to save.[2]

Meanwhile, a survey conducted on behalf of the Center for a New American Dream by Widmeyer Communications[3] found that Americans don't think we, as a society, are living in a manner consistent with the values we consider to be important—among them, protecting the environment. Eighty-seven percent of those surveyed agree that we should be more focused on protecting the environment through better daily choices.

Together these surveys show that an overwhelming majority of Americans are struggling to reconcile their income and expenditures with savings and investment goals—and struggling to reconcile their lifestyle habits with their values and concern for the environment. Wouldn't it be nice if we could live our green values and achieve a higher level of savings at the same time? Well, we can!

Although many don't realize it yet, going green is a wonderful way to save money. If that doesn't surprise you, what may surprise you is how *much* money you can save when adopting a well-rounded green lifestyle. It's not an overstatement to say that greening up your life can make you thousands of dollars richer in just one year. Depending on your lifestyle and the changes you are willing and able to make, you could be substantially better off than you are today within just a few months of living the green life!

A green life today is a mixture of the best parts of traditionalism and modernism: traditionalism without the hardship and modernism without the waste. Put another way, green living is a marriage of sensible practices and modern ingenuity—a life that's part sensible and part ingenious leaves little room for the kinds of mistakes that lead to excessive waste that can undermine our future.

Saving the most through green initiatives is not about a handful of things you can accomplish and be done with it. It's about lifestyle changes—changes to your home, how you eat, how you get around, and how you behave as a consumer.

If you're worried you can't make the changes that will translate to rich rewards, don't be. First, saving money is a powerful motivator, which you will do when you eliminate several planet-unfriendly habits that you didn't realize are draining your bank account. Second, we all have it in us to live a greener life, because a greener life is less complicated and more fundamental, less material and more satisfying, less stressful and more joyful, less sedentary and more invigorating, less toxic and more healthful, and less wasteful and more gainful. Who wouldn't want to know more about a life that can be all that—and begin to live it!

This book will guide you every step of the way, showing you how to spot and stop wasteful acts and spending and empowering you to confidently pursue change, knowing your bank accounts will grow as a result.

If you're curious to learn just how much money you could save with this book as your guide and a commitment to following its suggestions, take a peek at chapter 8. If saving that kind of serious money sounds appealing to you, what are you waiting for? *Go Green, Spend Less, Live Better.*

DISCLAIMER

The information presented in this book is designed to provide helpful information on the subjects discussed. All acquisition costs, installation costs, rebates, incentives, operating costs, and savings projections expressed in this book are estimates based upon data and information from a variety of reputable sources, and they are provided for comparison purposes only. Your costs and savings will vary depending on several factors, including but not limited to your consumption habits; the location and size of your home; existing home systems, appliances, and use patterns thereof; local utility rates; vehicles and travel habits; and your current diet. The use of any information provided in this book, for whatever purpose, should not absolve any third-party user from due diligence to verify the information for themselves, this being their full responsibility.

The author's opinions and conclusions are her own and should any third party decide to act upon said opinions and conclusions, they do so knowing full well that their results may differ from those shared in this book.

Any suggestions related to diet are for informational purposes only and not intended to be taken as nutritional advice or as a substitute for medical advice. Before you make any changes to your diet, a conversation with your healthcare practitioner is advised.

The publisher and author accept no responsibility or liability whatsoever for adverse effects, loss, or damages suffered, or alleged to be suffered, by any third party as a result of decisions made or not made or actions taken or not taken based on any information contained within this book.

GREEN LIVING IS . . .
NOT EXCLUSIVE

Many people incorrectly believe that meaningful green living can best be achieved by the upper middle class who can afford to buy a hybrid electric vehicle, build a green home, and shop at a pricey organic market. Such actions have become modern-day testaments to green living, and when done right, they are praiseworthy. However, too often a closer look reveals bad driving habits, an oversized house, and organic food shipped from hundreds of miles away, then carted home in plastic bags—details that undermine otherwise good intentions.

Green choices that aren't accompanied by green values and green actions are more indicative of affluence than stewardship. *Affording* some of the trademarks of a green lifestyle and *living* a green lifestyle aren't necessarily the same thing because earth-friendly living is based much, much more on wise use than having all the latest green products and accoutrements money can buy. The difference between buying a quasi-green-lifestyle and living a truly green lifestyle is that the former decreases our wealth and benefits the earth little while the latter increases our wealth and benefits the earth much. That's right: a truly green lifestyle *increases* our wealth. And not through huge sacrifice and hardship, but by shrewdly reducing the waste and misuse that together drain our own resources and the earth's.

Not to be too dismissive, green products *do* help make up a greener lifestyle—and many important ones are recommended throughout this book—but to be the most beneficial they must be used thoughtfully and responsibly as they were intended, not overused and overscaled as they so often are.

Whatever green products or technologies we purchase, our intention should be to do the least harm, meaning mindfully engaging ourselves not just in proper use but also in deferring disposal for as long as prudently possible. This treatment of our stuff is how we lessen the effects of collective consumption and use as well as how we save the most money.

The average income earner can achieve much more than they may have thought possible once they fully understand what it IS to be truly green.

FOUR GREEN "ISMS"
Green IS . . . Action

Anecdotally speaking, only about 10 percent of green living is about the products and technologies that can help you achieve your goal of creating an earth-friendlier home and way of life. The rest is all you and what you do or don't do. Your actions in the form of deeds, conduct, and routines play the bigger role in how you manage your personal impacts and the impacts of the things you use.

Although lots of the bigger solutions take time (like improving the fuel efficiency of our auto fleet and overhauling our transmission grid to accommodate a build-up of renewable energy), you can carry out smaller initiatives right now that will make a difference. Opportunities to green up occur several times throughout the course of an average day. From the time we get up until the time we go to bed, every decision, every act is a chance to do better, and personal actions are no small potatoes in the grand scheme of things: Individual actions from millions of ordinary people have cumulative effects, and when the shift in the way we do things becomes a groundswell, change that began inside homes, alongside roadways, in backyards, and within communities can drive the sweeping changes and reforms our living planet desperately needs.

Green IS . . . Earning Rich Returns on Green Investments

Green products and technologies are often a sound investment. Even though upfront costs for products that use advanced technology to achieve greater efficiency are higher than conventional products, those that use less energy and/or less water can save their owners up to 70 percent in operating costs. To help you perform a cost-benefit estimate of new equipment purchases, EnergyStar.gov provides savings calculators. And cost-benefit comparison tables detailing payback periods and net savings for a range of upgrades are provided in chapter 3 as a general guide before doing further research. The upside to doing the research and perhaps investing in high-efficiency products is the return on investment, which can rival and often exceed the returns earned from the stock market.

If your bank account is not ready for significant earth-friendly upgrades around the house—like beefing up insulation in the attic or replacing inefficient appliances—that can change as soon as you start to implement all the *no*-cost and *low*-cost recommendations in this book, which may save you thousands of dollars in a short amount of time, depending on your current lifestyle and how much room for improvement there is. If you're already a model green citizen, this book is a good opportunity to review yourself, improve your weak areas, and save a little more money each month, but the typical American can save much, much more—up to several thousand dollars. Then, when it is time for you to open your wallet—whether it's to re-place a burned-out light bulb or a broken down furnace—it will be fatter and better equipped to buy a high-efficiency unit that will consume less energy, create less pollution, and return your investment through yearly savings in operating costs.

Green IS . . . Getting More for Your Money

Often, affording greener versions of things like food and con-sumer products isn't about saving up for them—it's about choices and budgeting. We don't always need to make more money; we just need to spend the money we already have more wisely.

Take food for example: Today households earning between $30,000 and $50,000 spend an average 38 percent of their food budget on food purchased away from home—from restaurants, fast food establishments, vending machines, concessions, and the like.[4] Eating at fast food restaurants in particular appeals to self-described "price sensitive" individuals because they per-ceive it to be cheaper than eating at home. Overall, consumers below middle-age are more likely to turn to fast food during recessionary times,[5] but fast food is not the value dining option its users perceive it to be. The average amount spent by a pa-tron at a fast food establishment is $10.16,[6] but even someone spending less than $5 is throwing money away along with co-pious amounts of paper and plastic served with every meal.

The reality, if you are willing to give up the obvious con-venience of fast food, is that $10, $5, or even $3 could buy more food—and better quality food—if spent at the market instead of the drive-through lane.

Healthy, earth-conscious meals can cost less than $10 a day per person. That's an average cost of just $3.33 per meal! This price point doesn't account for a diet that includes two-to-three servings of meat per day or supersized portions, but it does account for moderate amounts of meat as well as delicious, wholesome, and healthy foods from other important food groups, all in calorie-appropriate portions. Through a combination of commitments that include cooking with seasonal, whole ingredients; eating less meat; growing some of our own food; and making the most of the food we buy, we can get more food, nutrition, and enjoyment from our food dollars. Chapter 6 lays it all out: how to make home-cooked, healthful meals a budget-friendly, gratifying, and everyday occurrence.

Green IS . . . Money in the Bank

Rising consumption doesn't just put increasing pressure on the natural regenerative capacity of the earth; it also puts increasing pressure on our finances. We pay for nearly everything we consume, and prices are increasing for everything from fuel to food to water. Of course we stand to save greatly when we reduce our consumption of resources that are only getting more expensive.

Americans waste millions of dollars every day when they fail to correct their misuse of resources. Perhaps you are losing $400 a year guzzling water packaged in plastic bottles while drinking water flows freely (or nearly so) from your tap; or you are wasting $210 each summer by permitting a flawed sprinkler system to pump thirty thousand gallons of treated municipal water directly into the street and storm drains; or you are spending an extra $100 a year by hanging on to an inefficient refrigerator. Such examples are just the tip of the iceberg. A closer look at our habits and homes can reveal hundreds of examples of waste that, if corrected, would conserve natural resources, decrease pollution, and reduce expenditures.

When approached as a way of life, green living is more than accessible and affordable—it is a viable means of achieving greater wealth. Of course saving money is neither the most important nor the most rewarding part of greener living, but it's an added bonus. If this fact helps you achieve your financial goals while improving the environmental outlook at the same time, everybody wins.

FIVE REASONS YOU WILL LIVE BETTER AND SAVE MONEY WHEN GOING GREEN

Every day lots of people spend money they don't need to when they fail to appreciate or realize the full financial cost of all their choices and the money-saving opportunities that elude them. Greener choices in particular that conserve resources and defend environmental health have so much potential to save us money that when we start to live green, our green capital just continues to grow. The discussion that follows is an overview of five reasons why green lifestyles lead to more savings and a better life. The following chapters will provide much more information—and proof—that living green is synonymous with saving green!

1. Less Affords More

The last decade has seen some of the worst personal savings rates among U.S. citizens in modern times. This has plunged many of us into debt, thwarted our ability to save for the future, and caused more stress and arguments over money—this is no way to live.

There are many reasons one might experience financial stress, and a distinctly American precursor is overspending. It's not just bank accounts, retirement plans, college funds, and relationships that suffer under the burden of overspending: when we buy things we don't need we are participating in the unnecessary consumption of vital resources and ignoring environmental implications from the production, use, and disposal of whatever it is we consume. Earth-friendly living is predicated upon avoiding overconsumption, so it handily reduces expenditures and provides more opportunities for saving money.

Every decade since the 1970s, Americans have spent a growing share of their disposable personal income on consumer expenditures (the amount spent on goods and services at the household level) and a shrinking share on personal savings. The personal savings rate has plummeted since the 1970s, falling from 9.59 percent in that decade to an average 3.3 percent between 2000 and 2009.[7]

With the obvious financial gains from reducing consumption, you'd think it would be the easiest of all green behaviors to espouse, but this clearly is not the case. In the U.S., scale and quantity are national problems. Over the last several decades just about everything man-made has gotten bigger or has multiplied out of sync with population growth or basic human needs. Antithetical to sustainability, our homes, stores, material ownership, debt, sofas, TV sets, cars, suburbs, highways, portion sizes, and so on have exploded.

Restricting excessive or conspicuous consumption is fundamental to reducing our environmental impact; and, contrary to being a deprived state of existence, making do with less enables us to put more money aside so we can achieve a better standard for the things we eventually acquire in our lives. For example:

Own an Economy Car, Rent Luxury or Brawn

Compared to a midsize SUV crossover like the Mazda CX-9 (MSRP $29,725 and 19 avg. mpg), a lighter, smaller, fuel efficient car like a Honda Fit (MSRP $15,325 and 30 avg. mpg), not only costs much less up front, but the fuel savings alone—$861 a year at a constant average fuel price of $3.72— would make it possible to rent a larger car once or twice a year, as needed, or to pay for occasional delivery fees for bulky purchases and still have money left over. Factor in the savings in depreciation, financing, and insurance when owning a smaller car and you can easily save upwards of $16,000 over five years![8]

Own a Small Home, Green the Renovation

Today Americans occupy three times as much living space (about 980 square feet per household member) as people did sixty years ago. But over-sizing our homes has significantly and needlessly increased the built environment's use of raw materials and waste from building-related construction and demolition debris[9]—it has also increased the financial burden of owning a home and doing renovations. Furthermore, when we spend our entire budget on square footage, we sacrifice the dream of making our home a true reflection of our tastes and values.

If you want a beautiful, green home but don't have a fortune to spend, buy a small home that is *beneath* your budget, then spend some of the difference to bring it up to green standards—an investment that will improve the home's efficiency and increase its value. A small home (see table 1) will not only cost less to renovate, it will cost significantly less to furnish, heat, cool, light, and maintain compared to an over-sized home.

Table 1: Small Home Guidelines

Members in household	Approximate square footage needed
Up to four	About 600 sq. ft. plus an additional 200 sq. ft. per member
Between five and nine	About 600 sq. ft. plus an additional 250 sq. ft. per member

Own Less Furniture, Enjoy Greater Quality

A smaller house as suggested above will automatically limit the amount of furnishings you need, so the furniture budget can go toward quality instead of quantity. But if your dwelling has more rooms than you honestly need, those extra rooms have either already led to—or could soon lead to—buying more furnishings than you use on a regular basis. Filling a home—especially a large one—from top to bottom with furniture isn't conducive to saving money, nor is it respectful of the resources sacrificed for every chair, hutch, and accent pillow that crosses the threshold.

If you already find yourself with too much furniture, sell some of it. If you are reading this book, you are already trying to improve your financial condition, and this can instantly help you. If you are just beginning to furnish a home, fight the urge to over-furnish rooms you hardly use. For example, why have two dining sets if you dine at the kitchen table most of the year? Why furnish a room for guests if it only gets slept in once or twice a year? Why fully furnish two "living" rooms if you spend the majority of your time in just one? If you can, own a single dining set that can easily go from everyday-casual to special-occasion-formal. A roll-away bed or an inflatable mattress is fine for occasional guests. And a thinly furnished "formal" living room can borrow seating and lamps from other rooms if and when it is needed for entertaining.

With less furniture to buy, you'll save more and be able to afford the nicest, highest quality furnishings for the rooms you live in every day as well as put more money aside for other things.

2. Secondhand Discounts

You know how giddy you can get when you save 30 percent off the suggested retail price for something? Well, this is small potatoes compared to the discounts you can find in the secondhand, or reuse, marketplace! But, reuse isn't just about saving money—it's green, because reuse stops the waste of still-useful items and reduces unnecessary production of new goods.

Reuse retailers are in every community, but recently interest in reuse has taken off. The quantity and variety of pre-owned goods, increased ways to advertise them and the number of sellers are all helping to turn reuse shopping into an increasingly viable means of acquiring durable goods. With the success of www.ebay.com and www.craigslist.org—two very different websites with a common goal of connecting buyers and sellers of pre-owned goods—and Amazon.com's entry into the used market, the supply of used goods for the budget- and earth-conscious buyer is growing by leaps and bounds.

Following are a few of the reasons why more and more eco- and money-savvy shoppers are rejecting new goods, and their higher price tags, and instead enthusiastically searching for others' castoffs. For much more detail and resources on this topic see chapter 7.

High Quality, Low Prices

"Quality" and "used" are not mutually exclusive terms. People don't just get rid of junk. There are lots of reasons why people get rid of nice, quality items as well: for example they might be downsizing, redecorating, upgrading, moving, or liquidating an estate. Sometimes quality goods are sold off because the need for something has disappeared or to obtain fast cash.

Higher quality pre-owned goods tend to come from private sellers found through local or online classifieds and at upscale consignment stores and antiques stores, but don't forget that pawn shops and swap meets—especially those in large metropolitan areas—can offer good quality used merchandise too.

Competition among Sellers, Great Deals for Buyers

Anyone with a computer and Internet connection can market their unwanted items to interested buyers via an ever growing number of buy/sell websites—the most popular averaging a staggering ninety-seven million unique visitors per month in 2011. Online marketplaces are so popular, in fact, that www.amazon.com, www.ebay.com, and www.craigslist.org all receive more unique monthly visitors than the websites of powerhouse retailers like Walmart and Target.[10]

The sheer number of sellers operating in the online marketplace requires competitive pricing strategies. For eBay.com sellers to attract buyers to auctions, sellers may set starting bids very low or offer free shipping or both—creating deals in the making for lucky bidders. If you don't win what you're bidding on, there's always another auction!

The Donations of Others, Dirt Cheap

If you're looking for dirt cheap prices for clothing, linens, toys, kitchen wares, small home and office accessories, or furniture that you can repurpose or refurbish, visit local charity thrift stores that sell donated items to earn money for charity. You may come out empty-handed on your first trip, but new items typically arrive daily, so visit often.

Bartering Is Back, Goods and Services Flow FREE-ly

Bartering—trading goods or services without using cash—is back. From local barter exchanges to Internet websites to classified ads, there are a number of ways to advertise goods or services you can offer in exchange for something you need. Bartering sites (also called swap sites) may be relatively new and generally unfamiliar to U.S. consumers, but if they take off here as they have in the U.K., online swap sites could become serious rivals to auction sites such as www.ebay.com or retail sites such as www.amazon.com.[11]

3. Longevity Gives Back

Durable, high-quality, and satisfying products that are made to last and that you will want to keep around for the foreseeable future can substantially reduce replacement and repair costs that inevitably follow strictly sticker-price motivated buying decisions. Not to mention the valuable resources that will be spared an untimely death trying to keep up with frivolous replacements of so many lower quality and unsatisfying products.

Shifting from a throwaway society to one that values permanence is a two-part commitment. First it requires that we generally reject flimsy and disposable products in favor of ones that have staying power. However, nothing is immune to the effects of time—especially things that are well loved and well used. And this hints at the second commitment for seeking longevity from our stuff: we need to take care of it. And on the occasion when something soils, breaks, tears, squeaks, or just needs to be "refreshed," channeling your grandparents' fix-it mentality can get you a few more years out of something you've already gotten great mileage from, saving you even more—as long as the solution has a reasonable price.

Of course nothing lasts forever: products and materials wear out and products we use must keep up with consumer safety standards and sustainability goals. When the time comes to buy something new, having extra savings from years of deferred replacement costs will make the occasion much more gratifying, because you'll have more money to afford the kind of quality and special features that will lead to another lasting purchase.

No More Throwaway Products, No More Throwing Away Money

We are in large part a society that values convenience, and unfortunately we don't mind using things up in one use and throwing lots of stuff away if it affords us a bit more convenience. From throwaway countertop wipes to disposable diapers to plastic food wrap, Americans threw away 22.3 million tons of nondurable paper and plastic (excluding containers and packaging) in 2010.[12] About 339 pounds annually for each U.S. household!

These conveniences trash the planet and clean out your pocketbook. A year's worth of disposable cleaning wipes can cost three and half times what a small collection of reusable rags and a bottle of non-toxic cleaner costs;[13] a year's worth of disposable diapers can cost *five* times more than a home-cleaned cloth diapering system;[14] and a year's supply of disposable plastic food storage bags and wrap can cost six times as much as a set of reusable containers. Reusable substitutes are also one-time purchases, so the long-term savings compared to their disposable counterparts is huge!

Invest In Quality and Beauty, Have It Forever

Surround yourself with things that you've carefully chosen for your life now and for the future. This includes choosing everything from high-quality, attractive furniture that will take abuse and have lasting appeal to versatile home accessories that can be adapted when redecorating to sturdy mops and brooms that hold up to tough housekeeping chores indefinitely.

Making choices that we can live with for years to come sometimes takes a bit more time and money up front, but if the goal is to save money in the long run and do better by the environment, well then choosing carefully really pays off.

Consider an $800 sofa that's attractive primarily due to the price point. It probably comes with limited choices for fabrics, a 10-year warranty and it may utilize less than healthy or eco-sensitive materials. Now consider a $1,700 sofa whose price tag makes your palms sweat a bit, but it's love at first sight! It also comes with a lifetime warranty, the frame is certified sustainable and it's been put together with VOC-free glues.* If the means to afford it are there, the higher priced sofa could last three times as long and end up saving you $700 over the life of the sofa.

Applying the same buying conviction to all your purchases—made in moderation, of course, for the things you need—is a winning strategy for reducing expenditures over the long haul.

Extend Its Life, Save a Bundle

As a culture, we've become accustomed to replacing items that have fallen into disrepair or out of favor, even if something can be repaired or renewed easily and economically. It's a shameful waste of money and valuable resources.

Before we became consumer zombies who automatically cast off injured possessions for the chance to buy something new, repairing stuff was the norm. A half century ago, any American homeowner wouldn't have thought twice about dragging out the toolbox or a sewing machine to put something that had fallen apart back together again—sometimes better than new!

When it's possible to extend the useful life of something by cleaning, fixing, refurbishing, reconditioning, repurposing, rearranging or generally renewing it, we can usually save signifi-

---

* VOCs are organic chemical compounds (including formaldehyde, toluene, acetone, ethanol and isopropyl alcohol) that can be released into the air by everyday products and materials containing them. They are considered a pollutant, and their presence indoors can adversely impact the health of people that are exposed.

cant money; avoid hasty waste of salvageable things; and protect valuable resources from being frittered away for the
production of avoidable replacements.

If you're up for a do-it-yourself (DIY) project from time to
time there's no shortage of instructional books and web videos
out there to teach you how to transform just about anything in
need of a makeover. And if you lack a proclivity to fix things,
there's a business out there that wants to help.

> By weight, almost one quarter of landfill waste is made up of
> durable goods.[15]

4. Smaller Energy Bills

Energy use in this country keeps climbing, and so do the prices households pay for it, whether due to spiking commodities
markets or increasing demand. Gasoline prices have skyrock-
eted to over $4.00 a gallon more than once in recent years,
proving that the petroleum market is volatile and when prices
are low, they don't stay low. And when it comes to the major
home heating fuels, between 2002 and 2011, residential retail
prices for heating oil rose 320 percent, natural gas rose 43 percent and electricity rose 40 percent.[16]

Rising fuel costs can put a huge financial strain on American families that rely too heavily on the most expensive fuels.
The average household earning between $30,000 and $50,000
a year spent $5,639 on energy-related expenses in 2007; for
those earning over $50,000, energy-related expenses totaled an
average of $6,188.[17]

Our rising energy costs are something to be concerned
about, but even more alarming are rising global temperatures
and incidents of climate disturbance caused by the buildup of
greenhouse gases (GHGs) in our atmosphere. The recent rise

in GHGs has resulted largely from energy-related carbon dioxide emissions from increases associated with electric power generation and transportation fuel use.[18] Slashing energy consumption at home and on the road will ease climate-altering greenhouse gas emissions while also reducing our energy expenses.

Efficiency Up, Energy Costs Down

The inevitable, elective and mandatory uses of all kinds of things in our lives that consume energy make their efficiency critically important in our effort to reduce energy costs. Something as seemingly insignificant as the light bulbs in our home can cost us either roughly $400 a year to power or closer to $100, based on their efficiency. The amount of money that can be saved by achieving optimal efficiency not only from our light bulbs, but from our vehicles, homes and all within them should not be underestimated.

Most people would see the occasion of a major home appliance going on the fritz as most unwelcome. But the breakdown of an old appliance that has been costing you extra money in operating costs due to its inefficiency is an opportunity to replace it with a new energy-efficient appliance that will cost much less to run, saving you money with every use.

Combined, the transportation and residential sectors account for more than half of all energy-related carbon dioxide emissions in the United States.[19]

Lower Use, Lower Expenditures

The quickest way to slash energy-related expenses is to use less energy (duh, right), and while increasing the efficiency of our vehicles, major appliances, heating and cooling equipment, electronics, lights and so forth has great merit, we can also just use them less!

When learning passive home cooling tricks or hanging clothes out on a line to dry, we can turn air conditioners and dryers—two of the most used appliances in the home—into two of the least. And when we turn off lights and don't idle the car, with the flip of a switch and the turn of a key, we save energy and money.

> The total distance traveled by Americans exceeds that of all other industrialized nations combined.[20]

5. Fewer Health Risks

Obesity, heart disease, respiratory illness, neurological impairment, hormonal disturbance, allergies, headaches . . . are these indicators of a lifestyle that isn't green enough? They could be. For example, car dependence has contributed to an increase in sedentary lifestyles, impairing our physical fitness; hazardous household products from oven cleaners to solvents to insecticides pose serious risks to human health; conventional food grown and raised with harmful chemicals could be making us sick. Sooner or later, environmentally undesirable practices and products that impact health undermine our efforts to be well. And what does undermining our health have to do with our ability to protect our earnings and our ability to save? For starters, developing an illness can lead to lost income due to missed days at work, medications to ease our suffering and, in the worst cases, hospitalization. Even if you have health insurance, uncovered expenses can add up to hundreds of dollars or more in a year if you are frequently seeking medical attention for one or several problems.

An ounce of prevention is worth a pound of cure, and that ounce of prevention is a greener lifestyle. Lifestyle choices that look out for the earth's well-being bode well for us too: utilizing non-motorized transportation, reducing our exposure to chemicals and eating a diet rich in naturally grown fruits and vegetables is more preventative against poor health and disease, so our spirits, stamina and bank balance won't be drained!

Two thirds of the adult population aged twenty years and over are overweight or obese;[21] and obesity and inactivity is a risk factor in one quarter to one third of cancer deaths.[22]

Walk More, See the Doctor Less

The overweight are at far greater risk of developing serious health problems, such as diabetes and heart disease, and other chronic diseases; and while there are many contributing factors to obesity, inactivity makes every list.

The automobile is one culprit of inactivity, having taken away peoples' inclination to walk or ride a bike. Americans use the automobile for 87 percent of all daily trips[23] taken, yet one in four is a mile or less.[24] The fact that so many of us choose to sit down to get places, near as well as far, is expanding waistlines, oil consumption, GHG emissions, pollution, and an auto-dependent infrastructure that is paving over green space.

Ignoring opportunities to walk is only one contributing factor to bodies that are underworked and unfit, but studies show that a thirty-minute walk every day can lower LDL ("bad") cholesterol, raise HDL ("good") cholesterol, lower your blood pressure and reduce your risk of diabetes.[25] Replace a car trip with thirty minutes of walking every day, and burn calories instead of gas!

Replace Toxic Products, Eliminate Serious Health Risks

The U.S. Environmental Protection Agency (EPA) warns that every day humans are exposed to thousands of the more than 80,000 chemicals in use today, either singly or in various combinations through air, drinking water, food and dust.[26] It's impossible for us to shield ourselves from all the industrial compounds, pollutants and other chemicals that we're exposed to every day just from walking around, but we can control our immediate environment—our homes.

The last thing we should do is bring dangerous chemicals into our homes, pop the lids and start liberally spreading them around—releasing toxic fumes and agents that can make us sick—in some cases seriously so. A safer home and safer environment depend upon detoxifying the products we keep inside our cupboards for household chores and projects.

Finding non-toxic substitutions for everything from paint to household cleaners to pest controls is becoming easier, but the buyer still needs to beware of false claims. The Federal Trade Commission (FTC) has produced a guide—www.consumer.ftc.gov/articles/0226-shopping-green—to help consumers sort through environmental claims found on product labels.

> The human body contains an estimated 700 industrial compounds, pollutants and other chemicals due to our inhalation, contact and ingestion of toxic consumer products and industrial pollutants.[27]

Eat Right, Live Healthier

The conventional, industrial food machine of today is an energy-intensive, chemical dependent and often inhumane enterprise that has strayed exceedingly far from the agricultural model prior to WWII. Spraying crops with massive amounts of poisonous agents, promoting atypical growth in livestock with synthetic hormones, raising animals hock-deep in their own waste and processing nutritionally inferior foods are all common practices that are eroding either environmental health, human health or both.

The more conventional foods in your diet, the higher your risk of ingesting contaminants, additives and foods themselves that are known or suspected of causing health problems. Whether your diet makes you feel lethargic, causes mild discomfort or allergic reactions, disrupts hormonal or endocrine functions, or worse, these afflictions can be debilitating and expensive to treat.

Conventional U.S. food producers, on the whole, no longer turn out the best food in the world. The best food now comes from organic and sustainable producers who provide much-needed alternatives to conventional foods and their problems. Eating more foods that were raised as nature intended, without so much interference from science, will decrease your exposure to man-made synthetics and additives that have no dietary benefit and could make you very sick.

It's much less expensive to invest in healthy foods that come with fewer possible risks and actually promote good health.

Since the 1950s, the nutritional quality of produce in America has declined substantially, according to U.S. Department of Agriculture figures.[28]

GETTING OFF TO
A GOOD START

Whatever attitudes, habits, behaviors, and possessions make up our lives, there is always room for improvements that can save us more money and ease environmental strain. Improvements can come from an immediate shift in our thinking followed by a simple adjustment in consumption—like when deciding to drink tap water again after months (or years) of carting water home in plastic bottles. Then there are improvements that can come only after careful research and monetary investment, such as replacing an electric hot water heater with a solar one. And in between these two extremes are hundreds if not thousands of other practical ways to help the planet *and* save money.

The following chapters in this book show ways each of us can live and use technology to reduce our impacts, and they will provide details that confirm our opportunities to save money when making decisions with the earth's—and our own—well-being in mind. But before we get into the details on a subject by subject basis, it may help to look at some super basic ways to immediately reduce spending and provide some financial cushion that can be put to good use later.

WAYS TO BE GREEN THAT DON'T COST ANY GREEN

There's no better way to start going green than by adopting some behaviors that take absolutely no money to follow through on. And no green behavior goes unrewarded! Depending on your current habits and expenditures, you could save several thousand dollars—yep, several *thousand* dollars—in one year by following the advice in this chapter alone. And all the money-saving tips in this section save resources and reduce pollution, so you can feel good about the difference they will make while you watch your bank account grow.

Drink Tap Water
Estimated Annual Savings (Per Capita): $208–$1,281

One third of Americans drink bottled water regularly[1]—water that costs between $1.42 and $8.82 a gallon when consumed from the tremendously popular half-liter bottles. Compare this price per gallon to what the average American pays per gallon for tap water: less than a penny! But bottled water often *is* tap water, or at least 48.7 percent of it is; and according to Food and Water Watch, that percentage is growing. What began as a niche market of overpriced natural spring water has turned into one big scam. The bottled water industry sells U.S. consumers more than half a billion bottles of water a week. In 2010, Americans spent $11 billion for a product they don't need.[2] For a product, in fact, they already own—as long as they are current on the water bill, that is.

The savings of giving up bottled water are significant. Let's assume an average adult drinks 50 ounces or 1.5 liters of water a day purchased in half-liter bottles. When purchased by the case, each bottle of plain old American water costs about $0.19, when not on sale; spring water from halfway around the world costs about $1.17 per bottle. If you're grabbing a single bottle from a convenience store, domestic water costs about $0.69 and foreign water about $1.65. For this exercise, we'll take a blended average of the four prices and estimate the average bottled water drinker to be spending roughly $0.52 per half-liter bottle. At this price, in a year consuming 1.5 liters per day adds up to $568.

No one is arguing that bottled water isn't convenient, and that's really what people are paying for, but just how *inconvenient* is it, really, to refill our own reusable bottle from a convenient tap source. Save your money, save the earth and get a reusable bottle. Tap water in this country is frequently tested and tightly regulated—in fact, it is more regulated than bottled water! That said, if you only want to (or need to) consume filtered water, you don't have to rely on a bottling company to do it for you. Purchase a pitcher filter for less than $30 or spend a bit more for either a countertop or undercounter filter that attaches to your main tap. Any of these home filtering methods is more economical than paying for bottled water on a regular basis.

If you want to understand bottled water better, watch the excellent animated short film (just nine minutes long) *The Story of Bottled Water* at www.storyofstuff.org/movies-all/story-of-bottled-water.

Each year, making the plastic water bottles used in the U.S. takes enough oil and energy to fuel 1,000,000 cars.[3]

Brew Your Own Coffee
Estimated Annual Savings (Per Capita):
$625–$1,467

More than half the U.S. population drinks coffee daily, and more and more of that coffee is being purchased by the cup from retail coffee houses, carts and kiosks where the average price for an espresso-based drink is $2.45 and the average price for brewed coffee is $1.38.[4]

Daily coffee consumption among coffee drinkers increased from 2.5 cups in 2005 to 3.1 cups in 2010,[5] largely due to the dense concentration of coffee shops that have made it extremely convenient to get a hot cup of gourmet coffee nearly anywhere, any time of day. And an unintended consequence of the success of coffee shops is that Americans are throwing away an unprecedented number of paper and Styrofoam cups each year.

Not everyone buys three overpriced cups of coffee in the course of a day, but all it takes is one $2.45 beverage per day, served up in a disposable cup, to drain $894 from your pocketbook and waste 365 cups and their lids in a year—and perhaps a hundred or more coffee sleeves too!

Brew coffee at home or at the office using a low-waste system like a French Press. With the money you save you'll be able to afford organic, fair trade coffee (about $11/pound). Carry coffee with you in a stainless steel thermos mug and it will stay hot for an hour or more (vacuum-insulated stainless steel keeps hot drinks hot for four hours!).

McDonald's serves more than 500 million cups of coffee each year within its U.S. restaurants.[6]

Adjust the Thermostat
Estimated Annual Savings (Per Household): $100–$210

The average homeowner spends about $1,000 on heating and cooling,[7] but it's possible to save 10 to 21 percent of this expenditure just by using energy-saving temperature settings on the thermostats that control heating and cooling devices for at least eight hours at a time, such as at night while you sleep. If your house is empty during the day, you'll save the most by adjusting the thermostat for the eight hours you are away as well.

Follow these recommendations (degrees expressed in Fahrenheit):

	At Home	Asleep	Away
Winter	65°–68°	57°–60°	55°–57°
Summer	78°–81°	82°–85°	85°–88°

Take Reusable Bags to the Store
Estimated Annual Savings (Per Household): $21–$62

Using reusable shopping bags can earn you up to a $0.10 per bag discount at the supermarket. And now that some cities are charging between $0.05 and $0.10 for each plastic bag you take, there's even more incentive to turn down plastic and use your own bags brought from home.

Reusable bags are often larger and always sturdier than disposable plastic bags—one can tote two to three times the bulk and weight of a flimsy plastic bag. This means you may be able to get by with a set of just four to six reusable bags at a modest cost. The best part is you'll be protecting landscapes and wildlife from a ubiquitous and hazardous source of litter.

With reusable bags, you get what you pay for. Some cheap bags marketed as "reusable" won't last a year. Buy good quality bags that can stand up to years of consistent use. Look for heavyweight fabric and carrying straps as well as reinforced stitching. For the best prices on sturdy bags, head straight to the thrift store where you can always find a variety of totes that make excellent reusable shopping bags.

Americans throw away 145 times more plastic today than we did in 1960.[8]

Make Less Garbage

Estimated Annual Savings (Per Household): $36–$324

The latest data on the U.S. municipal solid waste stream reveals that the average American creates nearly four and a half pounds of garbage each day, and it doesn't get hauled away for free. Some communities charge fixed rates for garbage collection or collection costs are included in property taxes, but more and more communities are switching to variable rates—charging households based on the volume of waste generated. Cities that levy variable rates may charge residents based on the size and/or number of bins (or bags) used, or based on how often a bin is put out for collection.

Generally, downsizing from a larger to a smaller bin will save variable-rate customers between $3 and $7 per month, and switching from two to one bin can save between $10 and $20.[9]

You can reduce garbage by composting, giving up disposable versions of products for which a durable alternative exists, choosing products that come with the least packaging, and recycling everything you can (check the website www.earth911.com if you are unsure about how or where to recycle something).

Waste-burning incinerators are the leading source of dioxin in the environment. Dioxin is one of the most toxic chemicals known to science.[10]

Don't Light the Day
Estimated Annual Savings (Per Household): $34-$137

Two 60-watt porch lights left on during daylight hours can waste 526 kWh of energy and $68 a year, on average. The typical home, however, has not two but four exterior lights: that number of 60-watt bulbs costs an average $137 to run during daylight hours all year long. Even when using energy-efficient, 15-watt CFLs, leaving those fixtures on all day will cost an additional $34 in a year.

Be sure to turn all outdoor lights off each morning, or install automatic lighting controls to help, which cost very little to install (see chapter 3, part III).

Pay Lower Prices for Energy
Estimated Annual Savings (Per Household): $10-$322

If your electricity provider has an off-peak pricing program, you could save money by running large appliances and performing some of your electricity-consuming activities during non-peak hours when energy prices are lower. Shifting energy usage to off-peak hours also benefits the environment. When extra power generators are needed to supply high peak demand, the backup generators used are often the oldest and least efficient—the ones the power company would prefer not to use. When demand for power is more evenly distributed, only primary generators are needed to supply customers during a twenty-four-hour period.

Enrolling in such a plan includes the installation of a new meter that records time-of-use data, but there is usually no charge for this. Contact your utility to inquire about off-peak pricing rates and plans.

Pack Leftovers for Lunch
Estimated Annual Savings (Per Capita): $1,070.68

According to a study by the International Council of Shopping Centers, office workers eat out 2.9 times per week and spend $7.10 per lunch on average.[11] Over a year, that adds up to $1,070.68, not including the tips. A hundred and fifty takeout lunches per office worker per year in this country also produces considerable trash from Styrofoam, paper and plastic serving ware.

A "free" lunch could be as close as your dinner plate. Studies have shown that Americans consistently overestimate portion sizes of foods[12] and are consuming 24 percent more calories today compared to forty years ago.[13] So, if you think your dinner might be supersized, start putting aside some of your dinner for lunch the following day.

Fast food outlets are our country's primary source of urban litter.[14]

Ask to Borrow Something
Estimated Annual Savings (Per Household): $347

Average annual expenditures for miscellaneous household equipment was $657 per household in 2010,[15] but lots of items that fall into this category sit in a closet or garage most of the time. How often do most of us use luggage, an electric mixer, a cordless drill or an extension ladder? The occasions to use many consumer products are rare enough that it makes more sense to borrow them than buy them.

Don't Buy Anything but Necessities for Four Months
Estimated Annual Savings (Per Household): $1,115

A study of Commerce Department data reported in the *Wall Street Journal* suggests that 11.2 percent of all consumer spending in 2010 was for nonessential stuff,[16] and the study did not count luxury items, so the figure is likely a realistic picture of what ordinary people spend on stuff they don't absolutely need.

Also in 2010, the average annual expenditures for a U.S. household earning between $20,000 and $50,000 was $29,883, putting estimated nonessential spending at $3,346 per household.[17] Clearly a little nonessential spending makes life more fun, but much of it wastes resources and money.

To recover some of that money, try only buying yourself and your family what is absolutely necessary for four months. Two things can happen: given time to think about something you don't permit yourself to buy at once, you'll either a) realize you don't really need or want it after all; or b) you'll realize you really do need or want it, in which case you can buy it after the four months have passed. It's the purchases in the first group that you are trying to prevent—the impulsive, emotional ones that result in something you can easily live without.

From air conditioners to microwave ovens to cell phones, Americans now perceive many consumer products once considered luxuries to be necessities today.[18]

Dust Off Your Bike
Estimated Annual Savings (Per Capita): $35–$500

Miles traveled by motorized vehicle are at an all-time high. Today we drive almost everywhere, even when distances could be covered in five to twenty minutes by bike or on foot. This fact underscores an absurd dependence on the automobile that overrides our most apparent opportunities to get exercise and reduce fuel costs.

So, ask yourself, "Where do I regularly travel within one to five miles, one way?" If you answered anything but "nowhere" you can start saving from $0.07 to $0.20 for every mile you cover on a bike when it replaces a trip in a hybrid or gas-motorized vehicle.[19]

With your doctor's blessing, biking, walking or rolling to a destination instead of driving is better for the environment and a healthful way to save money.

Walking or cycling the recommended amount for daily exercise could reduce U.S. oil consumption by as much as 38 percent when replacing driving.[20]

Don't Be Impulsive
Estimated Annual Savings (Per Capita): $740

Cars make it so easy to run out for things on a moment's notice that in fact we do. The average person makes more than 16 non-work-related trips* each week for things like shopping, social visits, recreation and errands, burning extra fuel when we retrace our steps.[21]

Keep a running list of things you need from the store and errands you need to run; hold off until you can tie trips together with an appointment or a meeting. Sure there will be situations that require an unplanned bolt to the store or somewhere else, but going from 16 trips each week down to 8 will save the typical driver 4,476 miles and 199 gallons of fuel a year and also keep 3,979 pounds of the global warming gas CO_2 (carbon dioxide) out of the atmosphere.

---

* The National Household Travel Survey defines a trip as each time a person travels from one address to another.

Clean Less
Estimated Annual Savings (Per Household): $75–$99

Many of us have the wrong impression of how clean is clean enough. Keeping a clean house is important, but there is such a thing as too clean—over cleaning backfires on us and the environment. First, over cleaning with daily applications of chemical antibacterial and disinfecting products puts us at risk because immune systems—especially those of children—need to be regularly stimulated by bacteria in order to develop, and many antibacterials and disinfectants pose serious health risks. Second, chemicals that get flushed and rinsed from our homes pollute the environment when municipal wastewater, still contaminated with household chemicals that could not be removed, is discharged into waterways.

Frequent dusting, sweeping, vacuuming and wiping-up aside, limit cleaning to about once every two weeks for average households.

Clean the Old-Fashioned Way
Estimated Annual savings (Per Household): $125

The typical household spent $150 on laundry and cleaning supplies in 2010.[22] This amount is much more than necessary when you consider that inexpensive household staples that can be used to clean the whole house may be sitting in your pantry right now. White vinegar, baking soda, washing soda, lemon juice and salt—the same natural ingredients used by our grandparents to clean—are effective and best of all cheap and safe.

So why do so many pay so much for commercial cleaners? Marketing: advertisements have convinced consumers that they need a different cleanser for every surface in the house (e.g., window cleaners for windows, shower cleaners for showers, floor cleaners for floors and so on). Those same advertisements tell us we need chemically enhanced products to clean effectively: neither is true.

We use more product—and more dangerous product—to clean our homes than is necessary or wise. For recipes of natural cleansers you can make for pennies, go to www.greenmatters. com/green-tips/housekeeping/.

> The average home can accumulate as much as one hundred pounds of hazardous substances including cleaners, pesticides, oils, solvents, paint and batteries.[23]

Pay Your Bills Online
Estimated Annual Savings (Per Household): $28–$54

According to the U.S. Postal Service's Household Diary Study for 2010, postal customers mailed 8.1 billion payments or 62.4 payments per household that year. Preceding those payments the post office delivered 22 billion paper bills and statements to U.S. households.[24] All those bills, statements, checks and envelopes consumed an estimated 992 million pounds of paper.

The average household today mails 5.2 payments per month, but some households are still paying all their bills with paper checks or about ten per month on average.[25] If you're still sending checks to your collectors by mail, you're not only wasting paper, you're wasting money—$28 to $54 a year at the first-class postage rate of $0.45.

Sign up for electronic bill pay today, and if you haven't already, sign up for electronic billing and statements too. Some banks will charge their customers to set up automatic e-payments unless they maintain a minimum balance of $5,000 at all times. To avoid bank charges, set up automatic payments through payee websites instead. You often have a choice of whether to allow them to bill your credit card or withdraw money automatically from a checking account.

Turn Unwanted Items into Cash
Estimated Annual Earnings (Per Household): $930

Nielsen Customized Research reports that the average American household is hanging on to 50 unused items for which they paid a total of over $3,100.[26] What's sitting in your attic, basement, garage or the back of a closet right now that you haven't used in months—or years? If its current market value is over $20, it may be worth selling. Previously-owned items that are passed on from one person to another save resources and pollution by avoiding the production of that item in a new form, so why not clean out your attic and garage and have a sale!

How much money you can make selling items you no longer want depends upon the desirability of the item, how much use it has received, its age and its condition.

Reduce Your Federal Tax Liability
Estimated Annual Savings (Per Taxable Entity): $25–$350

Donating items to charity is a good way to keep useful things out of the landfill and support a good cause at the same time. Items donated to charity are also a tax deductible expense as long as they are in good or better condition, itemized and made to a qualified organization.

Tax deductible donations can reduce your taxable income by the amount of your qualifying contribution and lower your federal tax bill. For example, if you donate $1,000 in clothes, furniture and housewares to Goodwill Industries and you are in the 17 percent tax bracket, your tax savings will be $170.

Take your donations to a donation center during business hours and request a receipt. Fill out the details of your donation right away. When it comes time to claim your deduction, the IRS will require a description of what was donated, its fair market value, the name and address of the charity and the date you made the donation. You can read more about this topic at www.irs.gov/publications/p526/ar02.html.

Say It in an E-Card
Estimated Annual Savings (Per Household): $172

Have you shopped for a store-bought greeting card lately? The cost typically ranges from $2 to $4 per card. If you send an average amount of greeting cards out each year, spending a few dollars here and there can really add up.

Approximately 7 billion greeting cards are purchased by U.S. consumers each year,[27] or 47 cards per household. At a median cost of $3.66 each (including tax and postage), sending paper greetings can end up costing $172 a year.

Save trees and money by sending free electronic greeting cards (e-cards), as well as electronic versions of invitations and announcements, to those for which you have an email address. E-cards are an acceptable way to send a happy greeting. Just search the Internet for "free e-cards" and have fun browsing!

The pulp and paper industry is the world's fifth largest industrial consumer of energy and uses more water to produce a ton of product than any other industry.[28]

Dematerialize the Holidays
Estimated Annual Savings (Per Capita): $535

Frenzied and overindulgent spending during the holidays seems to be a tough habit to break. Consumer spending over the holidays has risen each year since 1995 when the National Retail Federation started tracking holiday spending with the exception of 2008 and 2009, when unusual economic concerns caused sales to decline just slightly. On average, holiday sales have increased 2.6 percent a year for the last ten years. Just how carried away do we get? The average holiday shopper spent $713 on holiday gifts and seasonal merchandise in 2011.[29]

> The amount of household garbage in the United States generally increases by 25 percent between Thanksgiving and New Year's.[30]

The waste produced by all the extra packaging and gift wrap during the holidays generates literally tons of extra trash, but there's a lot more to the typical holiday binge and purge cycle than wrap and packaging. The gifts themselves—which account for the largest share of a holiday shopper's budget—may be the bulk of the problem. According to the short documentary *The Story of Stuff*, only 1 percent of what we buy survives after just six months. It's a fair assumption that holiday gifts are a part of this grim statistic. Truth be told, the majority of gifts we give are just not what the recipient would have picked out themselves, and the gifts often end up in the trash bin.

Get control of the situation: Draw names so that within a gift-giving circle or group (e.g., family, friends, and coworkers) each person gives and receives just one gift. And consider gifting experiences (art class, rock-wall climbing session, music lessons, massage, etc.) instead of material things.

Downgrade Disposables
Estimated Annual Savings (Per Household): $277

Disposable products were invented to waste your money—truly. They are a cash cow for the producers who know that consumers will have to replace disposable products hundreds or thousands of times in their lifetime. It's no wonder manufacturers keep inventing new products you can use once and throw away!

Today we throw away disposable versions of hundreds of products from razors to serving ware to toilet brushes. To keep up with the constant replenishment of throwaway paper and plastic products, more and more trees and petroleum resources are consumed and pollution proliferates. It's also a waste of money: our most popular throwaway indulgence—the paper towel and napkin can cost a typical family over $3,690 by the time the first child moves out of the house (see table 44).

In your own home, review the disposable products you use, and then count up how many times you'll go to the store this year to buy replacements. The time and money it takes to run out and replace things over and over really adds up.

WANT TO SAVE EVEN MORE?

No-cost improvements like those described above—and more to be revealed in subsequent chapters—can immediately lower your impact on the planet and start saving you money. Then you'll have a choice to make: how much of that saved money can you and will you put into a savings account and how much can you and will you invest in earth-friendly upgrades that will save you even more money? You will probably have to spend some money to be as green as you can be and, ironically, to save more than you do today. Anyone who wants more money in five, ten or fifteen years than they have today needs to invest, and many green upgrades are *very* good investments.

This book is about practices and products that save resources and about putting them to work in our lives to improve the world and our financial well-being. So, if you're ready, it's time to dive into the remaining chapters to discover many more ways you can live green and save big.

ENERGY EFFICIENCY PAYS

The modern American home isn't what it used to be. Our homes are bigger and loaded with more lighting, appliances, and electronics than anyone could have imagined sixty years ago when the average home was half as big as the average new home built today and families owned just one television set. Our bigger homes cost more to heat and cool, and the slew of appliances and electronics we fill them with takes a bite out of our budget every time we turn them on, and as you'll read later—in some cases—even when they're turned off!

Major increases in fuel oil and natural gas prices, plus modest increases in electricity prices over the past decade, have also contributed to higher residential energy expenses. In 2001 families with gross annual incomes between $30,000 and $50,000 spent 3 percent of their average after-tax income on household energy bills. In 2012, these households are projected to spend twice as much, or 6 percent, of their average after-tax income on residential energy.[1] The increasing share of family income devoted to energy diverts needed funds away from other necessities and makes it more difficult to save and invest for the future.

On average, Americans spend roughly $2,000 per household on residential energy each year. However, energy expenses can be considerably higher for homes heating with expensive fuels, for inefficient and wasteful homes, and for very large households. With so much money going toward energy expenses, reducing the home energy load is a money-making proposition. According to the Department of Energy, the average home can reduce energy use by 30 to 40 percent when practicing energy-saving habits and making energy-efficiency upgrades. That would mean an annual savings of $600 to $800 for the average household. And every time we shave another energy unit off our monthly utility bill, we reduce industrial pollution and greenhouse gas emissions that are altering the climate. Saving money while cleaning up the environment is a beautiful thing!

U.S. households produce 21 percent of the country's global warming pollution.[2]

This chapter is divided into three parts that provide an overview of many of the products, technologies and practices that can enable you to create a more energy-efficient home. In addition, starting here in chapter 3 and continuing to the end of the book, you'll find tables that detail efficiency upgrades by highlighting the costs and savings associated with the implementation of each. This way you can estimate, at a glance, which upgrades will be the most aggressive in terms of achieving efficiency, how much money you might need to spend on an upgrade and ultimately how much you could save in the near and long term. There are two types of tables used for this purpose: **Product tables** and **scenario tables**. The former compare yearly and lifecycle costs (acquisition cost plus yearly operating costs) of inefficient and efficient home and lifestyle products. They highlight *costs*, so the *lower* the number under the Lifecycle Costs heading, the better the product is for saving money. Scenario tables compare the relative costs and savings within a category of products or actions to a "typical" scenario. These tables focus on the *savings* among the scenarios analyzed, so the *higher* the number under the Net Savings heading, the better the scenario is for saving money.

Annual energy savings: Difference between annual energy costs associated with our typical scenario and those associated with an alternative greener scenario.

Scenarios:
Ownership and use scenarios include a "typical" scenario to which two or more greener scenarios are compared. The darker the scenario is shaded, the earth-friendlier it is relative to the typical scenario.

Payback period (in years): How fast the savings from an upgrade will offset the initial cost is referred to as the payback period, It's a simple calculation of initial cost divided by annual savings.

10-year net savings: Subtracting the payback period from 10 and multiplying that number by the estimated annual savings gives you your 10-year net savings. Calculations are not adjusted for inflation and assume no investment of the money you are saving. If you are able to invest some savings, chapter 8 discusses this topic.

Table 18 Estimated Savings from Automating Exterior Light Fixtures

TYPICAL SCENARIO Human-powered switches + Incandescent bulbs (on 18/7)	($204)					
GREENER SCENARIOS	**Initial cost**	**↑Annual energy costs↓**	**Annual energy savings**	**First year ROI**	**Payback period (in years)**	**10-year net savings***
Photosensors + CFLs (on 14/7)	($55)	($34)	$170	309%	0.3	$1,730
Timers + CFLs (on 12/7)	($106)	($29)	$175	165%	0.6	$1,752
Motion sensors + incandescent bulbs. (on 1/7)	($84)	($11)	$193	230%	0.4	$2,098

Initial cost: May include purchase price (excluding sales tax) and installation cost minus incentives like rebates and tax credits. Numbers are shown in parentheses to represent a debt or expense.

Annual energy costs: Based on typical usage and the current national average cost of a kilowatt hour (kWh), therm and gallon of water (including sewer charges): $0.13, $1.08, and $0.0075, respectively.

First year ROI* (Return on investment): The ratio of money gained (or lost) relative to money invested expressed as a percent. Any positive ROI indicates a capital gain and the higher the ROI the better.

Note: Headings may vary.

*   On average, a long-term investment (twenty years or longer) in the stock market, based upon the DJIA (Dow Jones Industrial Average), earns a total return per year of 9–10 percent. A 10 percent ROI is considered very good, so if investing in a green upgrade can earn you an ROI greater than 10 percent—in less than twenty years—it is an *exceptionally* good investment.

The information provided in product tables is pretty straight-forward, but scenario tables contain more analysis, so the info-graphic on page 39 explains one in more detail. If you ever get confused as to what all the headings and numbers mean, come back to the infographic for clarification.

How much you save when implementing what you learn from this chapter will vary depending on many factors includ-ing the product or course of action you choose, available incen-tives for efficiency upgrades, local installation costs (if applica-ble), current appliances and systems, patterns of use and local utility rates.

Whatever efficiency upgrades you determine you should and are able to make, within this chapter you'll find a range of solutions and basic information that will help you make deci-sions that are well-informed and economically and environ-mentally beneficial. If you're not ready to make major upgrades to your home's efficiency or replace any major appliances, pay particular attention to the "Do Now and Save" sidebars that provide no- and low-cost strategies that can bring down your energy costs the moment you put them into action.

PART I: WALLS, WINDOWS, DOORS, AND ROOF—A.K.A. YOUR HOME'S "ENVELOPE"

Keeping your home warm in the winter and cool in the summer can be a huge expense for those living in severe climates and in homes that weren't built to keep the weather out and expensive heated or cooled air in. An underinsulated, leaky home will suffer heat loss and air infiltration, causing moderate to great discomfort and accounting for a third of heating and cooling costs, estimates the U.S. Department of Energy (DOE). That can mean a loss of hundreds of dollars in one heating and cooling season.

The solution to an underinsulated and leaky home is weatherization: this involves improving insulation wherever you can and sealing cracks throughout the home. Weatherizing a home is one of the easiest and most affordable ways to improve your home's energy efficiency and there are big savings to be gained. According to the DOE, on average, weatherization reduces heating bills by 32 percent the first year following installation of weatherizing products. If you improve the energy efficiency of windows at the same time, you can save even more, and if you rely on mechanical cooling in your home, you can save still more!

Weatherizing Essentials

Preventing the escape of heated and cooled air from your home is critical to protecting energy dollars. The first step is to locate where heat loss and infiltration is occurring. Professional energy auditors have sophisticated equipment for detecting air leaks and heat loss in a building's envelope. An energy audit will cost from $200 to $400 but can also include an evaluation of your major appliances and heating and cooling system to determine the overall energy efficiency of your house as well as recommendations for improvements that will make your home more energy efficient and save you money in the long run. If you qualify as a low income household, you may be eligible to receive a free energy audit through your local utility or another program. If you don't qualify for a free energy audit and can't afford to hire an auditor, there are steps you can take to find many, but maybe not all, leaks in your home (see the sidebar, "Resources for Weatherizing Your Home").

Depending on what you find during a professional or do-it-yourself energy audit, the five major remedies include: filling gaps, repairing ductwork, adding insulation, improving windows and assessing ventilation.

Resources for Weatherizing Your Home

Find State-run programs providing weatherization assistance:
www.eere.energy.gov/wip/wap.html

Index of energy raters:
www.resnet.us/directory/raters.aspx

DIY energy audit tool:
www.hes.lbl.gov

Tips on selecting and applying different types of caulk and weather-stripping:
www.nrel.gov/docs/fy01osti/28039.pdf

Insulation R-values for different areas in your home:
www.ornl.gov/sci/roofs+walls/insulation/ins_16.html

Button It Up

Because warm air naturally moves to cooler spaces, expensive heated air inside a home will leak right out through cracks and gaps around windows, doors and penetrations (e.g., holes made for vents, wires and plumbing). And heat gain through those same leaky spots in the summer will cause air conditioners to work harder.

There are lots of products for filling gaps around the house and which one you choose will depend on the location and size of the gap as well as the mobility of things around the gaps.

Acrylic Latex or Silicone Caulk

Caulk can be used around window and door casings where cracks may or may not be evident. It certainly won't hurt to caulk every window and door in the house, inside and out. Caulk is meant to be semi-permanent, so don't use it on any part of a door or window that you wish to open again!

There are two primary choices for caulk, acrylic latex (or just "latex") and silicone. Latex has a somewhat shorter life than silicone, but it has key advantages: latex caulk is easier to apply, can be painted, is more easily removed and cleans up with water. A distinct advantage of silicone is that it is more flexible, and therefore better suited for gaps that will expand and contract.

Rope Caulk

Rope caulk is a Play-Doh-like material that is so easy to use. You just peel off sections of "rope" and press it into cracks by hand. Rope caulk can be removed at the end of the heating season so it's ideal for cracks around a window's moving parts. Technically rope caulk is reusable, although with every season it gets a little dirtier and harder to work with, so most people will find it easier to start with fresh product after just one or two uses. The reference to Play-Doh might give you the idea to let your kids help, and it's a good one! This could be considered a chore for adults, but fun for kids (ages 7–12 or so).

Weather stripping

Weather stripping refers to permanent or semi-permanent products that are designed to fill gaps around the moving parts of doors and windows and space under doors. Here's where things get a bit more complicated. There are *many* types of weather stripping ranging in price, installation ease, effectiveness and durability. It can be overwhelming trying to figure out which type is best for your application. It's a good idea to photograph your window casings, door jams and thresholds—anything that needs weather-stripping—to visually explain your needs to the salesperson at the home improvement store.

It's easy to spend very little on weather stripping, but this is no time to be cheap. Even the higher-end weather stripping products aren't expensive and paying for and installing highly effective and durable products will save you the most time and money over the long run. (For a guide to different types of weather stripping see the sidebar, "Resources for Weatherizing Your Home," on page 42).

Expandable Foam

Wherever wires, pipes or vents penetrate the walls or roof of your home, you could have gaps that need sealing. The often irregular shape of these gaps and mobility of wires and pipes makes expandable foam the ideal product to seal out drafts in this situation. There are two types of expandable foam—polyurethane and latex. The latter is less toxic and can be cleaned up with soap and water.

Chimney Balloon

If you have a chimney damper that no longer closes properly, inserting an inflatable chimney balloon just below the damper during periods of non-use will prevent cold drafts from entering a home and stop heat and air conditioning from escaping out through the chimney. Chimney balloons are advertised as reusable, but only a high quality one will last after repeated reuse, so invest accordingly.

· Since 1949, energy use in the residential sector has more than quadrupled.[3]

Tighten the Delivery System

In forced air systems, ducts move conditioned air throughout the home. If ducts aren't tight they can lose up to 20 percent of the air your system is working to heat or cool.[4] Tightening ducts requires making reconnections as necessary then sealing all connections with mastic—not duct tape.

Impede Temperature Transfer

Without proper insulation your house won't be very good at limiting the transfer of heat and cold through the walls and roof. The walls and roof can heat up or become cold and transfer that temperature to the inside of your home through radiation. Insulation slows this process down.

Attic/Roof

The roof is where a home will gain and lose much of its heat. Typically a lack of insulation, or an insufficient amount, at the top of your dwelling means that on a hot summer day 35 percent of your heat gain can radiate in through the roof, and during a cold winter 35 percent of heated air can be lost via ceilings and attics.[5] If you're prioritizing where to improve insulation first, this is the place to start if you have access.

Walls

Uninsulated walls can account for 25 percent of heat loss in the winter.[6] To determine if your walls are insulated, remove the face plates from some electrical outlets around the house. Then using a flashlight peek (don't poke) into the gap between the wallboard and the electrical box. Can you see any insulation? If you can't confirm whether or not you have insulation in your walls, schedule an appointment with an energy inspector who can determine your insulation levels and requirements as well as identify air leaks, making them easier to address.

If finished walls need insulating, it can be a relatively noninvasive procedure if you opt for a blown-in product, like recycled cellulose.

Ducts

Insulating ducts that run through unconditioned spaces in your home is very important. Heated air, for example, traveling through long runs of uninsulated ducts, cools down considerably by the time it reaches a room's register. When the air you paid to heat comes out of the register cool, you are not getting what you paid for. This holds true for cooled air too that can lose its desired temperature as it travels through ducts that have been warmed from ambient air.[7]

Green insulation products to consider include blanket insulation in the form of batts or rolls made from pre-consumer recycled cotton, formaldehyde-free sealed fiberglass, or mineral wool; loose-fill insulation made from recycled newsprint (cellulose); and spray insulation including both bio-based open cell spray polyurethane foam (SPF) and HCFC-free closed cell bio-based SPF. The effectiveness of these different types of insulation at slowing down or blocking the transfer of heat is measured in R-value. The higher the R-value, the better the insulation. Closed cell SPF has the highest R-value at 6.5 per inch, compared to 3.2 to 3.7 per inch for all the rest; it's also fairly expensive. SPF can be worth the investment, however, if you have long cold winters with lots of snow (which can lead to ice dams on under-insulated roofs), and high heating costs.

Many homeowners try to install insulation themselves. If you decide to try, you will save money up front, but correctly installing insulation is trickier than it looks. Batt insulation, for example, if not installed properly will leave voids greatly reducing its R-value. To ensure that insulation will perform as it's designed and lower your energy costs by the maximum amount, hire a qualified installer; or at least carefully follow all manufacturer directions when installing insulation yourself.

Table 2: Structure Thermal Performance with and without Insulation

Source	Heat flow with poor or no insulation		Typical reductions in heat gains and losses when beefing up R-values or sealing air leaks	Reduction in heating and cooling bill
	Winter heat loss	Summer heat gain		
Gaps	15% to 30%	5% to 15%	60% to 90%	3% to 27%
Walls	15% to 25%	15% to 25%	30% to 50%	5% to 13%
Roof	25% to 35%	25% to 35%	30% to 60%	8% to 21%
Windows	10% to 20%	25% to 35%	15% to 50%	2% to 18%

Sources: www.sustainability.vic.gov.au, www.flintenergies.com, www.consumerenergycenter.org

Improve Your Windows' Defenses

Inefficient windows can account for 10 to 25 percent of the heating and cooling bill depending on your current windows and how many are in the house.[8]

If you have single-pane windows, they have an insulation value (R-value) of around 1. When you consider that an insulated wall has an R-value between 13 and 21, it's easy to see that windows make lousy climate barriers. There's a limit to how energy efficient windows can ever be, but we aren't about to wall ourselves in, so here's what can be done: Old windows can be replaced with Energy Star–qualified* windows that are

---

* Energy Star is a program developed by the U.S. Environmental Protection Agency and Department of Energy to assess the energy efficiency of appliances and household products. Products earning the Energy Star label outperform competing appliances in energy efficiency by significant margins.

twice or even five times more energy efficient; or for a fraction of the cost of replacement windows you could install storm windows, heat-shrink film or insulating shades.

Replacement Windows

Replacement windows, at a cost of around $300 to $700 per window on average, will be a large investment and often a bad one, from an energy standpoint that is, because in most cases what you could save in energy costs won't justify the expense—no matter what the window salesperson tells you. Unless your windows are particularly bad (single pane, aluminum framed), you have lots of them, and you live in a harsh climate, consider less invasive and more economical upgrades to existing windows (see below).

If you have the type of home that would benefit from having its windows replaced, and the money to go for it, keep in mind that each increase in R-value provides a lower return. In other words you'll see a big savings between R-1 (U-0.98*) and R-2 (U-0.5) windows, but less between R-2 and R-3 (U-0.33), because there are diminishing returns with each added increment in R-value.

Storm Windows

Good storm windows will add an R-value of 2.0 or better to your windows for a combined R-value of 3.0 when added to single-pane windows. That's as good as high-end replacement windows will perform but you'll pay a lot less for the storms.

Exterior mount storm windows can be very inconvenient and somewhat dangerous if you have second-story windows—climbing a ladder with a large window of glass and positioning it into place is more than a bit awkward. Also, ex-

---

* R-value measures heat resistance and *U-value (or U-factor) measures* heat transfer. The higher the R-value and lower the U-value a window has, the better it is at slowing down or preventing heat loss through it.

terior mount windows are not usually considered an aesthetic enhancement. Enter interior storm windows! Interior storm windows are easier to take in and out as the weather changes, they don't alter the outside appearance of your home, and they tend to cost less than exterior storms because they don't have to withstand winter weather. Interior storms can cost between $100 and $150 for an average-sized (12.5 square foot) window, but do-it-yourself kits sell for as little as $55 for a 60" × 30" window. Another option is to make your own interior storms which can cost about $3 to $4 per square foot for a Plexiglas-based frame.

Because homes typically have many windows, even do-it-yourself kits can add up to $1,000 or more by the time every window is outfitted. Storm windows, therefore, will be the best investment for homes with a long heating season and high-cost heating fuels. For others, the payback period will be quite long. For the same or almost the same R-value effect, heat shrink film is a real bargain.

Heat-Shrink Film

Heat-shrink film creates an insulating air space between the window and the room by applying it over the surface of the window frame with double-sided tape and shrinking it taut with a hair dryer. These kits, available at most hardware stores, will add an R-value of about 1 to your windows.

To help prevent pulling paint off your window frame along with the tape in the spring, use a hair dryer to warm the tape (and its glue) first.

Interior Shades

Shades can provide some help for inefficient windows, but they must be tight-fitting, insulating, and remain closed to really make a difference. If all three of these things can be accomplished, shades can improve R-value by 1–2. Shades will block solar heat gain and natural light, so consider how and where they will be an advantage. (For more summertime solutions that reduce heat gain through windows, see "Passive Cooling" beginning on page 85.)

Table 2 shows the winter heat loss and summer heat gain that is typical in homes without proper weatherization and insulation. Cutting heat losses and gains in half through applied weatherization and insulation can cut your heating and cooling bill substantially. How substantially depends on the current state of your home's thermal performance, whether air gaps were sealed properly and on the increase in R-value you achieve. Table 3 shows what is possible, and likely, for a home that is suffering from many air leaks and no insulation.

Table 3: Estimated Savings from Some Weatherizing Scenarios

TYPICAL SCENARIO Heating and Cooling	($1163)					
GREENER SCENARIOS	Initial cost less rebates and incentives	↑Annual energy costs↓	Annual energy savings	First year ROI	Payback period (years)	10-year net savings
Apply heat-shrink film to windows	($44)	($1,105)	$58	132%	1	$522
Stop air leaks	($100)	($945)	$218	218%	0.5	$2,071
Insulate exterior walls and attic with loose-fill cellulose*	($2,175)	($844)	$319	15%	6.8	$1,021

* The specific type of insulation that is best for your situation depends upon a number of factors including your attic's construction and whether it is vented or unvented and houses any heating and cooling equipment. Always consult a professional before beginning a project.

Spotlight on Savings

A typical household in need of insulation and basic weatherization can reduce their heating and cooling bill by half, or about $595, when improving the efficiency of windows, sealing air gaps in the home, and adding insulation.

Protect Air Quality

Although it's hard to make a house truly airtight, once you've sealed up gaps and cracks, a controlled ventilation system is strongly recommended to ensure that adequate fresh air is still getting in and stale or humid air is not getting trapped inside your home. Stagnant indoor air can get pretty toxic. Chemicals from furnishings and household products, carbon monoxide from combustion appliances and other pollutants quickly degrade indoor air when a building doesn't have good ventilation. If your home doesn't already have a ventilation system, there are several options ranging in complexity and price. Begin your research at www.energy.gov/energysaver/articles/whole-house-ventilation.

PART II: MAJOR APPLIANCES AND SYSTEMS

Combined, major appliances (including the refrigerator, washing machine, clothes dryer and dishwasher), a water heater, and heating and cooling systems account for the majority of home energy use, or about 75 percent. (Lighting and electronics make up the majority of the balance and they are discussed in Part III of this chapter.)

We can reduce energy costs associated with running major appliances and home systems in three ways: by learning to use them wisely, by finding alternatives for their use in some cases and by increasing their efficiency.

Many of us have at least one appliance, and maybe a few, that are nearing the end of their service life and therefore inefficient—in some cases severely inefficient by today's standards. If this describes your situation, you'll want to begin preparing for the replacement of inefficient appliances. Don't panic. Yes, new high efficiency appliances are expensive and buying an appliance is a big decision that can be complicated by all the different brands, models, sizes and features to choose from. That's where this book, and this chapter specifically, can help. This book was written to help you spend less, in part so it will be easier to save up for things like energy-efficient appliances that, through their use, can improve the environment and ultimately save you even more money. This chapter will provide answers to questions like:

- How do I know when it's time to replace an old appliance or system?
- How can I bring the cost of a new appliance or system down?
- What do I look for to make sure I'm getting the appliance or system that uses the least energy and will save me the most money in annual operating costs?

- What can I expect to pay for a new appliance or system?
- How much can I expect to save each year over what I am paying now with my current appliance or system?
- How much can I expect to save over the first ten years of the appliance's or system's life?

What you will not find in this chapter is a discussion of solar electric (photovoltaic) or wind turbine systems. Solar and wind systems can cost, on average, $5,000 and $3,000, respectively, per installed kilowatt for a residential-sized system prior to available credits and rebates. Based on 2010 installation data, the typical residential system is close to 6 kilowatts, making the starting price point for an average system $18,000 and above. At current prices, these systems are considered beyond the financial reach of this book's target audience who is looking for ways to reduce energy costs through lower-cost upgrades that come with shorter payback periods. That said, through 2016 the federal government is offering to pay 30 percent of the cost of a photovoltaic or wind turbine system, and several states offer their own tax incentives—some paying for as much as 25 percent! Getting almost half of a renewable energy system paid for is pretty great, so if your state is playing ball, and you can swing it, swing away!

Home appliances are the world's fastest-growing energy consumers after automobiles.[9]

Old Can Be Costly

Most people's instinct is to hang on to an appliance until it dies a slow death—believing that postponing the purchase of a new one will save them money in the long run—not true. Due to the inefficiency of older appliances, they can cost their owners anywhere from 10 percent to 75 percent more to run than a high efficiency appliance of equal size or capacity.

Although shelling out money for a new appliance isn't fun, the energy consumed by major appliances has been greatly reduced due to new technology and minimum federal efficiency standards, so you'll save money every year through lower annual operating costs—as long as your use patterns remain the same or decline.

When to Replace

Energy efficiency in appliances and heating and cooling equipment is increasing so fast that even units manufactured within the past eight years are likely to be less efficient than a new ultra-efficient model. That doesn't mean you should automatically replace every appliance that is eight or more years old, even if you could afford to do such a thing.

Before deciding to replace an appliance or a heating or cooling device, weigh the costs and benefits of doing so. It takes raw materials and energy to make new products, and disposing of the old to make room for the new has ramifications that need to be considered and offset.

Determine Age

The service life of an appliance depends on how much use it received; whether or not it has been maintained and serviced according to the manufacturer's recommendations; and—in the case of dishwashers, clothes washers, and hot water tanks—the quality of your water (mineral deposits from hard water or sediments from old pipes can shorten the life of appliances that use water). Use table 4 to determine when an appliance is at or nearing the end of its useful life. If you aren't the original owner and don't know how old an appliance is, the date of manufacture should be written on the sticker or plate that bears the model and serial numbers. If there is no date,

Table 4: Average Life Expectancy of
Various Home Appliances and Equipment

Appliance	Service life in years
Refrigerator	13–15
Clothes washer	9–11
Dryer	15–18
Dishwasher	9–11
Forced air furnace	15–20
Boiler	25 (steel) 35 (cast iron)
Heat pump	16
Central AC	12–15
Room air conditioner	10
Evaporative cooler (swamp cooler)	15–20 Depends upon monthly and seasonal maintenance. Replacement parts can extend life and are inexpensive.
Hot water storage tank (gas or electric)	6–13 Depends a lot on use, water conditions, and whether or not maintenance was performed.
Solar hot water system	15–30
On demand hot water heater	20 Many of its parts can be replaced to extend service life.
Heat pump hot water tank	20 The maintenance on these units can be high.

contact the manufacturer. With the model and serial numbers, they can tell you when it was manufactured.

Compare Energy Efficiency

If you want to know how an older machine measures up to a newer appliance in terms of efficiency, compare its energy specifications to that of an energy-efficient, Energy Star appliance. To do this, visit www.energystar.gov and click on the appliance category to view the spreadsheet of qualified products. Scan the spreadsheet for a model that is comparable to yours in size or capacity and energy source (e.g., gas or electric). Compare that model's energy use (usually expressed in watts/hour, kilowatts/hour (kWh), kWh/year, or BTU/hour—in each case lower is better) or energy rating (higher is better) to that of your current appliance (see table 5). There will be much more discussion of energy ratings for specific appliances throughout the chapter.

You'll find energy specifications for your appliance in the owner's manual, and possibly somewhere on the appliance. If you don't have the manual, or the information seems to be missing from it, again, call the manufacturer to get the specifications you are looking for.

If your appliance has both exceeded its estimated service life and is less efficient than a newer Energy Star model, it's time to start planning to replace it in the near future.

Table 5: Energy Ratings for Various Home Appliances and Equipment

Energy ratings: The ratio of energy supplied (e.g., in heat) relative to the energy consumed (e.g., in electricity or gas)	Applicable appliances
SEER (Seasonal Energy Efficiency Ratio)	Central air conditioners and heat pumps
EER (Energy Efficiency Ratio)	Room air conditioners
AFUE (Annual Fuel Utilization Efficiency)	Furnaces
HSPF (Heating Seasonal Performance Factor)	Heat pumps
MEF (Modified Energy Factor)	Clothes washers
EF (Energy Factor)	Dishwashers, storage water heaters, tankless water heaters, clothes dryers
SF or SEF (Solar Factor or Solar Energy Factor)	Solar water heaters

Call In the Energy Inspector

If you're still unsure about what machines in your home really need replacing, you can hire an energy inspector to perform a home energy audit. As mentioned earlier in this chapter, an energy audit will include much more than an evaluation of your major appliances and heating and cooling system. It will also include diagnostic testing to pinpoint where and how your home can be made more energy efficient. Read part I of this chapter beginning on page 41 where we initially discussed energy audits—if you haven't already—before deciding for or against one.

Prioritizing Replacements

If several appliances seem to be reaching the end of their useful life at the same time, you may need to prioritize which ones to replace first based on their energy consumption. Those that use the most energy—and are powered with conventional energy sources—cost more to run, create more air pollution and consume natural resources faster, and therefore should top your list for replacement as soon as you have the funds.

An appliance's energy use, or consumption, is a factor of the watts or BTUs (both measurements of energy) it consumes per hour and the amount of use it receives. Table 6 reflects average household energy consumption by end use, but keep in mind that your household energy consumption could break out differently. You can bet that inefficient, oversized, undersized and heavily used appliances are consuming a nontypical share of your household's energy expenditures and driving up your energy costs overall.

For example, if you operate two refrigerators all year long, they could make up 14 to 22 percent of your household energy expenditures—possibly costing you more to operate than the hot water tank, washer, dryer and dishwasher combined! If your hot water tank is oversized for your needs or just very

Table 6: Home Energy Consumption by End Use

End use	Energy use averaged over one year
Space heating	29%–41%
Space cooling	11%–13%
Water heating	13%–20%
Refrigeration	6%–8%
Clothes washing and drying	5%–8%
Lighting	11%–15%
Small appliances and electronics	11%–15%

large to accommodate high hot water demand, it could account for 20 to 25 percent of home energy costs. And if you live in a severe climate with a long heating or cooling season, heat with oil or propane, or have an old leaky house, you can probably double the figures below for space heating or cooling.

Dealing With Sticker Shock

You can expect energy-efficient appliances to have higher sticker prices relative to models that don't match their higher efficiency. The models that stand to save us the most money through lower energy use don't come cheap up front, but there are two costs to consider when evaluating new appliances: the purchase price and the operating cost. Energy efficient-appliances save consumers money every year through lower annual operating costs which can more than offset their higher purchase price. Take a look at the following example in table 7, which shows that the machine with the higher price tag and higher efficiency will end up *saving* its owner $500 to $600 over its lifetime.

Reducing Costs

Everybody likes a good deal, and when making large purchases it's especially important and worthwhile to look for ways to bring the total cost of the purchase down. Knowing what

additional savings to look for, and *ask* for, could save you some
serious money.

Table 7: Washing Machine Comparison

Appliance	Initial cost less rebate	Annual operating costs*	Lifecycle costs (initial cost + annual costs over 11 years)*
Conventional washing machine (31.07 gal. per load)	($500)	($174)–($198)	($2,240)–($2,480)
Energy Star washing machine (14.38 gal. per load)	($700)	($104)–($118)	($1,740)–($1,880)

Source: www.energystar.gov

*The first figure accounts for gas water heating, the second electric water heating.

Promotions

Retailers and manufacturers routinely offer in-store and online
promotions, and to reach more customers they register these
promotions with websites like www.promotionalcodes.com,
www.couponmountain.com, www.retailmenot.com, and
www.offers.com. Don't be tempted to use a coupon for an item
that isn't the energy-saving model or size your research deter-
mines is best for your needs.

Rebates and Other Offers

There are two kinds of rebates to search for: rebates from the
manufacturer and energy efficiency rebates from your utility,
city or state. The website www.energystar.gov/index.cfm?
fuseaction=rebate.rebate_locator makes quick and easy work
of tracking down the latter, as well as other special offers like
tax exemptions or credits. The site at www.dsireusa.org is another good source of information on state, local, utility and federal incentives that promote energy efficiency. If you miss this

step, not to worry: appliance stores usually promote rebates and offers to help move the merchandise. When you buy a qualifying appliance, you'll receive all the paperwork you need to apply for the rebate or offer.

Sales

Stores often know ahead of time when they will be having sales. See if you can find out when a store's next big sale is and plan to purchase your new appliance during the sale. You probably won't get a salesperson to give you the dates of a future sale, since they are usually forbidden to leak the sale date. Make it possible for them to tell you, without breaking any rules.

For example, here's one way of asking:

You: When is your next big sale?

Them: I can't reveal that.

You: OK. Can you tell me if it would it be wise to wait until June to buy a dishwasher?

Them: Maybe sooner.

You: May?

Them: Yes, sometime around then would be a good time to buy your appliance!

Doesn't always work, but it's worth a try!

You can also try to predict a sale with the following information: According to MoneyCrashers.com, major appliance manufacturers ship their newest models to stores in May (if refrigerators) and in September/October (other major appliances). At these times, retailers will be discounting older models to make room for the new inventory. You can also expect sales over holiday weekends, such as Presidents' Day, Memorial Day, and so on.

Recycling Incentives

Scrap metal is worth cash, and the typical appliance consists of about 75 percent steel according to the Steel Recycling Institute. All appliances containing steel can be recycled when they have reached the end of their useful lives—and should be in order to keep metals, as well as toxic components that may be present, out of the landfill.

In a good year, scrap metal recyclers will pay around $30 per ton for appliances that do not contain refrigerants or coolants (e.g., CFCs and Freon). Since a typical washing machine weighs around two hundred pounds, or one tenth of a ton, you won't make much cash recycling appliances, but it should be enough for gas money to haul it to the recycling facility.

An old refrigerator could earn you more if there is a bounty on freezers and refrigerators in your community. Many utility companies offer up to $35 for old refrigerators and freezers both as an incentive to replace inefficient ones and to see that refrigerants are disposed of properly.* Incentives can be offered for recycling inefficient room air conditioners for the same reason.

Recycling appliances doesn't always earn you cash: depending on where you live, appliance recycling could be offered for free (appliance retailers may offer to remove your old appliance for recycling when they deliver your new one) or cost between $5 and $15 per appliance. Regardless of whether you make a little cash or pay a little cash, recycling old appliances is essential, and often mandated, to reduce solid waste and environmental pollution (see the sidebar, "Resources for Recycling Appliances").

Resources for Recycling Appliances

www.recycle-steel.org
www.energystar.gov/recycle

---

* U.S. law prohibits the release of ozone-depleting refrigerants into the atmosphere during the service, maintenance, or disposal of refrigeration and air conditioning equipment.

By using recycled steel scrap, in one year, the steel industry saves the equivalent energy to electrically power about 18 million households for a year.[10]

THE RIGHT APPLIANCE AND THE RIGHT WAY TO USE IT

Lots of things impact an appliance's operating costs—its technology of course, its size or capacity, its features, where it is located in the home and how much use and maintenance it receives. The remainder of part II of this chapter will help keep you focused on all the considerations that go into making a decision about a new appliance, so you'll end up with an appliance that will conserve the most energy dollars possible while still meeting your needs.

Kitchen and Laundry Appliances

Heating and cooling equipment consume the bulk of home energy, but despite maybe adjusting a thermostat a few times a week (we'll get to that later), it's largely background equipment: as long as it is doing its job of keeping our home comfortable, it's pretty much off the radar. Kitchen and laundry appliances, on the other hand, are fixtures in our everyday lives; we interact with them regularly and rely on their capacity and features to help us manage our household and to simplify our lives. So let's begin with these hard-working appliances.

The (Energy) Elephant in the Room

The refrigerator rarely, if ever, has to be turned on and off, so we don't often consider how much energy it uses, but if your fridge was new in the 1980s or early 1990s, or heaven forbid in the 1970s, you need to get acquainted with its energy use. According to the U.S. Department of Energy's Lawrence Berkeley National Laboratory, a refrigerator that is more than fifteen years old can cost twice as much to run as a newer energy-efficient model; and one that is more than twenty years old is very likely costing three times as much to operate.[11] Refrigerators can be expensive to replace, but with so many incentives (see under "Reducing Costs" beginning on page 58) to help ease the burden, this could be the time to take the plunge if your refrigerator is old and inefficient.

With every new appliance you buy, the first decision you'll need to make is what size is right for your household—and it's a big decision. The larger the appliance the more energy it will use. To gauge how much capacity you need in a new refrigerator, evaluate how well your current one meets your food storage needs. If things have been cramped, size up—but only if a larger refrigerator will fit the current space your old one occupied! If your refrigerator is usually half full, size down. If you're buying your first refrigerator plan on 12–14 cubic feet for one to two people and an additional 2 cubic feet for each additional person. (Use 12 cubic feet as your base if you don't typically store fresh foods and 14 cubic feet as your base if you often enjoy many fresh foods.)

When it comes to features, choose a model with the freezer either on the top or bottom: Side-by-side models are less efficient than either. And avoid through-the-door features, which increase energy use and add to the purchase price.

Every appliance you buy should meet Energy Star standards, at a minimum. Energy Star–qualified refrigerators are 20 percent more efficient than models that don't qualify, on average. However, don't rely on the Energy Star label alone, because each model bearing the label will vary in its energy efficiency. Also check the bright yellow EnergyGuide label*

---

* The EnergyGuide label is currently found only on clothes washers, dishwashers, refrigerators, freezers, water heaters, window air conditioners, central air conditioners, furnaces, boilers, heat pumps, and pool heaters. Each label states the estimated yearly operating costs and estimated yearly electricity use for these appliances and they can help you compare the energy use of different models as you shop for an appliance.

required on all refrigerators (and many other appliances as well) to compare the kilowatt hours (kWh) a particular model uses in one year. The lower the kWh usage the less you'll spend in energy costs.

Do Now and Save

- Set the fridge temp to 38° and the freezer to 3° (or 0° for long-term storage).
- If your refrigerator is less than half full, move some pantry items to the fridge (i.e., canned fruit, salad dressing, beverages). Your fridge should always be ¾ of the way full because it has to work harder to cool voids inside the box than objects that have already been cooled.
- If you operate two refrigerators simultaneously all year long, try to consolidate items into one box except for brief periods when you really need the full capacity of two refrigerators.

Estimated Annual Savings: $10–$145

To recap, the best new refrigerator will . . .

- be sized to accommodate your true food storage needs,
- either have the freezer on the top or the bottom,
- have the Energy Star label, and
- use the least kWh yearly among other similar models (compare EnergyGuide labels).

Table 8: Refrigerator Comparison

Appliance	Initial cost less rebates	Annual operating costs	15-year lifecycle costs
1991 side by side w/in-door dispenser (21 cu. ft.)	existing	($145)	end of life
2012 conventional non-dispensing top freezer (21 cu. ft.)	($949)	($67)	($1,954)
2012 Energy Star non-dispensing top freezer (20 cu. ft.)	($834)	($53)	($1,569)
2012 Energy Star non-dispensing top freezer (18.2 cu. ft.)	($714)	($50)	($1,404)

Spotlight on Savings

The typical household can save around $100 a year when replacing an old inefficient refrigerator with a new Energy Star model.

Cleaning Machines

When it comes to washing machines and dishwashers, energy efficiency is closely related to water efficiency: the less water these appliances use the less energy they will use to heat the water. The newest generation of washers and dishwashers has made major gains in energy efficiency primarily due to improved water efficiency; therefore you can find information on these machines in chapter 5.

> In the United States, the majority of power comes from fossil fuels that produce heat-trapping gases—chiefly carbon dioxide—and are causing severe and abnormal weather that is altering the planet's landscape and ecosystems.[12]

Blowing in the Wind

Clotheslines were once permanent fixtures in American backyards. Then the clothes dryer came along and changed all that. Eight out of ten households now have a dryer,[13] and they are one of the most expensive home appliances to operate. If you need a new dryer, an energy-efficient one can save you a bit, but if you really want to save money, use your dryer less. Sunshine is free and drying laundry outside for part of the year will help both your clothes and your machine last longer.

Gas and electric dryers can be comparable in efficiency, but if your laundry room has a gas hookup, consider a gas dryer that

Do Now and Save

- Use solar energy to dry laundry. Most of the country experiences average daily temperatures over 65 degrees for at least 5 months each year. This gives most of us ample opportunity to dry clothes outdoors, as long as a clothes line isn't prohibited by any CC&Rs* in your community.
- Install a retractable clothesline in your laundry room, or purchase a drying rack, for drying lightweight garments indoors all year long.

Estimated Annual Savings: $31–$74

can be cheaper to operate and less polluting wherever electricity at the local power plant is sourced from fossil fuels. Yes, natural gas is a fossil fuel, but direct combustion of a fossil fuel by a home appliance is generally more efficient than producing the power at a distant plant and delivering it to your home. See "Cleaner Combustion" on page 79 for more explanation.

Pick a dryer with a moisture sensor and cool-down feature: Both features conserve energy: the former by preventing over-drying and the latter by using residual heat inside the drum during the final minutes of drying. It's not always apparent from the dryer display if these features are included. Settings that sense dryness and automatically shut off the dryer can have proprietary, ambiguous names; and many permanent press (medium heat) cycles have a cool-down period at the end, but not all, so don't be afraid to grill the appliance sales person for an explanation of what all the dryer settings mean. You can save about 15 percent with a moisture sensing control. When using a cycle with a cool-down period, how much you can save depends on the ratio between the drying period and the cool-down period, but expect to save at least 10 percent when using this setting.

---

* CC&R stands for covenant, conditions and restrictions. Some properties are subject to CC&Rs that govern what owners can do, or not do, with or on their property.

You won't find either an Energy Star or EnergyGuide label on clothes dryers because energy usage across dryers is considered too close to warrant the analysis. You can, however, compare the Energy Factor (EF) of different models: the higher the EF number, the more energy efficient the dryer.

To recap, the best new dryer will . . .

- be a gas dryer if your electricity comes primarily from fossil fuels or your laundry area is not equipped with a 240-volt outlet,
- be an electric dryer if your electricity comes primarily from clean, renewable energy or your laundry area is not equipped with an installed gas hook-up,
- have the highest EF number among similar models,
- have a moisture sensing setting (preferred to a temperature sensing control), and
- have a cool-down feature (often standard as part of the permanent press cycle).

Table 9: Clothes Dryer Comparison

Appliance	Initial cost less rebates	Annual operating costs	15-year lifecycle costs
1998 electric dryer	existing	($166)	end of life
2012 electric dryer	($599)	($124)	($2,459)
2012 gas dryer	($599)	($83)	($1,844)

Assumes 416 dryer loads per year.

 Spotlight on Savings

If you have a gas hook-up in your laundry area, a new gas dryer will save you an estimated $615 over its life compared to a new electric dryer.

Hot Water Heaters

A water heater is typically a busy piece of equipment. It typically accounts for 18 percent of home energy costs, but in homes with teenagers, who are known for taking long showers, a family can spend 22 percent of its energy budget to heat water. A four member household that uses 204 gallons of hot water a day (an average amount according to the EPA) can spend around $1,944 a year to heat their water with electricity depending on electricity rates and the efficiency of the unit!

Whether you have a small or large household, choosing an energy-efficient water heating system, and starting to conserve hot water daily, can make a considerable difference in your energy expenditures. Reasonably, you could cut your water heating bill in half.

Greenhouse gas levels in the atmosphere are higher now than at any other time in the last one million years.[14]

Storing Water

Storage tank hot water heaters are very popular, but not terribly efficient. The temperature of the water held inside the tank must be maintained at a preset temperature at all times whether that hot water is needed or not. Throughout the day water is heated, loses heat, and must be reheated, regardless of when you actually need it. Maintaining thirty to eighty gallons of water to a precise 120 degrees all day long is wasteful and costly.

Gas and Electric Storage Hot Water Tanks

If you have a gas line to your home, a gas-fueled storage tank can be cheaper to operate than an electric unit, and less polluting in areas of the country where the majority of electricity is generated by burning fossil fuels.

Features to look for that will save you money over the life of a hot water tank include built-in heat traps, thick insulation, and an Energy Factor of 0.67 for gas and 0.92 to 0.95 for electric. A condensing boiler can increase a gas hot water tank's efficiency considerably, but condensing units with energy factors of 0.80 and better were still not available at the time this book went to print. Keep your eyes open for these: Energy Star says a gas condensing unit can save a typical family of four $170 a year when replacing a standard storage gas water heater.

Standard storage water heaters are among the least expensive home appliances, so splurge on a tank with a longer warranty period. According to Consumer Reports, a unit with a 12-year warranty will cost you only an average $90 more than one with a 6-year warranty, but due to its longer expected life will save you the trouble and expense of replacing your hot water tank in half the time.

Do Now and Save

- Make sure the tank is set no higher than 120° F. Higher temperatures speed corrosion and waste energy.
- If the tank doesn't include an insulating membrane (consult the manufacturer if unsure), wrap the tank with an insulating blanket made especially for the size of your tank.
- Turn your electric hot water tank off when you leave town, and turn a gas tank down to low.
- Perform annual maintenance to extend its life by as much as ten years, including draining the tank until the water runs clear.
- Insulate bare hot water pipes.

Estimated Annual Savings: $31–$92

Heat Pump Storage Water Heaters (HPWH)

An ambient air-source HPWH works by pulling warm air from the surrounding room, simultaneously cooling the room it's located in. Since HPWHs use energy to move heat not to generate it, the energy savings can be up to 50 percent compared with standard electric resistance water heaters. The downside is that these systems require minimum ambient temperatures and space to work effectively and are expensive to purchase, install and maintain. Current prices range from $1,600 for a 50 gallon tank to $3,000 for an 80 gallon tank. Installation charges vary considerably due to many factors. A 2010 study by Lawrence Berkeley National Laboratory found installation costs can range from a low of $148 to a high of $2,784 and average $538.

A hybrid water heater that functions as a heat pump when ambient air is warm enough, but uses traditional electric heating elements when the heat pump can't keep up with demand, isn't much cheaper than a HPWH. Either one, however, could earn sizable rebates and incentives due to typical EFs of 2.0 and better. When one of these babies replaces a standard storage tank, in some states you can earn cash for your old tank plus rebates or incentives worth hundreds of dollars to put toward the appliance and the installation.

Sizing a Storage Tank Water Heater

Tanks come in different sizes, and their capacity is usually what people base their buying decision on, but a storage water heater's FHR, or first-hour rating, is more important. The FHR tells you how much hot water the heater can deliver in an hour. Calculate how much hot water your household uses during peak demand, and match the hot water tank's FHR to that demand. The better your household is at staggering hot water demand, the lower FHR you will need and the more money you can save.

Use the following worksheet to estimate hot water use for various household activities during your family's peak demand. Calculate only peak demand water use, leaving the other boxes empty. If our estimates for how much water flows each minute from showerheads and faucets do not match your true flow rates, change the figures in the worksheet before making your final calculations. (Chapter 5 provides comprehensive information that can help you determine flow rates from different existing fixtures you have, as well as information on changing fixtures to reduce water use. Or refer to table 10 on page 74 for typical flow rates for various household devices.) If you have lots of company, make sure to include the demand from overnight guests in your calculations.

Worksheet to Determine Peak Demand Hot Water Use

Peak demand hour: _____ **(e.g., 7 a.m.–8 a.m.)**		
Showering	2.2 gallons per minute × number of people showering × length of average shower in minutes	=
Kitchen sink chores with water running (e.g., washing and rinsing dishes)	1.8 gallons per minute × minutes running over one hour	=
Bathroom sink chores with water running (e.g., shaving and hand washing)	1.1 gallons per minute × minutes running over one hour	=
Automatic dishwashing	8 gallons per load* × number of loads	=
Laundering with warm water	11 to 18 gallons per load* × number of loads	=
Total one-hour peak demand:		

* Hot water use will vary greatly based on your appliance. Check your owner's manual for water-use details.

To recap, the best new storage tank heater, depending on your fuel source, will . . .

- be a standard gas tank or electric tank with a minimum EF rating of 0.67 or 0.92, respectively, if your budget is under $1,000 and space is limited,
- be an Energy Star–qualified condensing gas unit if your budget is $1,500 to $2,000 and space is limited,
- be an Energy Star HPWH if your budget is $2,000–$3,000 and you have a location for the tank that remains in the 40°–90°F range year-round and provides at least 1,000 cubic feet of air space around the water heater,
- come well insulated (modern hot water tanks come from the manufacturer with good insulation, but some are better insulated than others),
- have built-in heat traps to prevent convective heat loss through the inlet and outlet pipes,
- have the longest possible warranty among similar models, and
- have an FHR that does not exceed your household's peak hot water demand (including times when guests may be in the house).

Going Tankless

A tankless hot water system, unlike a storage hot water system, heats water only when needed, or on-demand. The huge advantage of these systems is that you don't pay to heat water you're not using, saving potentially hundreds of dollars a year on water heating costs. These systems are becoming quite popular in new, small home construction, but don't always work for larger homes or existing homes that don't have the proper infrastructure to make their installation economical.

Whole-House Systems

A whole house system can be pricey, and adding them to an existing home isn't always feasible, or at least not economical.

For example if you use electricity to heat water, residential wiring generally will not support a large capacity tankless water heater; and if your home came with a gas tank water heater, you probably don't have a gas line sized properly for a tankless water heater.

If you are building, this could be the system for you, but it's not exactly a no-brainer: whole house systems achieve the most energy-cost savings, compared to traditional storage heaters, in homes that use less than forty gallons of hot water a day. In households with higher demand, the cost savings will not be nearly as high, according to the Department of Energy. Not only are they best for low overall users, but the amount of water used at any one time cannot exceed the unit's maximum flow rate, measured in gallons per minute (usually 3 to 5 GPM, depending on the starting and ending temperature of the water). Table 10 shows typical flow rates for various household devices.

However, whether or not a tankless system will work for your new home is more complicated than the number of people in your household and use patterns. Your fuel source, water pressure, and the temperature of water entering your house are all critical to determining if you can benefit from a tankless system. Ideally you'll want natural gas service, water pressure in the range of 15 to 150 PSI (pounds per square inch), and an incoming water temperature of 50 degrees Fahrenheit or higher.*

Tankless systems are hot (as in fashionable), but they must be given careful consideration. If you can't make one work for your household, a superefficient condensing gas storage tank—which is comparable in efficiency and life cycle costs to a dreamy on-demand system—may be your best option for a whole house system.

---

* Exact system specifications will vary.

Table 10: Typical Flow Rates for Various Household Devices (in Gallons Per Minute)

Device	Low-flow	Typical flow
Showerhead	2.0	3.0
Bathroom faucet	1.0	1.5
Kitchen sink faucet	1.5	2.5
Dishwasher	1.0	2.5
Clothes washer	1.5	4.0

Electric Point-Of-Use (POU) Heaters

POU heaters are usually installed to augment a tank system that is struggling to provide adequate or timely hot water to a particular fixture or appliance. The POU heater is installed very near the fixture or appliance and supplies it with instantaneous hot water—on demand.

It's possible for POU heaters to replace a tank system entirely, but this is most effectively done in a one- or two-person household with low hot water demand. Another consideration is when you use hot water. Electric on demand heaters require sudden, intense spurts of energy, so using POUs can increase peak energy demand back at the power plant, something it's important to reduce. So these units are best not only for homes that use very little hot water, but for which demand can be shifted to shoulder or off-peak hours.

According to the Department of Energy, you can achieve the greatest savings compared to a conventional storage hot water system—up to 50 percent—when installing a POU water heater at each hot water outlet. Typical applications might include a kitchen sink, an entire bathroom, and a laundry room; just remember, each unit can start at $179 but may require both an electrician and plumber to install, so the fewer applications you have the more affordable their implementation.

To recap, the best tankless system will . . .

- achieve optimal delivery and cost savings given your incoming water pressure and temperature,
- be sized to provide a minimum flow rate equal to the flow rate of any fixtures you will use simultaneously,
- be gas if it is for a whole house system, and
- have an Energy Star label (available for whole house gas systems only).

> It's estimated that U.S. homes waste between five and twenty gallons each day waiting for hot water to run from hot water taps, or approximately 1.4 billion gallons annually.[15]

Hot Water Courtesy of the Sun

In solar hot water (SHW) systems, solar thermal collectors heat the water, which is then stored inside a tank. SHW systems cannot operate alone, however. Typically between 50 to 70 percent of the daily hot water load is produced solely by the solar system so a backup system is needed to pick up the slack. The backup system can be either a tank or a demand heater that uses a conventional power source.

The feasibility of a SHW system depends upon such things as the amount of solar radiation at the site and your hot water usage. You can find a qualified professional to perform a site assessment through the Solar Energy Industries Association's website at www.seia.org.

Solar water heating can be a good investment if you have above average sun and above average fuel (or electricity) costs, but it's an expensive investment at current start-up and installation costs—typically $3,000 to $5,000 for a whole house system. But federal, state, city, and utility incentives could reduce start-up and installation costs significantly, and there's more: water heating costs can be reduced by 50 to 80 percent according to the DOE when a solar water heating system replaces traditional means of heating water; solar water heating also insulates you from rising fuel costs.

Don't forget about all the great environmental benefits. Solar water heaters use 100 percent clean, renewable energy. By investing in one, you will be reducing harmful air pollutants and wastes that are created when your utility generates power or you burn fuel to heat your water.

If you'd like to explore the feasibility of a solar hot water system, you could start with a site assessment, but you may want to know you can afford it first, so start by finding all state, local, utility, and federal incentives that can offset the costs of purchasing a residential solar system. If you learn you can recoup $2,500 of the cost of a system in the form of rebates and tax incentives,* well then, suddenly a solar system is no more expensive than some high efficiency storage tank systems!

To recap, the best SHW system will . . .

- be one that is preceded by a professional site assessment to correctly size and design the system,
- qualify for financial incentives that can offset 30 to 50 percent of start-up and installation costs (read qualifying requirements carefully),
- recover your costs in a reasonable amount of time (e.g., five to ten years), and
- have an Energy Star label (meaning that 50 percent or more of the total conventional hot water heating load is provided by solar energy).

---

* A tax credit, not to be confused with a tax deduction, is a dollar for dollar credit against taxes owed. If you underpaid and owe taxes to the government, a $1,000 tax credit would directly reduce the amount you owe by $1,000. If you overpaid taxes through withholding, a $1,000 tax credit would increase your refund check by $1,000.

Table 11: Water Heater Comparison

Appliance	Initial cost less rebates and incentives	Annual operating costs	12-year lifecycle costs *
2004 electric water heater, 0.59 EF	existing	($1,053)	end of life
2012 12-yr. electric water heater, 0.92 EF	($644)	($984)	($12,452)
2012 12-yr. high efficiency nat. gas water heater tank, 0.67 EF	($793)	($383)	($5,389)
2012 Energy Star HPWH, 2.0 EF	($1,938)	($417)	($6,942)
2012 Energy Star whole-house on-demand system (gas), 0.82 EF	($1,429)	($298)	($5,005)
2012 Energy Star SHW system, 0.5 SF w/auxiliary electric tank, 0.92 EF	($1,240)	($492)	($7,144)
2012 Energy Star solar hot water system, 0.5 SF w/auxiliary gas tank, 0.67 EF	($1,450)	($192)	($3,754)

Assumes four-member household using 102 gallons of hot water per day (half the national average—get that usage down!)

*SWH, HPWH, and On-Demand systems will last eight years longer and beyond with good maintenance, so they save much more compared to tank storage systems that have to be replaced every six to twelve years depending on the unit.

 Spotlight on Savings

A household heating 102 gallons of water daily with an inefficient tank storage system could be paying between $69 and $861 more each year to heat water than a household with an energy-efficient water heating system.

Heating Systems

The development of new technologies in the past decade has increased the types of heating systems available and drastically improved their efficiency. From active solar to geothermal to hydronic systems, there are more choices than ever before, and the highest efficiency systems can pay for themselves in energy savings. With so many choices, it was necessary to limit the following discussion to the heating fuels and systems that would have the most relevance to this book's audience. Most existing homes heat with a furnace or boiler, and the majority of them use gas or electricity (only 7 percent use oil and only 6 percent use propane). The next most popular way to heat is with electric resistance heaters including electric forced-air furnaces, baseboards, and wall heaters. Therefore, the following overview covers the most common systems available to gas and electric customers on a limited budget.

Based on estimates by the Energy Information Administration, over the winter of 2011–2012 natural gas customers spent an average $740 to heat their homes, while electricity customers spent $955 on average. But home heating costs can skyrocket depending on where you live, your fuel source, the size of your home and its thermal performance, your heating system, and your heating habits. Efficiency in home heating systems should be a priority for the dual purpose of saving money and reducing greenhouse gases.

Heating systems generally have a long service life, so most people won't be looking to replace their existing equipment right away. If you're in this group, you can still make energy efficiency modifications to an existing system by performing maintenance and installing retrofits that can improve efficiency without total replacement (see the sidebar, "Do Now and Save," on page 81).

If you'll need a new heating system within the next couple of years, start saving your money now. A high efficiency system is going to cost you in the neighborhood of $3,000 to $4,000 even after rebates and incentives. But the savings over the life of a new high efficiency system can be huge, especially when used with a programmable thermostat (see Tables 12, 13, and 14).

Cleaner Combustion

Most of the electricity in this country is produced by burning fossil fuels in generators that convert only about 30 percent of the fuel's energy into electricity, while the minimum efficiency of a gas boiler and furnace is 80 percent and 78 percent, respectively. Thus, heating with a combustion appliance is generally more efficient than heating with electricity.

A gas-fuel heating system can also cost much less to operate than an electric system because most U.S. residents pay higher rates for electricity than for natural gas.

Gas Furnaces and Boilers

Most homes use a furnace or boiler to produce heat, and energy-efficient models of either that replace an older model can increase efficiency by up to 40 percent, according to the DOE.

An Energy Star–qualified gas furnace and boiler uses 16 percent and 6 percent less energy, respectively, than a non-qualifying unit. But to get the most efficient unit compare the annual fuel utilization efficiency (AFUE) numbers which rate how efficiently a furnace converts its fuel source into heating energy: the higher the AFUE the better the unit's efficiency. For exam-

Table 12: Natural Gas Boiler Comparison—Northern Climate

System	Initial cost less rebates and incentives	Annual operating costs	25-year lifecycle costs
1987 Gas boiler, 0.65 AFUE	existing	($1,156)	end of life
Gas boiler, 0.78 AFUE	($3,000)	($964)	($27,460)
Energy Star boiler, 0.87 AFUE	($4,400)	($864)	($26,000)

Sources: www.energyexperts.com, www.energystar.gov, www.eia.gov

Assumes 95,000 to 100,000 BTUs, hot water boiler system.

Spotlight on Savings

Homes heating with a boiler that is more than twenty-five years old could save around $292 a year by replacing it with a modern Energy Star unit.

ple, an AFUE of 95 percent means that 95 percent of the energy in the fuel becomes heat for the home and only 5 percent is lost through the venting system or elsewhere. Electric furnaces will have AFUE ratings of around 95 percent as well, but this efficiency is deceiving: the AFUE only rates the efficiency of the unit itself, it doesn't factor in the efficiency of converting fossil fuels to energy at the power plant, which, as stated on the previous page, is only about 30 percent; and as electricity travels through power lines, some of it is lost. Therefore, high-efficiency gas units are preferable in areas with natural gas service.

Gas units with electric ignition and sealed combustion are the most efficient and especially important features for colder climates with long heating seasons.

Table 13: Natural Gas Furnace Comparison—Northern Climate

System	Initial cost less rebates and incentives	Annual operating costs	15-year lifecycle costs
Gas furnace, 0.78 AFUE	($2,200)	($1,034)	($17,710)
Gas furnace, 0.90 AFUE*	($3,100)	($896)	($16,540)
Energy Star gas furnace, 0.97 AFUE	($3,500)	($831)	($15,965)

Sources: www.energyexperts.com, www.energystar.gov, www.eia.gov

Assumes 95,000 to 100,000 BTUs, forced air furnace.

*In the Southern United States, furnaces with an AFUE of 90 percent are Energy Star approved, but in the Northern United States, only furnaces with a minimum AFUE of 95 percent qualify for the program.

Spotlight on Savings

When it's time to replace an inefficient gas forced air furnace, choosing one that is 97 percent efficient will save the typical household in a Northern climate $203 each year in operating costs.

Do Now and Save

- Have your system serviced to check for and repair any problems that may be impeding safe and efficient operation.
- Ask a serviceperson to recommend retrofits that can improve efficiency without total replacement, such as retrofitting a continuous pilot light with an intermittent ignition device. (Not recommended for aging appliances, however.)
- If your unit has a continuous pilot light, if possible, turn it off after the heating season, and have it relit in the fall. This service is usually provided for free by the utility company.
- For forced-air systems, repair, and insulate duct work.
- Refer to the Weatherizing Essentials section in this chapter and take necessary steps to improve house insulation and air-tightness.
- Install a programmable thermostat and turn your system down when away and asleep (see chapter 2 for settings).

Estimated annual savings: $54–$623

Improving Electric Heating

Homes that are heated with a form of electric resistance heating may benefit from upgrading to a heat pump. Heat pumps use electricity to move heat rather than generate heat and can use 50 percent less electricity for heating.

Heat pumps

In the case of an air-source heat pump—the most economical and popular kind—hot air is moved out of living spaces during the summer to help cool the space. During the winter the process is reversed and heat is captured from outdoor air, compressed, and delivered inside the home at a higher temperature. Because air-source heat pumps must extract heat from outside air when in heating mode, they work best in moderate climates where temperatures don't dip below 40 degrees Fahrenheit. Take this moderate climate thing seriously! If freezing temperatures are common where you live, the compressor will most likely fail to maintain the desired temperature (unless it's a Cold Climate Heat Pump), and the back-up heat strips will automatically kick in leading to energy spikes and higher energy bills.

The average American produces 20 tons of CO_2 a year—four times more than the world average of 4.5 tons per capita.[16]

For more extreme climates, or just better efficiency, geothermal heat pumps work not with outside air but with the more constant temperatures in the ground (ground-source) or water (water-source). Geothermal systems are quite expensive to install however, so given the purpose of this book, only air-source heat pumps are examined (see table 14).

A heat pump's Heating Seasonal Performance Factor (HSPF) measures heating efficiency while the Seasonal Energy Efficiency Ratio (SEER) and Energy Efficiency Ratio (EER) measure cooling efficiency. An Energy Star–qualified appliance will have a minimum HSPF of 8.0, and a minimum SEER and EER of 14 and 11, respectively. The higher the HSPF, SEER, and EER ratings, the more efficient the system and the more money you can save over the heat pump's service life.

Heat pumps are complicated mechanical systems; this makes them expensive—and expensive to repair. This is an investment that can pay off for the right home, but it requires plenty of due diligence.

Sizing a Heating System

Choosing the right size system is critical for achieving optimal efficiency and service life from heating equipment. Correctly sizing a system is complicated however and requires professional help. Ask a qualified HVAC contractor or your local gas or electric utility company to calculate furnace capacity using the ACCA Manual J Residential Load Calculation, which factors in climate, square footage, design, and construction. Contractors will often perform this service at no cost (see the sidebar, "Resources for HVAC System Selection and Installation").

To recap, the best heating system will . . .

- be sized by a qualified HVAC contractor using the Manual J Calculation,
- be an Energy Star unit with the highest AFUE you can afford if a gas or oil unit,
- have electric ignition and sealed combustion if a gas furnace, and
- be an Energy Star unit with the highest HSPF, SEER, and EER you can afford if a heat pump.

Resources for HVAC System Selection and Installation

Compare heating costs for different fuels:
www.buildinggreen.com/calc/fuel_cost.cfm

Tips for selecting a qualified contractor from the American Council for an Energy-Efficient Economy:
www.aceee.org/consumer/how-choose-contractor

Table 14: Electric Heating System Comparison—Mild Winter Climate

System	Initial cost less rebates and incentives	Annual operating costs	15-year lifecycle costs
1998 15 kwh electric furnace and blower	existing	($1,893)	end of life
2012 3 ton air-source heat pump, HSPF 7.7, SEER 13	($3,000)	($796)	($14,940)
2012 3 ton air-source heat pump, HSPF 9.2, SEER 16	($3,700)	($549)	($11,935)

Sources: www.energyexperts.org, www.energystar.gov

 Spotlight on Savings

When a heat pump replaces an electric furnace, it can reduce home heating cost by 58 to 71 percent or overall heating costs by $1,097 to $1,344 annually.

Cooling Systems

Whether you live in a hot and dry climate, a hot and humid climate, or a moderate climate that is only uncomfortably hot for two to four weeks out of the entire year, you probably fall into one of two categories: either you rely too much on air conditioning (two-thirds of all homes in the United States have one) when the heat becomes too much to bear, or you suffer without a cooling system. The first scenario creates high cooling cost, the second is just uncomfortable. This section shows ways to solve both problems.

It turns out there are nearly as many ways to cool a home as there are microclimates in the United States. And with the right cooling system, you can increase your comfort, save money, and help promote a cleaner environment.

Generating the electricity to power all the air conditioners in the United States releases roughly 100 million tons of carbon dioxide into the air each year.[17]

Passive Cooling

The first priority in reducing cooling costs is to reduce your building's solar heat gain. It's much harder and more expensive to cool a house that is being super heated due to exposure to the sun's intense rays. Sun hitting the roof, sides, and windows of a home can heat it to several degrees above outside temperatures, and once a home has absorbed heat from the sun, its mass holds on to that heat for several hours, forcing the air conditioner to work longer and harder.

Passive cooling is an alternative to mechanical cooling, the latter of which requires energy and often refrigeration technology. Passive cooling techniques that can be employed in existing homes include shading, insulating, reflecting, and ventilating.

Shading

According to the Consumer Energy Center, shading your home can reduce the temperature indoors by as much as 20 degrees on a hot day, reducing or eliminating the need for expensive mechanical cooling. There are both natural and man-made ways to increase shade, and though natural vegetation may provide the more attractive and less obvious sunscreen for our homes, plants and trees take time to grow and fill-in, so consider man-made solutions where instant shade can also provide instant relief and savings.

Vegetation. **Shade trees** in full leaf can block 70 to 90 percent of solar radiation and reduce air conditioning (AC) bills by 15 to 50 percent.[18] Plant trees mostly on the east and west sides of the house where, because of the lower angle of the sun in the morning and afternoon, trees don't need to be as mature before they'll block sun. For the best results, choose trees with a broad crown and plant them around 20 feet from the house. Any farther and they won't provide effective shade. Any closer and they could interfere with the siding or foundation as they mature.

Planting trees on the south side of a home is only advised in hot climates where the majority of energy dollars are used for cooling. In cold climates where heating appliances dominate energy use, trees on the south side of a home will impede beneficial solar heat gain in cooler months. Even deciduous trees that lose their leaves in the fall can block solar heat gain during cold winter months leading to higher heating bills. Northerners should use other shading techniques on south facing windows if solar gain in the summer is a problem, such as exterior solar shades or awnings—both discussed below under "Exterior Window Treatments."

Use the Arbor Day Foundations website for help choosing the best shade trees for your site, www.arborday.org/trees/index-choosing.cfm.

Besides shade trees, **trellises** and **arbors** can be strategically placed to provide very good shade when covered with dense-growing plants. Many fast-growing vines will reach a height and fullness capable of providing good shade in two to three years. In the meantime, the structure itself will provide some shade. Make sure the vine you choose is a hardy perennial that will last indefinitely.

According to the EPA, dark-colored rooftops can reach temperatures of 150 to 190 degrees Fahrenheit under the summer sun.

Exterior Window Treatments. If you don't have heat-blocking windows in your home, adding them will be an expensive undertaking (see the section on "Replacement Windows" in Part I of this chapter). If your budget won't allow for new windows, you can protect south facing windows with less expensive awnings or exterior solar shades—and to a lesser extent with interior shades.

A **fixed awning** will block the sun on the south side of the house when the sun is at its highest angle, reducing heat gain by up to 65 percent if properly installed.[19] An **adjustable awning** can block the sun at almost any angle and fully retract to allow for solar heat gain during the cool season. Generally, fixed awnings are best for homes with short cooling seasons while adjustable awnings are best in areas with long cooling seasons or where frequent high wind conditions could damage fixed awnings. As you may have guessed, adjustable awnings are generally more expensive than the fixed kind because of the built-in flexibility (lots of moving parts). Awnings can cost from $100 to $500 for a standard window, but you can reduce costs if you do the installation yourself, and midrange awnings can pay for themselves in just a couple of seasons.

Exterior solar shades that install on the outside of the window sash are another option, and they will block up to 70 percent of the sun's solar energy when installed on any window. They cost around $150 per window, so you will probably only want them outside high-use rooms where the sun is a problem.

As good as awnings and shades can be at blocking solar heat gain, they are not part of many energy efficiency rebate programs explicitly focused on windows—even in the south. Window films are much more likely to earn you a rebate, depending of course on where you live. This is curious since awnings and shades stop the sun from ever hitting the window, while window films reflect back a portion of solar heat gain and generally aren't as efficient. More on window films in a minute.

To recap, the best shade solutions will . . .

- target windows on the south or west sides of the home that receive direct sun for three or more hours a day,
- be film or retractable awnings if local weather patterns (i.e., wind) could turn some awnings and shades into sails, and
- include trees because trees have a *much* longer "service life" than any man-made product and will achieve the highest savings in the long term.

Table 15: Estimated Savings from Various Energy Efficiency Upgrades Focused on Windows for a Home with Higher Than Average Cooling Bills

TYPICAL SCENARIO Exposed, single-pane windows	($820)					
GREENER SCENARIOS	**Initial cost less rebates and incentives**	**↑Annual energy costs↓**	**Annual energy savings**	**First year ROI**	**Payback period (in years)**	**10-year net savings**
Window film (professionally installed)	($725)	($722)	$98	14%	7.4	$255
Fixed awnings	($900)	($648)	$172	19%	5.2	$826
Adjustable awnings	($1,800)	($615)	$205	11%	8.8	$246
Exterior solar screens	($825)	($615)	$205	25%	4	$1,230
Shade trees	($700)	($672)*	$148*	n/a	7.3†	$776

Assumes 100 sq. ft. of south-facing windows.

*Since the real benefits of trees, even fast-growing ones, won't be realized for up to three years, this represents the average annual savings over ten years or roughly 18 percent. Keep in mind, however, that once shade trees reach a sufficient height and width, they can reduce home cooling costs by as much as 40 percent.

†Adjusted to compensate for growth.

Spotlight on Savings

Blocking or reflecting the sun's rays on exposed south- or west-facing windows by an average 60 percent can reduce cooling costs 21 percent, resulting in an average savings of $172 annually.

Insulating

Insulation is discussed under "Weatherizing Essentials" starting on page 41, but it warrants special mention here because adding insulation to an uninsulated or underinsulated attic—easily done in existing construction with flat ceilings—is so important for beating summer heat.

Most rooftops in the United States are dark-colored and unreflective, and according to the EPA these rooftops can reach temperatures of 150 to 190 degrees Fahrenheit under the summer sun—heat that can radiate into the attic space, superheating it, which then radiates heat into your living space. Under such conditions, cooling costs can increase by as much as 40 percent to make up for the heat gain.[20] Adding a thick barrier of insulation (between R-30 and R-49 depending on where you live) on the attic floor can be an affordable way to improve the inside temperature of your home and cut AC bills (see the sidebar, "Resources for Weatherizing Your Home," on page 42).

Reflecting

Products that reflect heat that reaches your home back toward its source are called radiant barriers, and they can prevent overheating of homes in sunny climates. Radiant barriers include window films, sheets of reflective material (usually aluminum) for use in attics, and even light-colored house paint.

Reflective Window Film. Inefficient, single-pane window glass has very little solar heat resistance. To improve window glass efficiency at a minimal cost, window film can be applied to the inside to reduce the amount of heat the window lets through. Typically, residential window film reflects 33 to 66 percent of solar heat gain.[21] This means it will block heat gain in the winter as well, so they are best for climates that have hot summers and mild winters. It is possible to install window film yourself, but to get the best performance and aesthetic result, hire a professional installer.

Attic Radiant Barrier. Attics in very warm and sunny climates could benefit greatly from a radiant heat barrier placed over attic insulation or stapled to the roof rafters. While thermal insulation *absorbs* radiant heat and slows down the rate at which it travels, the addition of a barrier that *reflects* heat before it reaches the insulation will provide more protection. When a highly reflective and low-emissive barrier is installed in the attic, as much as 97 percent of the heat radiated from the hot roof is reflected back toward the roof keeping the top surface of the insulation cooler and reducing the amount of heat that migrates through the insulation into the house. In hot climates, radiant barriers can lower a cooling bill by between 5 and 10 percent.[22]

Research radiant barriers carefully so you get the right kind for your application. For example, if you want to lay the barrier directly over insulation, you'll need a product that allows water vapor to pass through it.

To recap, the best reflective solutions will . . .
- reflect 50 percent or more of solar heat,
- meet qualification standards for available rebate programs,

Table 16: Estimated Savings from Various Energy Efficiency Upgrades Focused on the Attic for a Home with Higher Than Average Cooling Bills

TYPICAL SCENARIO Uninsulated attic	($820)					
GREENER SCENARIOS	Initial cost (installed) less rebates and incentives	↑Annual energy costs↓	Annual energy savings	First year ROI	Payback period (in years)	10-year net savings
R-30 loose-fill cellulose*	($790)	($697)	$123	16%	6.4	$443
R-38 open cell bio-based spray urethane foam*	($1,400)	($648)	$172	12%	8.1	$326
R-30 cellulose insulation* plus radiant barrier	($850)	($640)	$180	21%	407	$954

Assumes 800 sq. ft. attic floor.

* The specific type of insulation that is best for your situation depends upon a number of factors including whether your attic is vented or unvented, houses any heating and cooling equipment, and its construction. Always consult a professional before beginning a project.

- be installed by a professional to protect the integrity of the product and the location where it will be located, and
- be supplemented by tree-planting wherever solar impacted surfaces are within the reach of a tree's mature shade and native or climate-adapted species are used.

 Spotlight on Savings

In warm and sunny climates, adding the recommended amount of insulation to an uninsulated attic along with a radiant barrier can cut cooling costs by 22%, saving the typical homeowner $180 a year.

Ventilating

After you've taken steps to reduce solar heat gain, the next strategy is to use naturally cool air, in place of mechanically cooled air, when available, to save money.

When outside air temperatures are within or below your comfort range, natural ventilation through open windows can be used in lieu of air conditioning to keep a home comfortable, especially when planting leafy vegetation outside windows and adding fans.

Evapotranspiration It turns out trees and plants don't just provide beauty and shade. Leafy vegetation cools surrounding air due to the evaporation of moisture from plant leaves. Planting leafy shrubs and small trees outside windows will cool the air that passes through their branches and into your home.

Do Now and Save

- Create drafts. Open windows only 2–3 inches on one side of the home's second floor and on the opposite side of the home's first floor. This will create a draft that will suck hot air from lower floors to the upper floors and out of the open windows.
- Catch a breeze. Move your desk or bed out of the corner and next to a window where you can be cooled by natural breezes as you work or sleep.
- Dry clothes on an indoor clothesline. As the water evaporates from the clothes it will cool the air temperature.
- Don't heat your home every time you turn the lights on. Replace heat-producing incandescent bulbs with cooler CFLs.
- Heat-producing appliances, like the dryer, dishwasher and kitchen stove can raise a room's temperature by 10 degrees. Don't use the dryer, run the dishwasher at night with the no-heat dry setting selected, and cook outside or prepare "cool" meals such as salads and sandwiches.
- Close window treatments on southeast and southwest windows to cut down on heat gain.

Estimated annual savings: $57–$246

Fans Though mechanical, fans use a fraction of the energy that active cooling systems do and they are often used as part of a passive cooling system. Fans are very effective at expelling hot air, in the case of whole house fans, and cooling room occupants in the case of ceiling and portable fans. A room can feel four to six degrees cooler to its occupants just by turning a fan on in that room. Obviously, if you can feel cooler at a higher thermostat setting or without AC, you will reduce your cooling bills.

Active (Mechanical) Cooling

Active cooling systems are energy intensive—some more than others—and where appropriate, should be used to *supplement* passive cooling strategies, not to replace them altogether.

Central Air Conditioner

Central AC is an energy intensive way to cool a home, costing the typical homeowner in the Northeast $250 a month. With many other cooling systems to choose from with similar up-front costs yet lower operating costs, central air conditioners should be reserved for only the hottest and most humid climates.

If you're installing a central AC, your HVAC contractor should use a design load calculation to size the unit to your home. Even if you're replacing an existing unit, don't assume an identically sized unit is the correct way to go. Choose an Energy Star–approved model with a Seasonal Energy Efficiency Ratio (SEER) of 14 or better for good cooling efficiency and the best energy-cost savings.

Make sure the unit is shaded. Sun beating down on an AC unit for several hours a day forces it to work extra hard, as you can imagine. Nothing could make less sense than locating your AC in the sun, so find a shady location or make shade somehow.

Room Air Conditioners

For households that have a limited number of rooms that need cooling, using room air conditioners can allow you to create zones in the house that are air conditioned and others that are not, saving energy and money.

The cooling capacity of a room AC must be carefully chosen to match the size of the room. Too little capacity and the AC will not effectively cool the room. Too much capacity and the unit will cycle on and off frequently, wasting energy and failing to properly dehumidify a room. You can calculate what cooling capacity (BTUs) you need for individual rooms based on each room's square footage. Energystar.gov provides a chart for quick calculation at www.energystar.gov/index.cfm?c=roomac.pr_properly_sized.

Units that carry the Energy Star label are at least 10 percent more efficient than standard units. Compare units' EER (energy efficiency rating) as well. The higher the EER, the more efficient the air conditioner and the less it will cost to run.

Do Now and Save

- Add ceiling or floor fans to the most often occupied rooms. Any room with a fan will feel cooler at a higher thermostat setting.
- Set a programmable thermostat higher by five to seven degrees when you are away.
- Shade an outdoor unit with an awning, arbor or tree.
- Wear lightweight fabrics, short sleeves and short pants indoors so you can set your thermostat no lower than 78° Fahrenheit.
- Have a central AC system serviced by a professional every other year to keep it well-tuned.
- Repair and insulate duct work if needed.
- A room air conditioner filter should be checked for cleaning or replacing every couple months.

Estimated annual savings: $21–$184

Evaporative Cooler (a.k.a. Swamp Cooler)

If you live in a hot climate with low humidity, a swamp cooler is a low-cost alternative to refrigerated air conditioning. Swamp coolers use about a quarter of the energy of a comparably sized air conditioner, and due to their simple technology, they cost less as well.

Swamp coolers use evaporation to cool air: a motor pulls fresh outside air through the unit and across a water-soaked material; the air passing over the water is cooled by as much as 30 degrees and the cool air is blown into the room.

Consider a swamp cooler only if you will need to cool your home when the outside relative humidity is low (30 percent or less is ideal) since they are not effective at cooling humid air. Also, some larger swamp coolers use up to fifteen gallons of water per day, so in extremely drought-prone areas, they aren't the best choice.

The size of a swamp cooler is measured in cubic feet per minute or CFM. Whether you need a larger unit that can cool an entire house via a duct system, a medium-sized unit to cool a large open area or a smaller unit to cool an individual room, there is a simple calculation to determine the proper size. Take the cubic feet of space you want to cool (square footage of room(s) or house multiplied by ceiling height in feet), and then divide that number by two. The resulting number will give you the minimum CFM rating for a proper-sized swamp cooler. For example, if you want to cool a 250 square foot room with 8 foot ceilings, the calculation would look like this: $250 \times 8 \div 2 = 1{,}000$ CFM.

Try to stay away from systems with a bleed-off valve that purges water frequently to avoid mineral build-up. Such systems use an additional five gallons of water per hour. If mineral build-up is a legitimate concern for you, given your water quality, consider installing a whole-house filter or choose a more water-efficient dump pump which empties the cooler pan at regular intervals, but less frequently than bleed-off valves.

To recap, the best whole house mechanical cooling system will . . .

* supplement passive cooling techniques to reduce energy use and costs,
* be sized by a qualified HVAC contractor,
* be a heat pump in moderate climates with light cooling and heating loads,
* be a refrigerant AC in hot, humid climates or in hot, dry climates where water is scarce,
* be an evaporative cooler in hot, dry climates (30 percent or less relative humidity) where water is in good supply throughout the summer,
* be an Energy Star model with the highest SEER you can afford, if a refrigerant AC or heat pump, and
* come without a bleed-off valve, if a swamp cooler.

To recap, the best room by room mechanical cooling system will . . .

* include standard room air conditioners in humid climates or severely water-scarce regions,
* include evaporative coolers in dry climates (30 percent or less relative humidity) where water is in good supply throughout the summer,
* be sized using available online charts and equations (see page 94),
* be an Energy Star model with the highest EER you can afford, if a standard air conditioner, and
* come without a bleed-off valve, if a swamp cooler.

Air Source Heat Pump

An air source heat pump should really be called a heat/cool pump, because all heat pumps (which you read about under *Heating Systems on page 81*) have a cooling mode. In cooling mode, a heat pump takes heat from inside a home and trans-

> ## Resources for Finding Professional Contractors by Specialty
>
> www.acca.org/consumer/find-a-contractor/
> www.homeadvisor.com/category.Heating-Cooling.10211.html

fers it to the outside air through a condensing unit, leaving your home cooler.

Whether or not you should invest in a heat pump for cooling really depends on how much sense it makes for you as a heater, because a heat pump will save you the most money in heating mode (30 to 70 percent in a mild climate), but it will not save you that much in cooling mode. It might not save you *any* money in cooling mode, as a matter of fact, so its benefits as a heating unit need to justify the investment.

As stated earlier, a heat pump's Seasonal Energy Efficiency Ratio (SEER) measures cooling efficiency while the Heating Seasonal Performance Factor (HSPF) measures heating efficiency. An Energy Star–qualified appliance will have a minimum SEER and HSPF of 14 and 8, respectively. The higher the SEER and HSPF ratings, the more efficient the system and the more money you can save over the heat pump's service life.

 ## Spotlight on Savings

Compared to a conventional central air conditioner, a higher priced Energy Star central AC will cost $182 less to operate annually, offsetting the higher price point and paying for itself in just three cooling seasons, on average.

Table 17: Mechanical Cooling Systems Comparison

System	Initial cost less rebates and incentives	Annual operating costs	15-year lifecycle costs
3 ton central AC, 12 SEER	($2,469)	($597)	($11,424)
3 ton central AC, 14.5 SEER	($3,019)	($415)	($9,244)
3 ton electric air-source heat pump,* SEER 13	($3,000)	($708) [cooling mode only]	($13,620)
3 ton electric air-source heat pump,* SEER 16	($3,700)	($520) [cooling mode only]	($11,500)
Swamp cooler (6,000 CFM)	($700)	($366) [$252 energy + $114 water]	($6,190)
			10-year lifecycle costs
Room air conditioners (3 averaging 8,000 BTUs each), 9.8 EER	($1,017)	($420)	($5,217)
Room air conditioners (3 averaging 8,000 BTUs each), 10.8 EER	($1,047)	($381)	($4,857)

Source: www.energystar.gov

Assumes Southwest coast home.

* The annual energy cost savings when replacing an electric appliance (air conditioner and furnace) with a heat pump is greatest when operating in its heat mode. See table 14.

PART III: LIGHTING AND ELECTRONICS

At one time, lighting and electronics made up a tiny fraction of home energy use, but all that has changed. Now, combined, they can make up a third of home energy use—as much as space heating or water heating in some homes! That was unheard of thirty years ago, but today homes are bigger, requiring more light sockets; and there are few products for the home more popular than those that are electronic and have the ability to connect us and entertain us.

Although a single light bulb and laptop computer use very little energy, the cumulative effect of increased home lighting use and home electronics ownership makes this area one to pay attention to. If you don't, it'll cost you.

Lighting

Since 2001, residential energy used for lighting has almost doubled.[23] The increase can be attributed to a combination of factors including the inefficient use of light fixtures, energy inefficient bulbs and the fact that our homes have gotten bigger. The average U.S. household now has over 40 sockets for light bulbs[24], providing ample opportunity for improvements and savings. Improving lighting efficiency can save an average household over $200 a year, so what are you waiting for? Here are some bright ideas to save you money.

Lights Out

When it comes to wasting lighting energy, perhaps our biggest offense is leaving lights on long after their use is not required. Nowhere is this more evident than outside the home. Forgotten exterior lights, still burning long past day break, are far too common.

Indoor lights get left on too, especially in households with children. But the very children which are so bad at remembering to turn lights off—with a little work—can be turned into enthusiastic and effective light monitors. Making the task of turning lights off a fun activity for kids is the cheapest way to save energy, but not likely the most effective. Thankfully, many inexpensive products exist that regulate light automatically, ensuring that lights come on and stay on only when needed.

- **Photo sensors**, for outdoor applications, detect ambient light and turn lights on at dusk and off at dawn. From season to season they never have to be adjusted.

- **Motion sensors** are made for exterior and interior applications. Those made for exterior fixtures are less sensitive and turn lights on when something moves within its range of detection. When no one, or no thing, is around to cause motion, the light turns off. Obviously the intended purpose is lost if, say, the movement from a porch swing or blowing branch causes the light to remain on throughout most of the night, so before installing them, make sure no such predictable triggers exist.

- **Timers** allow users to control the exact time lights come on and off. Timers are available that replace standard switches or plug into an outlet: virtually any light can be put on a timer.

- **Occupancy sensors** turn lights on when people enter a room then automatically shut lights off once the room has emptied. Sensors using *passive infrared* technology detect heat energy and work best in rooms without high obstacles between it and the room's occupants. Another option, *ultrasonic* sensors, transmit pressure waves and work by sensing the change in waves based on motion in the room. They work fine when barriers are present. Sensors that utilize more than one technology perform better, but also cost more.

Since bulbs used in connection with photo sensors and timers—and some occupancy sensors—will generally remain on for several hours at a time, it's important to find brands that work with energy-efficient compact fluorescent lamps (CFLs). Recently, this has become much easier to do. And if the CFL will be used in an outdoor fixture, make sure it's rated for outdoor use—some CFLs don't work well in subfreezing applications.

Bulbs used in outdoor fixtures equipped with motion sensors generally come on infrequently and for short periods (one to two minutes typically), so they are made for compatibility with incandescent bulbs primarily. CFLs aren't practical in motion sensor light fixtures due to their warm-up period; and when subject to frequent on/off cycles CFLs can wear down much faster than normal.

Table 18: Estimated Savings from Automating Exterior Light Fixtures

TYPICAL SCENARIO Human-powered switches + incandescent bulbs (on 18/7)	($204)					
GREENER SCENARIOS	**Initial cost**	**↑Annual energy costs↓**	**Annual energy savings**	**First year ROI**	**Payback period (in years)**	**10-year net savings***
Photosensors + CFLs (on 14/7)	($55)	($34)	$170	309%	0.3	$1,730
Timers + CFLs (on 12/7)	($106)	($29)	$175	165%	0.6	$1,752
Motion sensors + incandescent bulbs (on 1/7)	($84)	($11)	$193	230%	0.4	$2,098

Assumes average 12 hours/day of darkness, four exterior sockets, 800 lumen-equivalent for bulb or lamp.

*Includes the net gain in bulb replacement costs.

Spotlight on Savings

Timers set to turn outdoor lights on at dark and off at first daylight can pay for themselves in the first year. Over ten years, they can save the average home $1,752 in energy costs.

Lighting with Renewable Energy

If you need to light an outside area continuously, consider solar lights. Solar lights get all their energy from the sunlight—a renewable and free resource!

Solar lights have either a built-in or separate solar panel made up of photovoltaic cells that convert sunlight into energy which is stored in the light's rechargeable battery. To work effectively, solar lights must receive plenty of sunlight throughout the day. As long as your site receives the hours of sunlight each day recommended by the light's manufacturer, solar lighting can work for you. Look for lights that use energy-efficient, long-lasting LED (light emitting diode) light bulbs to conserve the batteries' stored energy. Speaking of batteries, before you purchase solar lights, check the type of battery included. Since all batteries can be recharged only a limited number of times, you want to buy fixtures that come with Nickel Metal Hydride (NiMH) or Lithium Ion batteries that supply thousands of charges and hold a charge for a good long time. These batteries also have the advantage of being easily recyclable.

Also check for lumens (or light output). With most LED outdoor lights you will get low lumens compared to halogen or CFL floods. For example, the output of a two-light flood with 50w halogen bulbs is around 1,100 lumens. To match that output you'll probably need to spend over $100 on an LED solar light, but the long-term savings can be worth the investment since you won't be paying electricity to run it or spending money on replacement bulbs (see table 19).

Table 19: Comparison of Exterior Security Light That Is Continuously On for an Average 12 Hours Per Day

Type of light	Initial cost	Supplies	Annual operating cost	10-year lifecycle cost
Halogen spot with two 50 watts (1200 lumens equivalent)	($35)	($16) [bulb replacement every year]	($57)	($765)
LED solar security light (1200 lumens equivalent)	($189)	($17) [NiMH battery replacement every two years]	$0	($274)

Look for a solar light with a photo sensor feature, so lights come on at dusk and turn off at dawn.

If you can't or aren't willing to buy a quality solar light that will provide adequate illumination and last for several years, don't waste your money. Low quality solar lights just aren't worth it.

 Spotlight on Savings

A good quality, properly installed solar light that is used in lieu of halogen spots can save the typical household $50 a year, on average, over the life of the light.

Lighting High Use Areas

In a typical home, the rooms that use the most lighting energy, in order, are kitchens, living rooms and family rooms.[25] With lighting use in these rooms averaging four hours per day, assuming ten sockets between these three rooms, each with a 75W incandescent light bulb, the typical home would spend $142 annually just to light up three rooms. If those same ten sockets used 18W CFLs, energy costs would drop to $34—a savings of $108 in an average home.

Compact Fluorescent Lamp (CFL)

Love 'em or hate 'em, CFLs have won. In 2012 (earlier in California) incandescent bulbs between 40 and 100 watts began a nationwide phaseout pursuant to a Bush-era law. These bulbs won't disappear for a while yet; the phaseout won't be complete until sometime in 2014, and in this political climate, don't be surprised if the law ends up being challenged and repealed. But let's hope cooler heads prevail.

Phasing out the most energy inefficient light bulbs will save an estimated $13 billion in energy costs and prevent 100 million tons of carbon dioxide from entering the atmosphere.[26]

Despite their energy efficiency and long life, CFLs have their critics. If it's not their cost or their perceived cold light or confusion over light equivalency that consumers object to, then it's probably their mercury content. Seems everybody has a bone to pick with CFLs. Let's take it one thing at a time and see if we can learn to accept the squiggly things, reduce our greenhouse gas emissions and save some money!

Although the initial cost of CFLs is higher than that of incandescent bulbs, they use roughly one quarter of the energy and last up to 10 times as long as a standard light bulb, making them cost-effective both for the energy saved and the replacement costs avoided through their use.

Consumers who don't want the cool, white light they associate with fluorescent tube lights are in luck. CFLs come in a range of color temperatures, measured in degrees Kelvin (K). The warmer the light (orange/yellow) the lower the Kelvin: the cooler the light (whiter) the higher the Kelvin. A 2700K lamp closely matches the color of a standard incandescent bulb while a 5000K lamp closely matches daylight.

Table 20: Light Output Equivalency

Incandescent light bulbs	Minimum light output	Common CFLs
Watts	Lumens	Watts
40	450	9–13
60	800	13–15
75	1,100	18–25
100	1,600	23–30

Source: www.energystar.gov

In terms of light output (lumens), to estimate the CFL you want relative to the familiar light output of an incandescent bulb, refer to table 20.

Packaging for all light bulbs manufactured after January 1, 2012, must now contain lumen and Kelvin information.

When it comes to mercury in CFLs, yes, they all have it. Low-mercury light bulbs are available, but whether the mercury content in a typical CFL is 5.0 milligrams or 3.0 milligrams, we need to put that amount into perspective. It's not just mercury and CFLs that go together. Coal-fired power generation and mercury go together as well. For every 1 kwh of electricity produced by a coal-fired power plant, 0.0234 mg of mercury—and other pollutants—is emitted into the environment.[27] Thus, comparing two light-output equivalent bulbs—one being a 75-watt CFL and the other an 18-watt incandescent—the one that uses four times as much energy is also the one that will produce four times more pollution through its use. Here's the math:

$$\frac{8{,}000 \text{ hrs. of use} \times 75 \text{ w per hr.}}{1{,}000} \times 0.0234 = 14.04 \text{ mg mercury}$$

vs.

$$\frac{8{,}000 \text{ hrs. of use} \times 18 \text{ w per hr.}}{1{,}000} \times 0.0234 = 3.37 \text{ mg mercury}$$

At the end of a CFL's life the mercury inside can be captured for responsible disposal through CFL recycling programs, so replacing a 75w standard bulb with an 18w CFL *reduces* mercury emissions by 76 percent. Even if the mercury within a CFL were to escape, over its life it would still contribute 5.67 fewer milligrams per bulb of mercury into the environment.

So, are you ready to change some light bulbs? All fixtures that are continuously on for one hour or more each day should use an energy-efficient bulb to save energy. That can be either a CFL or a light emitting diode (LED) bulb (more on LEDs in a bit). For "short-use" lights that typically aren't on for more than five to fifteen minutes at a time—like those located in stairwells, closets, garages and half baths, for example—CFLs are not necessarily the best choice. Most CFLs have a slight warm-up period and their life is reduced when frequent switching occurs, so long-life incandescent bulbs or halogen bulbs may be preferable where lights are needed quickly and briefly. Halogen bulbs (which are only slightly more efficient than incandescents) get very hot, however, and should not be used where there is a risk they could burn someone or ignite textiles.

Light Emitting Diodes (LEDs)

The future of household lighting could soon be energy-efficient LED light bulbs. LEDs that can replace standard light bulbs and CFLs are already lining shelves at home improvement centers. LEDs give off roughly the same lumens per watt as CFLs making them comparable in efficiency, but they can last up to five times as long (see table 21). A 25,000-hour life, as many LEDs boast, means avoiding lots of bulb replacements, adding up to significant savings (see table 22).

Table 21: Efficiency of Lighting from Least to Most

Technology	Typical lumens per watt (lm/W) in practical use situations	Life span in hours
Incandescent	12–15	1,000
Halogen	16–18	2,000
CFL	60–70	8,000–10,000
LED	40–60*	25,000–50,000

Source: www.eleekinc.com/eleekchart.pdf

*This is rapidly improving with technological advancements.

One important note about lumens and LEDs: because LEDs shine light in one direction, compared to conventional alternatives that shine light out to the sides, there is actually more "delivered light" from a 600 lumen LED than from either a 600 lumen CFL or incandescent. CFLs and standard bulbs can lose 30 percent of their light output to the fixture that houses them. This means that you can usually choose fewer lumens when choosing an LED without compromising on the amount of light that actually reaches the surface or area you want to illuminate.[28]

The big drawback to LEDs is their initial cost—about $40 for a 12-watt bulb (a 60-watt equivalent replacement). But high LED prices are expected to fall dramatically in just the next couple years.

To recap, the best light bulbs will . . .
- be CFLs or LEDs when they are on continuously for one hour a day or more, or
- be incandescents or halogen bulbs that use the lowest watts necessary for the application when the light is only used for minutes, not hours, during a day, but
- never be a halogen if the bulb could accidently contact a person's skin or a flammable home product.

Table 22: Estimated Savings Through Lighting Upgrades

TYPICAL SCENARIO Thirty-three 75w incandescent bulbs + seven 18w CFLs	($370)					
GREENER SCENARIOS	Initial purchase price	↑Annual energy costs↓	Annual energy savings	First year ROI	Payback period (in years)	10-year net savings*
Fifteen 18w CFLs, twenty-five 60w incandescents	($130)	($251)	$119	92%	1.1	$1,055
Thirty 15w CFLs, ten 60W incandescents	($190)	($149)	$221	116%	0.9	$2,082
Thirty 15w CFLs, six 60W incandescents, four 12w LEDs	($346)	($122)	$248	72%	1.4	$2,244

Assumes 40 lamps/bulbs per average household. Average hours in use per day, three.

*Includes the net gain or loss from replacement bulbs.

 Spotlight on Savings

When increasing the number of total energy-efficient CFLs in a home from 17.5 percent of all lighting to 75 percent of all lighting, the average home can save $221 annually in electricity costs.

Electronics

All one has to do is look around to see firsthand the great amassing of consumer electronic (CE) products in our lives. From MP3 players to Smartphones to e-readers to tablet computers to digital cameras, their pings and rings are now a spon-

taneous fixture in the auditory landscape. Although handheld
devices are the latest craze, consumer electronics for the home
are just as popular—including laptops, computers, monitors,
printers, multifunction devices, network devices, speakers,
HDTVs, gaming consoles, Blu-ray players, set-top boxes, DVRs,
DVD players and so on.

The average U.S. household spent $961 on CEs in 2011 and
has 24 CE products to show for it, according to the 14th Annual
CE Ownership and Market Potential Study conducted by the
Consumer Electronics Association. On top of that, keeping two
dozen CE products charged and operational consumes around
$183 to $264 per household.[29]

Due to the proliferation of CEs in the home, smart purchasing decisions and better use habits can save the consumer lots
of money over the lifespan of these products.

> According to the Consumer Electronics Association, CEs
> consumed 13.2 percent of residential electricity, with TVs,
> computers and set-top boxes for cable and satellite services
> accounting for the largest share of residential consumer
> electronics energy consumption.[30]

Ninety-Nine Percent of U.S. Households Have at Least One

According to Neilson Media, the average home today has more
TV sets than people living there. The average home has 2.9 TV
sets, while the average household is made up of only 2.3 people. This fact, combined with the trend in larger sets, the need
for set-top boxes and the presence of energy-sucking transformers (see Energy "Vampires" on page 117), has turned TV
sets into formidable energy consumers.

Tube TVs Lose Their Luster

Many conventional cathode-ray tube (CRT) sets are aging and their owners are saving up to purchase a more contemporary flat-panel display TV. However, before you rush to get rid of a fully functional CRT set, consider that many techies say that the technologies behind flat-panel televisions—plasma and liquid crystal display (LCD)—don't deliver pictures as clearly as traditional tube TVs do—though they are getting closer. CRT sets also use less energy than either of the newer technologies. A flat-panel TV will cost up to three times as much to operate. That said, consumers have voted with their wallets and seem to want the lighter and slimmer flat-panel displays.

If you are one of the rare few who both want a new TV and want it to use CRT technology, you're running out of time. As demand slips away for these sets, they are disappearing. There are however, likely to be many used CRT sets for sale for years to come through print and online classified ads. Just don't buy a tube TV that has aged to the point it will soon need a replacement tube—these are disappearing too!

When evaluating a used tube TV you want to see a sharply focused and bright picture with no bleeding at the edges within a minute of the TV warming up. CRTs fail slowly, so if the picture looks good today, it still probably has several good years left.

Flat Is In

In terms of picture quality and product life span, LCD and plasma TVs are very close in performance today, but when it comes to factors that impact the environment, LCDs have the clear advantage over plasmas: LCDs require substantially less power to operate than plasmas of comparable size, emit no radiation, and are much lighter than plasma TVs making the environmental impacts from shipping LCDs less.

When looking for a flat screen TV, there are two temptations to avoid: a sale on a plasma TV that makes it less expensive than an LCD, and buying a grotesquely large TV (a matter of opinion perhaps). The slight savings on that new plasma will quickly disappear due to its higher operating costs. And while tempting to upsize to a 52" set for a mere $50 more, you'll also pay for that decision in higher operating costs; and additionally, your viewing experience can suffer with a larger TV unless you have an adequately large room that can put sufficient distance between you and the screen.

There's a whole "science" to correctly matching screen size and viewing distance. You can easily find online calculators to assist you, but most of them calculate "optimal" distance for home theatre viewing, when you want to be immersed in the picture. For everyday TV watching and running occasional videos, figure on a viewing distance that is equal to three to four screen widths (see table 23).

Remember, manufacturers and retailers have an interest in selling you a larger, more expensive TV, so viewing distances are often underestimated to justify oversized screens for typically-sized rooms. In reality, very few homes have rooms large enough to accommodate a TV over 46 inches.

For some of the highest energy savings, purchase a set that's earned the Energy Star label and are, on average, over 40 percent more energy efficient than standard models. The most energy-efficient LCD TVs use LEDs, as opposed to fluorescent

Table 23: Matching Viewing Distance and Screen Size

Viewing distance in feet	Optimum screen size in inches
6.25–10	26 to 32
8.75–12.67	37 to 40
10–14.66	42 to 46
12.50–18.67	52 to 58

Assumes high-resolution TV with a 16:9 aspect ratio.

(CCFL) backlights. They are sometimes just referred to as LED TVs, and choosing one over a standard LCD could save you an additional $20 per year in operating costs.

To recap, the best TV is . . .

- a tube TV wherever still available if your budget is under $100,
- an Energy Star–qualified LED TV among flat screen options, and
- sized using table 23 as a guide if it will be used primarily for normal TV viewing.

 Spotlight on Savings

Yearly, a moderately-sized Energy Star LED TV will cost $133 less to run than a large plasma TV and $70 less to run than a large LCD TV in homes averaging eight hours of TV viewing a day.

Table 24: TV Set Comparison

TV type	Initial cost	Annual operating cost	20-year lifecycle costs
50" Plasma	($1,199)	($170)	($4,599)
55" LCD	($949)	($107)	($3,089)
40" Energy Star LCD	($499)	($60)	($1,699)
40" Energy Star LED	($699)	($37)	($1,439)
			10-year lifecycle costs
28" used CRT	($60)	($76)	($820)

Assumes 8 hours of TV per day per household.*

---

* According to Nielson Media's 2011 report on trends in media viewing, the average American watched 5 hours of TV a day in Q4 2010. Since the average household contains 2.3 people, and viewing by individual members can occur on different sets at different times, we estimate that aggregate TV viewing from multiple TVs totals 8 hours out of each day in the average U.S. home.

Home Computing

If there's one thing about computers you can count on, it's that they won't last long. It's not that they'll stop functioning in record time, it's that their technology, in a matter of a few years, will lag so far behind the newest generation's that consumers will feel that they need a new computer to keep up with the trend in faster, more versatile and more powerful computers. The impermanence of these machines is sometimes, cynically, called "planned obsolescence." Whether it's planned or simply inherent, manufacturers happily exploit it to create demand for new versions of old, still usable machines.

The reality that the average computer has a practical lifespan of only three to five years creates two problems. First, it compels us to spend money on new computers perpetually; and second, computers are loaded with toxic components that can pollute the environment if they are disposed of improperly. If you don't want to get caught up in a cycle of paying for and disposing of a computer every five years, consider whether you really need one at all. Can you use a library computer or share one to diffuse its impact? If the answer is no, keep reading for some pointers on getting the best computer for you and the environment; and if you'll be replacing an existing computer to make room for a new one, you'll need to deal with your old computer in an eco-responsible way (see the sidebar, "Resources for Donating or Recycling an Old Computer," on page 115).

Don't Shy Away From Refurbished

Refurbished can be a scary word. Most consumers assume that refurbished computers are older computers, and some are; but many refurbished computers, as reported by Gizmodo.com, were used for less than 30 days by the original consumer and returned, or are new computers just off the assembly line that had slight defects. In both cases, the computers have undergone a thorough inspection, had any detected problems fixed and are as good as new.

Websites like www.bestbuy.com allow you to compare different computers side by side, so use this feature to compare a refurbished computer to a new one and then make your decision. Refurbished computers from a reputable dealer will come with a warranty that is usually as good as the warranty on a new computer (one year). If this doesn't ease your mind, opt for the extended warranty—you'll still come out ahead since a refurbished computer is around 25 to 35 percent cheaper than a new one.

Older refurbished computers (last year's models) will be the best deal, and despite not being on par with a new computer in all respects, one may be plenty of computer for you, so be realistic about your needs. Paying extra cash for a new pumped up computer with massive memory, speed and graphics when you don't really need all those bells and whistles is a waste of your money and a perfectly good refurbished computer.

Do Now and Save

- Set power management features to automatically power down your computer and monitor or laptop during periods of inactivity to save energy. For instructions on enabling your operating system's power management go to www.energystar.gov/index.cfm?c=power_mgt.pr_power_mgt_users.
- Don't use a screen saver: They use extra energy to run and can prevent your computer from going into sleep mode. Modern CRT monitors and LCD displays aren't at risk of burn-in screen damage.
- Dim your screen. A computer screen on the brightest setting uses more energy.
- Plug your computer and its peripherals (printer, scanner, etc.) into a single power strip and shut off the power strip whenever the machines will be inactive for hours at a time.
- Install antivirus software. Undetected viruses and spyware running on your computer use extra energy and put your hard drive at risk. Antivirus software is often available for free from your ISP.

Estimated annual savings: $2–$227

> ### Resources for Donating or Recycling an Old Computer
>
> www.techsoup.org
> www.epa.gov/osw/conserve/materials/ecycling/donate.htm
> www.electronicstakeback.com

Reward Responsibility

Computers vary greatly not only in energy efficiency but also in materials used; and computer manufacturers vary in terms of environmental performance and their commitment to take end-of-life responsibility for the toxic and recyclable components in their hardware and machines. To find the most earth-friendly manufacturers and computers, visit www.electronicstakeback.com and follow their link to "tools for purchasers."

Taking a little extra time to find a computer (or any electronic product) that is part of a manufacturer-sponsored take-back program, for example, can save you money. In many communities, the closest computer recycling business may charge a fee to take an old computer off your hands, while many take-back producers do so for free.

Compact Computing

In this age of powerful laptops (with better track pads) and external storage devices and monitors, the desktop (tower) computer may be much more computer than many of us need. If you're still using a desktop computer, maybe it's time to take another look at laptop computers to see if one could become your primary computer. Laptops are 70 to 90 percent more energy efficient than desktop computers and they also use less metal and plastic than a desktop making them more material-efficient as well. Energy Star–labeled laptops have the most energy–efficient designs.

And computers just keep getting smaller. Tablet computers provide the latest opportunity to compact our computer. They are no substitute for a desktop, but they could replace a laptop for the user who does more web surfing and light computing.

To recap, the best computer will . . .
- be refurbished, preferably,
- have the least components (smallest) while still meeting your computing needs,
- be both Energy Star compliant and have a Bronze, Silver or Gold rating from EPEAT, and
- come from a manufacturer that will take back the computer at the end of its life for refurbishing or recycling.

Table 25: Computer Comparison

Type of computer	Initial cost	Annual operating costs	4-year lifecycle costs
Standard desktop computer with 23" LED monitor	($659)	($39)	($815)
Energy Star all-in-one desktop PC with 23" HD display	($775)	($22)	($863)
Energy Star 15.6" laptop computer	($549)	($5)	($569)
Tablet computer	($380)	($5)	($400)

Assumes computer is active for 6 hours per day, asleep for 3.5 hours per day, off for 14.5 hours per day.

 Spotlight on Savings

When downsizing from a desktop with a 23" display to a more energy-efficient laptop with a 15.6" display, you can save $294 over the life of the product.

Electronic waste, including computers, cells phones and TV sets, is the fastest growing component of municipal solid waste worldwide.[31]

Energy "Vampires"

If a machine hums, glows or feels warm to the touch even when turned off it's an indication that transformers are at work, keeping the machine in a constant ready, or standby, mode. Today, many consumer electronic products have transformers that suck energy from the power grid 24/7—as long as the machine is plugged into a viable electric socket. When you add up all the standby power losses from dozens of machines, appliances and gadgets—up to 35 for households with teens[32]—the impact isn't small: according to the Department of Energy, 75 percent of the electricity used to power home electronics is consumed while the products are turned off!

With the number of consumer products utilizing transformers expected to keep growing, they stand to consume an increasing share of household energy use and waste more energy dollars—unless consumers do two things: First, when buying new electronic appliances, choose products displaying the Energy Star label, indicating the use of low-voltage transformers that ensure low standby power use—in most cases one watt or

---

Do Now and Save

- Unplug wall chargers for rechargeable devices if not actively charging (e.g., power tools, cell phone, MP3 player, electric toothbrush, shaver, digital camera, handheld vacuum, etc.)
- Unplug appliances you aren't using (e.g., microwave, toaster, bread machine, coffee maker, etc.)

Estimated Annual Savings: $29

less. For products not included in the Energy Star program, the Federal Energy Management Program (FEMP) maintains a database of low standby power products at www.standby.lbl.gov/archives/1w-products.html. Second, implement the use of power strips as described below.

Electric power for appliances, including standby power when appliances are not being used, is the fastest growing form of energy consumed within households.[33]

Use Power Strips

Wherever you have energy users grouped together, for example within a home entertainment system or home office, plug equipment into a single power strip that is easy to access. Once items are grouped onto a power strip, depending on the power strip you choose, you can cut power to all connected or machines with the flip of a switch, or cut power to designated machines.

The most economical power strips (~$10) provide an on/off switch to supply or cut off power to any machine plugged into it. For a little more money (~$40), you can purchase power strips that have both "uncontrolled" outlets for devices that must be continuously powered (e.g., modems, routers, DVRs, set-top converter boxes, and clocks) and "controlled" outlets for devices that don't need to be powered while not in use. When the power switch is flipped off, only the controlled outlets will lose power until the switch is turned back on.

The most expensive power strips (~$90) "sense" when to turn off the strip. There's the kind that senses when the main machine, like a computer, has been turned off, and it automatically turns off the entire strip to which peripheral machines like printers and scanners are plugged into. There's also the kind that detect room occupancy and turn off the strip when the room is empty. The latter isn't ideal since the strip will remain on even if machines aren't being used as long as people are in the same room—and the opposite can happen as well. These "smart" power strips can save you the most money because they don't rely on you to flip the switch. However, due to the high price tag, they can take three times as long to pay for themselves compared to a standard power strip.

Power strips are not recommended for appliances with high power loads—plug that stuff directly into a wall outlet. They are also not recommended for things like set-top boxes and DVRs that need to download information from a service at regular intervals. Depending on your computing needs it may not be advised to plug modems and routers into them either.

Depending on how many machines you hook up and their respective standby power losses, you could save from $25 to $132 a year from the use of power strips.

 ## Spotlight on Savings

When hooking up your home media and office machines to power strips, the average household can save up to $132 from reduced standby power losses.

Setting Limits

Kids and adults spend more leisure time indoors these days than in previous years, and much of that time is spent watching TV and working or playing on computers and handheld devices.

A 2007 survey of youth risk behaviors conducted by the Centers for Disease Control found that one out of four students in the Untied States spends three or more hours out of each school day playing a video or computer game or using a computer for something that is not school work.[34]

According to the American Time Use Survey, the leisure activity that occupies the most time out of an average person's day is watching TV, while Americans spend the least time participating in sports, exercise and recreation. Specifically, according to Nielson Media Research, the average American watches nearly five hours of video a day—98 percent of that on a traditional TV, but with mobile devices and the Internet, most Americans can watch video whenever and wherever they want;[35] so get ready for the time that Americans spend sitting and staring at a screen to continue to grow.

All those hours "turned on" consume energy of course, but there are also unhealthy side effects. A study printed in the *Journal of the American College of Cardiology* suggests that sitting—which most of us do to watch TV and work/play on the computer—is bad for our health. The study found a link between prolonged sitting and an increased likelihood of having a heart attack, stroke, or other serious cardiovascular problem. The antidote to a life of marathon sit-ins at a screen is not simply to squeeze in a trip to the gym or playground here and there: to counter the ill effects of sitting, we need to sit less, says the study.[36] In the words of the First Lady, "Let's move!" Pull your kids and yourself away from the screen and just move.

The typical U.S. eight- to eighteen-year-old lives in a household equipped with three TV sets, three video players, three radios, three PDMPs (for example, an iPod or other MP3 device), two video game consoles and a personal computer.[37]

Install Parental-Control Software

A variety of different software programs are available that enable parents to control when and for how long their children can use the computer or be on the Internet. When the session expires, the computer will be blocked for that user until the next permitted session comes around. Except for basic time management software, most parental-control software will also allow you to restrict your child's access to certain websites and give you access to activity logs letting you know where they've been online. Check reviews and compare prices at a website like www.pcmag.com before deciding on a product.

Do Now and Save

- Try and limit leisure screen time (TV, computer, mobile devices) to no more than two hours per day per child in your household. (Recommended by the American Academy of Pediatrics.)
- Avoid putting a computer or TV in a child's bedroom or part of the home where supervision will be difficult.
- Schedule at least one or two afternoon activities with your family per week where exercise, culture or nature—not technology and not consumerism—is the focus.

Estimated Annual Savings: Priceless

GETTING FROM HERE TO THERE WITHOUT BREAKING THE BANK

On the whole, Americans love their cars . . . maybe a little too much. Americans own more cars, take more trips by car, and drive more miles per capita than any other industrialized nation. Some would say that our choice of what, how often, and how far we drive has nothing do with love but, rather, necessity. There are doubtless occasions when a vehicle is necessary, but let's face it, there's plenty of unnecessary driving going on out of choice and habit. We have come to either prefer or depend on the automobile to the gross exclusion of other alternatives even when that dependence doesn't make logistical or financial sense—and despite the grave risks and impacts of driving.

The environmental, societal, and personal impacts of our addiction to the automobile aren't pretty. For starters, our driving addiction feeds sprawl, intensifies congestion, uses up nonrenewable resources faster, adds tremendously to greenhouse gas emissions, degrades air quality, contributes to stress, and facilitates a sedentary lifestyle.

Cars are also expensive: Transportation accounts for 16 percent of a typical person's annual expenditures.[1] Only housing expenses take a bigger bite out of our annual budget. Cars put us in debt, divert needed funds away from other necessities, and thwart our ability to save and invest. The good news is, many uses of the car can be reduced or replaced, and if you're successful at seizing these opportunities your bank account can surge!

If you currently own a car, this chapter will show you how to use it less and use it wisely to save you hundreds or even thousands of dollars each year. Better yet, you may learn you don't need to own a car: a decision that can save the typical person $35,243 over five years.* Now that's more than pocket change!

> Transportation accounts for over two-thirds of the oil used in this country[2] and for nearly a third of all greenhouse gas emissions annually.[3]

REDUCING MILES DRIVEN

Sure, the conventional car itself is a polluting, greenhouse gas-emitting machine, but the real reason it is inflicting so much damage to our environment and quality of life is due to the huge number of miles driven. Between 1981 and 2007, the number of miles Americans drove increased every year. In 2008 and 2009, for the first time in twenty-seven years, the number of miles driven by Americans declined from the previous year.[4] Only months of record-high gas prices and a slowing economy in 2008 broke the 27-year swell. Regardless of the reasons for the first decline in miles driven, year-over-year, in almost three decades, it proves Americans *can* drive less when they put their minds to it.

---

* This figure is based on Edmunds.com's *True Cost to Own* calculations for the 2012 Toyota Camry sedan, the bestselling passenger car in America in 2010.

Driving less than you've become accustomed will be an adjustment, of course, but one well worth pursuing. Driving less can improve several areas of your life at once: it's an opportunity to reduce costly expenditures, relieve stress, improve fitness and gain time.

The growing reliance on the private car is the most significant contributing factor to rising energy consumption for transportation.[5]

Use Human-Powered "Transportation"

There's no cleaner or cheaper way to get around than by using people power—walking, biking, skateboarding, skating, scooting or rolling, for example. The extent of our individual abilities varies of course, but U.S. Census figures suggest that 95 percent of Americans over the age of fifteen are able enough to get themselves around without assistance.[6] Considering, it's a little unbelievable that although a significant portion of total personal travel consists of shorter trips, these trips are dominated by personal vehicles. On average, 6.7 out of every ten short trips taken in the United States take place in personal vehicles, even though in urban areas, 28 percent of trips are one mile or less, 44 percent are two miles or less and 53 percent are three miles or less—distances that can be covered on foot or by bike or a number of other ways not involving a car. Even in non-urban areas, 30 percent of all trips are two miles or less.[7]

Walking and riding a bike are the two most popular people-powered ways of getting around, but can they really be viable means of traveling for the average person? Yes—as long as your doctor agrees. Walking is a no-brainer, requiring little more than a comfortable pair of shoes, weather-appropriate clothing and something in which to carry personal effects.

Cycling requires more of a commitment, but also gives us much more range.

Bike Logic

There are lots of reasons one might be intimidated by biking, including the thought of sharing the road with bigger, faster vehicles or getting stranded with a flat tire or busted chain. It's good to be a little scared. Those that take off for their first city bike ride expecting it to be all thrills and chills will put not only themselves at risk, but others on the road as well. Biking on city roads requires knowledge and confidence. There are rules of the road and bike maintenance that must be learned and followed to stay safe and mobile; and confidence is what makes you able to relax and have fun!

The learning curve for becoming a good rider is short for most people and the pay-off is huge, so if you're able-bodied follow these four recommendations and start looking forward to better fitness and a fatter wallet!

1. Learn. Start by contacting your Department of Transportation or a local bike league for a copy of local and state laws and regulations for cyclists, but don't stop there; use the library and the web to collect sage advice from seasoned bike commuters who have been around the block several thousand times! (See sidebar, "Resources for Easier Biking," on page 127.)

2. Practice. Skill and confidence should both be mastered before riding on streets with vehicle traffic. If you've never ridden a bike before, begin by riding on off-street bike paths. Next, take short rides on secondary roads, starting with right turns only. Then add some left turns and go a few more blocks than you did the day before. Gaining confidence on the bike won't take long for most people, but it's imperative to have it before you peddle alongside traffic.

3. Be prepared. Bike trips need planning. You'll need to map your route (cyclists can have more or less options than drivers—either way you'll want the safest route), dress for the weather and have the necessary gear to fix a tire, chain or other equipment and to carry personal effects or purchases.

4. Be patient. Don't give up just because it's a little more work, because it's a whole heck of a lot more fun than driving once you get the hang of it!

Almost one third of Americans lead sedentary lives without engaging in any physical activity, and almost another one third are not regularly active.[8]

Covering the Distance

Many people think it will take too long to bike or walk, even to relatively close destinations. Well, it only takes the average person about fifteen minutes to walk one mile, or bike three miles, so where destinations fall within this range, non-motorized transportation is a viable choice. It's also a viable choice for longer distances, but starting out gradually is a good idea for anyone getting used to the idea of getting around under their own power.

When it comes to the speediness of a car to get us somewhere, compared to a bicycle or our own two feet, the car will often win, but not always. Getting from point A to point B by car can be frustratingly delayed due to routine occurrences such as traffic jams, red lights, road construction, refueling or lack of parking. Time yourself—door to door—the next time you get in the car to make a short trip. You may be surprised by the result. Even if riding a bicycle or walking somewhere takes longer, if it only takes five to fifteen extra minutes, that's not a lot of time. And there's this to keep in mind: when taking your time to get someplace, you just might find that the journey is more interesting than the destination.

Even when our legs or a bike could get us safely to our destination, sometimes we opt for a car due to its passenger seating, cargo space or weather conditions outside. When we're traveling in numbers, a backpack or bike isn't sufficient to carry our load, or the weather is damp or cold, climbing into a vehicle may just be the best choice. Biking and walking don't have to replace short car trips in every case to make a difference. That said, for the determined eco-traveler, there's all kinds of gear in the marketplace for making trips on foot and by bike safer and more comfortable in bad weather; and in the case of biking, there's also gear for towing kids, pets or heavy stuff (see sidebar, "Resources for Easier Biking").

Resources for Easier Biking

Biking to work tips:
www.activetrans.org/tricks-tips
www.commutebybike.com/cats/commuting-101

Bicycle trailers for kids, cargo and pets:
www.bicycletrailers.com
www.cycletote.com

LED safety vest:
www.ledtronics.com

Map your ride:
www.mapmyride.com

Folding bikes for bike/transit commuters:
www.commuterbikestore.com

Workhorse bikes and gear:
www.bikesatwork.com
www.worksmancycles.com

Find Others Going Your Way

Sadly, single occupancy vehicles rule the road! A whopping 76 percent of commuters drive alone to work each day, which translates to 105,476,000 single-driver commuter cars clogging roads and burning unnecessary fuel each day across America.[9] This certainly contributes to the unbearable traffic congestion plaguing most major cities, the pressure to expand freeways and soaring vehicle emissions.

All this single occupancy driving also drives up personal expenditures for transportation energy. The average household earning between $30K and $50K annually spends $3,657 on fuel alone (households earning over $50K annually spend only slightly more)[10]—a figure that could be substantially reduced by taking advantage of available public transportation or carpooling with others. If not every day, at least as often as you can make it happen.

Trade the Freeway for Free Time

Less than 3 percent of all trips nationwide are transit trips according to the American Public Transportation Association (APTA). Part of this reason is the fact that good public transit is not available to everyone. But even in cities where public transportation options are extensive, with the exception of New York City, the majority of residents in those cities rely on means other than public transportation to get to work.[11]

It may not be easy to break the habit of a personal vehicle that provides on demand transportation and the flexibility to come and go as you please, but trading a personal vehicle for public transportation isn't a hardship—it's just different—and different in several good ways: under- and above-ground trains never encounter traffic, statistically mass transit is a safer way to travel and public transit costs commuters a fraction of what driving costs. In addition, letting someone else do the driving reclaims the time you previously spent with your hands on the wheel and eyes on the road. Having this extra time and free-dom to read, knit, text, Tweet, sleep or whatever it is you like to do, is one of public transportation's best rewards. And as for the financial rewards: The APTA's report on public transporta-tion benefits estimates that a typical person who drives to work and pays for parking can save an average $8,400 per year by taking public transportation instead of driving. That's one heck of an incentive!

Resources for Public Transport

Plan a transit trip:
www.maps.google.com/help/maps/transit

Book a taxi from your mobile phone or the Web:
www.flywheelnow.com
www.taximagic.com

Fill the Seats

When public transit isn't an option, carpooling or ride sharing could be the next best thing. Carpooling isn't just for job com-muters, though. It's an ideal solution for many single occupan-cy trips to places people drive on a regular basis including church, school, the health club, etc. It also works for any outing that draws large crowds, such as a sporting event or concert taking place at a large arena. Every time you drive with a car buddy instead of going solo, you save money, and everyone in the car reduces their personal carbon footprint.

Like public transportation, ride sharing gives you time-off from being behind the wheel, and those extra minutes you get

Each year, public transportation use saves the United States 4.2 billion gallons of gasoline.[12]

back to be productive in other ways can be a real gift to busy people. But ride sharing offers us something that public transportation doesn't, necessarily. It's a way to meet others with common interests. Carpools in the south are called "hook-ups" and how appropriate that is: Carpools are indeed an opportunity to hook up with people who work for the same company, attend the same church, belong to the same gym and so on.

Carpooling can also get you to your destination faster if your route includes High Occupancy Vehicle lanes that allow your vehicle to travel in a less congested, faster moving lane. Even without HOV lanes, if you are sitting in a car with three others, that's three less cars on the road, and that can also allow traffic to move more freely along your route, especially in cities where ride sharing is really catching on.

Finding others from your neighborhood who are going your way has been helped by a number of websites that allow travelers to find each other (see sidebar, "Resources for Finding Car Buddies").

Resources for Finding Car Buddies

www.ridebuzz.org
www.zimride.com
www.erideshare.com

Work from Home (Telecommute)

If you can arrange it with your employer, telecommute at least one workday per week. Nothing reduces the emissions, expenses and aggravations of commuting like avoiding it entirely! If you think such a setup is a long shot, don't be so sure: Telecommuting is becoming more accepted by employers in the face of studies like the one published in the *Journal of Applied Psychology* that found that allowing employees to work from home increases morale and job satisfaction; it also lowers employee stress and turnover.[13]

And what's good for the employee is good for the employer and environment. According to the Telework Research Network, U.S. companies could collectively increase their bottom lines by between $525 and $665 billion a year as a result of savings in real estate, absenteeism, turnover, and increased productivity. In several real-world cases, worker productivity has increased 20 to 45 percent due to telecommuting. Taking millions of workers out of the commuter pool would substantially reduce our dependence on oil and cut greenhouse gas emissions.

Whatever you spend on a daily commute, be it for driving or public transportation, it becomes money in the bank if you never have to leave the house. But working from home isn't entirely free, so if saving money is your primary goal, weigh the costs of working from home with the savings in fuel and vehicle maintenance or public transit fare.

The Work from Home Trade-Off

Being able to go to work in your pajamas may be what some consider the best part of working from home, but it can also save you money in more ways than one: if you are a car commuter, saving on gas—and tolls and parking if they are part of your daily commute—is just the beginning. Driving fewer miles can lower insurance rates if the reduced mileage is significant enough to bump you to a lower bracket. And expenditures related to vehicle maintenance will go down too. The trade-off is that you will need a home office—the expense of which may or may not be covered by your employer.

What will you realistically need to furnish a basic home office? You can probably get by with a laptop computer, cell phone, Internet connection, desk, chair and multifunction printer. Staring with nothing, it could cost you around $1,150 to start up a home office and $150 a month for the cell phone plan and Internet connection. However, if you already have an Internet connection at home—plus a personal computer and cell phone that you are willing to use for work—you could spend as little as $360 for a basic multifunction printer and some used furniture. Furthermore, you may be able to take a tax deduction for your home office that will lower your tax liability. (Consult a tax attorney to find out the best way to go about it.)

As long as the off-set commuting expenses are higher than what you pay out of pocket to be able to work from home, telecommuting is not just a part of the solution to overcrowded roads and global warming pollution, it's part savings plan! Of course if you can get your employer to pay for your home office expenses then you are really coming out ahead.

In 2010, the average commuter spent thirty-four hours sitting in traffic—at a cost of $713 in lost fuel and productivity.[14]

Better Manage Trips

The average person takes more than sixteen non-work-related trips every week. The bulk of the average driver's weekly trips are used for shopping, personal business, and social and recreational appointments, with an average trip length of eight miles.[15] Work routes and schedules are usually not that flexible, but when it comes to non-work-related trips like visiting friends, going to the gym, seeing the doctor or taking care of shopping and errands, we have more control over when and how we go. Using this control wisely can be the difference between squandering time and resources or saving them up.

Plan Ahead and Consolidate Trips

If driving is unavoidable, ideally, schedule appointments, errands and shopping trips for the week in a way that minimizes driving. You'll save time, mileage and money if you can plan trips to take place within a single afternoon. If car trips cannot be limited to a single day each week, so be it, but there is a compromise that benefits the person who needs to get some things done *and* the planet that is choking on car fumes. The compromise exists somewhere between driving back and forth between your home and points all over the city each day and making a circle around the city once or twice a week to cover those points with greater efficiency.

Consider someone who makes four separate trips in a day, returning home after each one: 3.6 roundtrip (RT) miles to the library; 10.2 RT miles to meet a friend for mid-morning coffee; 6.7 RT miles to make an afternoon dentist appointment; and finally, 3.5 RT miles to the grocery store before dinner. That's a total of twenty-four miles and approximately eighty-four minutes spent behind the wheel.* Instead, accomplishing everything in a single, well-planned trip, with minimal retracing of steps in between, could reduce miles driven by two thirds and reduce time behind the wheel by almost an hour. Now, who couldn't use an extra hour in a day? And the money saved on fuel—between $1.79 and $6.38 depending on what you drive—could pay for coffee or even dinner. You can see how habituating better driving habits *every* day can add up to big savings.

 Spotlight on Savings

The average driver taking sixteen non-work-related trips a week averaging eight miles each can save $733 a year by consolidating trips and reducing miles driven by two-thirds.

---

* Time calculated using www.maps.yahoo.com.

Map Routes

Are you sure you're getting from one place to another using the most efficient route? Enter a trip's start and end points into a mapping website like www.maps.google.com, www. mapquest.com, or www.maps.yahoo.com and see what route is recommended. The default setting typically searches for routes that take the "shortest time"—something that may be different than "shortest distance." That's because the goal of these websites is to find the *optimal* route for travelers, one that takes into account not just trip distance but trip flow based on routing algorithms.

There's another advantage to using an Internet connected device to map routes—avoiding traffic. A Google Maps application feature (available on compatible mobile devices) called "traffic view" allows travelers to assess current traffic along their route, and select an alternate one. Google Maps Navigation (in beta development at the time of this printing) goes further by applying knowledge of real-time traffic conditions to *automatically* route drivers around traffic.

Prioritize Proximity

Many trips we take can be shortened by selecting stores, service businesses, healthcare providers, etc. that are closer to home. Do you still have the same dentist you chose when you lived in another part of town? Are you in the habit of driving to the mall seven miles away to pick up yarn from a chain store—bypassing the small yarn boutique that just opened two miles from your home? Have you put off transferring your gym membership to the new facility that is closer to you? Make some changes that will close distance gaps between you and the places you go and people you see to save time, fuel and money.

Complete Errands the Twenty-First-Century Way

Nowadays, trips can be completely eliminated for many errands that once required them: banking, renewing a driver's license, renting DVDs, buying stamps, renewing library books, and browsing competing stores' selections and sales can be accomplished using the Internet.

Modern technology and entrepreneurism will continue to create uses for the computer and web to serve our needs without leaving the house. On a local scale, this can help cut down on individual car trips by the millions, and that means less congestion and pollution. In fact, the type of driving typified by running errands—idling, lots of starts and stops—is especially fuel inefficient, so reducing the errand load makes a big impact.

Table 26: Estimated Savings When Reducing Miles Driven

TYPICAL SCENARIO Vehicle miles: 12,000 annually	($1,984)		
GREENER SCENARIOS	↑Annual fuel costs↓	Annual fuel savings	6-year fuel savings
10% fewer miles (10,800)	($1,786)	$198	$1,188
33% fewer miles (8,000)	($1,323)	$661	$3,966
50% fewer miles (6,000)	($992)	$992	$5,952

Assumptions: 22.5 MPG, $3.72 per gallon for gas

 Spotlight on Savings

Implementing a plan to reduce miles driven by a third can save the average driver $661 a year in fuel costs alone.

Take the Car-Free Challenge

Every day you own a car, whether you move it or not, it costs you money. The tab is always being run up by oil changes, tire rotations, loan payments, insurance payments, refueling, licensing fees and so on. Cars are money pits and horrible investments, depreciating to a quarter of their original value by the time most of us want to sell (in the sixth year). Why would anyone elect to keep one around if they could figure out how not to? Perhaps the answer is, nearly no one bothers to figure out how not to. Ask yourself the following questions (you may need to do a bit of research before answering):

- Do you live within four miles of all of your customary destinations? And if so, are there bike-friendly routes available?
- Do you have access to public transportation that picks you up and drops you off within walking or biking distance to all of your customary destinations?
- Do you have access to a rental car company, a car-sharing network or live within a car-sharing community that could provide a car for occasional needs? (See "Learn to Share.")
- Can you identify a ride-sharing opportunity through a ride-share website for your most routine trips (e.g., work, school)?
- Do you or can you work from home?

If you discover that it would be possible to replace your car by using a combination of other transportation modes, the temporary inconvenience of implementing a car-free plan and establishing new habits may be tempered by the amount of money you could save: Even after paying for occasional rental cars for special trips, the average car owner who decides to go car free can save many thousands of dollars per year—*many thousands, per* year.

If you want to investigate car-free living further, pick up the book *How to Live Well Without Owning a Car*, by Chris Balish.

Learn to Share

If you own a car just to drive it once or twice a week and to make the occasional road trip, your fuel expenses may be enviable, but non-fuel expenses—$6,640 for an average driver[16]—can hardly be justified when there are other options. One option not so far discussed is sharing. Sharing a car with others can be an extremely affordable and low-hassle way of getting around if you drive only occasionally. There are up to four ways to share a vehicle to cut down on car ownership expenses:

1. Give up a car and purchase a membership in a car sharing network;
2. Give up a car and rent a car occasionally from someone nearby;
3. Keep a car and rent it out to others for extra cash;
4. Keep a car and sell an ownership share, splitting expenses with a co-owner.

If you're fortunate enough to live in a city with a car sharing network, you're in luck: joining up could meet all of your driving needs at a fraction of the cost of owning a personal vehicle, and everything is taken care of for you: gas, insurance and parking are included.

Most car sharing networks work something like this: You pick a plan based on how much you think you will drive, and pay either a monthly or annual fee to join. When you want to drive, you reserve a car in advance (online or by phone), choosing among several vehicle types parked at different locations throughout the city. Next you choose to pay by the hour or the day for that vehicle, plus something for each mile driven. All the specifics of your reservations are coded into the vehicle, so when you show up to drive it, you simply unlock the vehicle with an electronic key and drive off. When you're done with the vehicle you simply return it to its original parking space.

If you live in a city without a car sharing network, there's a relatively new trend in car sharing where ordinary people loan their car out to complete strangers—community car sharing, if you will. Websites set up to help connect those in need of some wheels with those with wheels and in need of cash are more or less in a pilot phase (see sidebar, "Resources for Car-Sharing," page 139); their success will determine how fast and far this idea spreads.

Sharing a car in either of the above ways will reduce car-related expenses, but also, in all likelihood, you'll end up driving less when you have to reserve a car and pay by the hour or mile for its use; this means the environment will win too.

You can also share a car the old-fashioned way and co-own one with one or more people. If you would consider this, be diligent in setting terms and conditions for everything from how it will be paid for, insured, stored, maintained and shared to deciding how to dissolve the agreement and sell the vehicle. In fact, it would be wise to hire a lawyer to draw up the agreement. This may sound a bit extreme, but it's just smart to put all the rules and what-ifs in unambiguous language.

Table 27: Estimated Savings for a Light Driver Substituting a Car Sharing Arrangement for an Owned Vehicle

TYPICAL SCENARIO New Toyota Camry (single owner)	($5,220)*		
GREENER SCENARIOS	↑Avg. yearly true cost↓	Average annual savings	Average 5-year savings
Co-own (50% share) new Toyota Prius hatchback	($2,943)*	$2,277	$11,385
Car sharing network	($2,105)	$3,115	$15,575

Assumptions: 2,000 annual miles driven, $3.72/gallon

*Includes estimated depreciation, finance charges, fuel, insurance, maintenance & repairs, taxes & fees (amortized over five years).

Spotlight on Savings

Sharing ownership and expenses for an ultra fuel efficient hybrid car can save the light driver more than $2,200 a year compared to owning a standard sedan alone.

> ## Resources for Car-Sharing
>
> **Business-to-people car-sharing:**
> www.zipcar.com
> www.car2go.com
>
> **People-to-people car-sharing:**
> www.wheelz.com
> www.getaround.com
> www.relayrides.com

SIZING UP CARS

If owning a car is mandatory (or just your personal choice), it's going to cost you, as you may well already know. At the minimum there will be the initial cost or down payment, insurance, license and registrations fees, maintenance and fuel. But expenses typically also include interest on a loan, unplanned service and repairs, traffic fines, parking fees, parking citations and tolls. Owning a passenger car or light truck/SUV can cost its owner $35,243 or $55,178 over a five-year period, respectively.* Imagine what you could do with that kind of money!

It doesn't have to cost that much to own a car, however. It's possible to lower expenses substantially by driving the most fuel-efficient vehicle you can afford, buying a previously owned car, and of course, taking as many opportunities as possible to leave the car at home—as described above.

---

* Based on Edmunds.com's *True Cost to Own* calculator for the number one selling passenger car and light truck in America: the Toyota Camry and Ford F-150 Truck, respectively.

Reality Check

Cars have become much more than vehicles for transport, perhaps deepening our love for them: They can navigate us, entertain us, respond to voice commands and connect us to the Internet. Some can climb rocks or pull a freight car! But vehicles loaded with extra options and power come with a higher price tag and lower fuel economy.

Don't make the mistake of buying more car than you need or more of what you need in a car. A safe, reliable car with good fuel economy will cost you much less over its life than one that is overbuilt. Perhaps an obvious point, yet Americans still seem to be hooked on gas guzzlers. Regardless of the money that can be saved by driving a fuel-sipper even when gas is only $2/gallon, it appears from historical vehicle sales data that it's only when gas prices threaten to hit $4/gallon that America's preference for larger vehicles diminishes.

If progress toward a cleaner environment and less dependence on foreign fuel is to triumph, car buyers need to take a longer view where their pocketbook is concerned. Gas prices, if down, won't stay down (yes, and vice versa); and alternative-tech automobiles, though more expensive than conventional ones, offer the greatest long-term savings.

Get Electrified

Electric cars aren't a new invention. Electric cars were among the first ever built along with steam and gas-powered automobiles, but the battery technology of the day didn't provide enough power or allow the car to travel very far, so electric cars were abandoned—along with steam engine cars—in favor of the combustion car. Finally, after 100-plus years of the internal combustion engine, this nation—and the world—is being forced to come to grips with the nasty impacts of gas-powered vehicles and look for alternatives.

Hybrid Electric Vehicles (HEVs)

Hybrid electric vehicles (more accurately, hybrid *gasoline* electric vehicles) use an electric motor in coordination with a gasoline engine to conserve fuel and emissions, and they are up to twice as fuel efficient as a conventional car of the same size and capacity. Small to midsized HEVs are the best deal with an average 2012 MSRP of $25,200 (excluding luxury models) and an average fuel economy of 41 mpg.

With all the excitement over HEVs, they haven't sold as well as expected—making up only 2.4 percent of all vehicle sales in 2011 despite more options. Two likely reasons for the poor performance are fear of higher repair costs associated with HEVs and their higher price tags compared to regular cars—about $3,400 difference between a 2012 Toyota Camry LE Sedan and 2012 Toyota Camry LE Sedan Hybrid, for example.

 Spotlight on Savings

HEVs can save heavy city drivers nearly $1,000 in fuel costs annually compared to a comparably sized conventional gasoline powered car.

On the first matter, repair costs for hybrid models have fallen in line with those of non-hybrids recently. Beginning with 2007 models, repair costs for HEVs are no higher, or only slightly higher, than for conventional cars;[17] so there's one less worry. On the matter of the cost gap, it's a gap that requires a longer view from car buyers and consideration of their driving habits. Someone that racks up 16,000 miles of mostly city driving annually will benefit the most. Compared to a new gasoline vehicle that gets 25 mpg in the city, assuming fuel prices of $3.72 per gallon, an HEV that gets 43 mpg/city could save a heavy city driver $992 in annual fuel costs. It would take over three years for the lower fuel costs to offset the higher MSRP of the HEV, but over six years—the average number of years an American keeps a new car*—the net savings would be $2,480. Holding onto the car even longer—say for ten years—would profit the average driver $6,448 at a consistent average price for gas.

Plug-In Hybrids (PHEVs)

A plug-in hybrid electric vehicle differs from an HEV in that it has a larger battery that moves the car along in an all-electric mode for much longer. A downsized gas engine recharges the battery en route and takes over as the source of propulsion during the recharge phase.

In 2012, several auto makers released their first generation PHEV, and at least one released their second. About in the middle of the pack in terms of price is the Chevy Volt, at $40,000. A chunk of change, for sure, but for the person able and willing to finance a PHEV, one offers substantial operating cost savings over a comparable gasoline-fueled vehicle. A study by the National Renewable Energy Laboratory found that when replacing a conventional vehicle, a PHEV can reduce gasoline consumption by 56 to 70 percent;[18] and recharging the battery, which can be done from a conventional 120-volt electrical outlet, costs on average less than $1 per charge.[19]

 Spotlight on Savings

When replacing a conventional vehicle, a PHEV can reduce gasoline consumption by 56 to 70 percent; and recharging the battery costs on average less than $1 per charge.

Speaking of batteries, how long will they last is a frequently asked question. The answer is, a long time. According to the nonprofit EV advocacy group Plug In America, Nickel-metal hydride batteries (NiMH) in the earlier EVs are proving to

---

* Average length of new vehicle ownership reached a record high of an average of 71.4 months, or almost six years, in 2011 according to Polk & Co., an automotive research firm.

have very long lives. Electric cars with over 100,000 miles have reportedly experienced no degradation in range. Newer generation EVs like the GM Volt and the Nissan Leaf offer warranties for their lithium-ion batteries covering eight years or 100,000 miles. Similar warranties are expected from other manufacturers.

Electric Vehicles (EVs)

All-electric vehicles, which use only an electric motor, come in basically two categories, those built for the neighborhood and those built for the freeway. EVs that travel at slower speeds (up to 25 mph) are called Neighborhood Electric Vehicles (NEVs). NEVs, whether in the form of a scooter, car, van or truck, typically average 35 miles per charge—plenty of range for the average commuter. EVs that travel at faster speeds (over 100 miles per hour in some cases) and have more range are rarer and come with much higher price tags than NEVs do.

If you can make an EV work—at either end of the price, range and speed spectrum—you'll pay only around $0.01 to $0.04 per mile—the lowest per mile cost for "fuel" of any other vehicle type on the market. If your interest is more than a little peaked, learn more about EVs for sale via PlugInAmerica.org's vehicle tracker (see sidebar, "Resources for Plug-In and All-Electric Vehicle Enthusiasts").

Resources for Plug-In and All-Electric Vehicle Enthusiasts

Find EV charging stations:
www.evchargernews.com
www.afdc.energy.gov/locator/stations

Plug-in vehicle tracker:
www.pluginamerica.org/vehicles

The average fuel economy of the U.S. auto fleet is dead last compared to other industrial nations.[20]

Greenhouse Gas (GHG) Emissions and Electric Cars

The question on everyone's mind: do EVs really reduce greenhouse gas emissions—even when driven in states that rely heavily on coal generated electricity? A 2007 study conducted by the Natural Resources Defense Council and the Electric Power Institute found that if EVs were charged entirely with electricity generated using 2010 coal technology, the result would still be a 28 to 34 percent reduction in well-to-wheels* GHG emissions compared to the conventional vehicle.[21] And it's going to get better: By year 2050, power plants are expected to be cleaner, relying on low emissions controls and more renewables, so in all likelihood, GHG emissions from EVs will continue to fall.

EVs are great, clearly, but their supply is very limited and the price tags can be high. The vast majority of drivers will be relying on gasoline fueled automobiles for some time. Drivers who can't afford the built-in mega efficiency that PHEVs and EVs offer will need to exploit all the ways of making their conventional vehicle more efficient if they want to reduce greenhouse gas emissions and save money at the pump. We explore these "exploitations" on the following pages.

Smaller Is Usually Better

A consumer's first buying decision with respect to a new car usually involves what type or class of car from which to buy

---

* Well-to-wheels analysis of vehicle technologies considers the energy use and greenhouse gas emissions associated with the fuel production as well as vehicle operations.

(e.g., compact, midsized, large sedan, wagon, minivan, SUV, truck, etc). The size of your vehicle and its fuel economy no longer have an absolute inverse relationship—meaning when the former goes up, the latter goes down. Hybrid technology has made some SUVs more fuel efficient than a standard mid-sized passenger car, but for the most part, compared to smaller vehicles, larger ones just burn more fuel. They also, generally, cost more, consume more resources in production, are heavier and thus harder on roads and create bigger disposal problems at the end of their life.

Consider carefully what size car you need on a consistent basis. If you determine that most of the time a smaller car is sufficient, and only occasionally a larger car is needed, buy the smaller, more fuel efficient car. On those rare occasions when you'll need a larger car, you can rent one. This strategy could save you hundreds, if not thousands, of dollars over the life of the vehicle.

Do Now and Save

- Change the oil and filter as recommended by the vehicle manufacturer—or as often as every 3,000 miles or three to six months if you do a lot of short trip driving, especially in cold weather.
- Check tire pressure monthly and inflate them if necessary.
- Reduce your vehicle's drag by removing objects that interfere with its aerodynamics. Remove roof gear you aren't using, keep windows rolled up at highway speeds and if you drive a pick-up truck, swap out the tailgate for a cargo net.
- Get regular tune-ups using a good mechanic and improve gas mileage from 4 to 40 percent.
- Practice good driving skills like accelerating and breaking gradually, observing the speed limit and using overdrive when traveling at speeds over 40 mph.
- Don't idle your engine. After ten seconds, idling uses more fuel than it takes to restart the engine. The only reason to idle a well-tuned car is to allow it a thirty-second warm-up on an extremely cold day.[22]

Estimated Average Annual Savings: $128–$278

Important Numbers

There are lots of numbers to consider when choosing a car: cylinders, liters, transmission, passenger volume, cargo volume, headroom, legroom—even crankcase refill capacity! But of all the numbers there for you to evaluate, those that give information about the environmental performance of a vehicle should be given special consideration.

> The personal automobile is the single greatest polluter in many cities across the country.[25]

Fuel economy

A vehicle's fuel economy measures its mileage per gallon. Every gallon of gas burned creates approximately twenty pounds of carbon dioxide[23], so a car that drives farther on less fuel has a smaller carbon footprint—or tire print. Good fuel economy also saves you money of course. Driving a vehicle that averages 50 miles to every gallon will save the typical driver $825 over a one year period and $4,950 over six years, compared to driving a vehicle that averages 26 miles to the gallon.

A vehicle's average MPG will be included on the vehicle sticker, or you can compare the fuel economy of several vehicles at once at www.epa.gov/greenvehicles or www.fueleconomy.gov.

Exhaust Emissions

Cars burning gasoline and diesel emit pollutants—and lots of them. Pollutants include carbon dioxide, carbon monoxide, nitrogen oxide, sulfur dioxide, hydrocarbons, volatile organic compounds and particulate matter.[24] Some of these pollutants are greenhouse gases (GHGs), considered by many scientists to contribute to climate change. But even if you're a climate change skeptic, vehicle emissions are a major cause of air pollution—the *leading* cause in many heavily populated U.S. cities. Some metropolitan skies have turned a near constant brownish-yellow color; and the high concentration of air pollutants and ozone from vehicle exhaust puts their inhabitants, especially children, at higher risk for acute respiratory problems.

It's important to purchase a car that emits fewer harmful pollutants and GHGs. The EPA maintains a database of new cars sold in the United States that includes their pollution and GHG score (10 being the best). Look up cars at www.epa.gov/greenvehicles.

Table 28: Vehicle and Fuel Cost Comparison

Vehicle and fuel economy	MSRP	Annual fuel costs	6-year fuel costs
2012 midsized SUV 23 city/30 hwy	($22,295)	($1,759)	($10,554)
2012 midsized sedan 25 city/34 hwy	($21,995)	($1,596)	($9,576)
2012 midsized sedan hybrid 43 city/39 hwy	($25,990)	($1,081)	($6,486)
2012 compact 26 city/35 hwy	($13,484)	($1,540)	($9,240)
2012 compact hybrid 51 city/48 hwy	($23,015)	($897)	($5,382)
2012 PHEV ($0.029/mile)	($39,195)	($348)	($2,088)

Assumptions: 12,000 annual miles driven, $3.72/gal, weighted 60 percent city and 40 percent highway driving.

 Spotlight on Savings

Driving a vehicle that averages 50 miles to every gallon will save the typical driver $862 over a one year period and $5,172 over six years, compared to driving a vehicle that averages 26 miles to the gallon.

Consider a Nearly New Car

Each year improvements are made in engine performance, so a new car is more likely to have better fuel economy and emit fewer emissions than a comparable earlier model used car. But a *nearly new* used car can come close to the fuel efficiency* of a new car, while costing $5,000 to $10,000 less for a typical midsized model. This huge discount is largely due to depreciation: in the first two years, a new car will typically lose 35 percent of its value, so the used car shopper can get a discount at least equal to the car's depreciation.† Besides the obvious financial advantage, buying a used car also conserves raw materials.

When considering a used car, to make sure you're avoiding anything more than a slight discrepancy between its fuel economy and that of a comparable new car, do a side by side comparison at www.fueleconomy.gov.

---

* According to the U.S. Bureau of Transportation Statistics, the average fuel efficiency of a passenger car sold in 2008 is 31.5 mpg; in 2009, 32.9 mpg; in 2010, 33.9 mpg; and in 2011 33.8 mpg.
† On average, new cars depreciate about 20 percent the moment you drive them off the dealership lot. The second and third year the vehicle will depreciate roughly 15 percent a year, thereafter which depreciation rates slow down.

STOP FLUSHING MONEY DOWN THE DRAIN

Unfortunately most Americans don't think about how much water they consume because it's always there when they go to turn on the tap, and because, for most of the country, water is cheap—too cheap. As a result, many cities across the country are planning rate increases to more accurately reflect the cost of providing clean water, which puts high demands on supply, wastewater treatment, and delivery systems. A 2010 report released by the U.S. Conference of Mayors says that water and sewer rates for American households will double to quadruple in some cities over the next twenty years. But, even with rate increases in store for much of the nation, water will remain relatively cheap. This fact, however, doesn't mean we can't save money through water conservation. We can! We can because we use so much of it, and up to 73 percent of water used inside the home is heated[1]—adding to the cost of its consumption.

Depending on your current appliances, fixtures, and practices, you can save a decent amount of cash when you work to bring water use in your home down. But there's a bigger reason why saving water is a good idea: water is *not* an infinite resource. Human consumption places very high demands on water, and when demand exceeds supply—due to drought, overuse, leaky infrastructure, or pollution—we face water shortages, even here in the United States. Making sure we will always have enough freshwater for human and ecosystem needs depends on managing water better.

CLOSING THE FLOOD GATES

Americans consume seventy gallons of water per capita per day on average for indoor household uses alone.[2] If that sounds like a lot of water, you're right, it is: it's about *four* times the daily water required by someone living in a water-conserving home and practicing wise use.

Inside the home, aside from the water we use for drinking and cooking, we use water primarily for flushing and washing. A family of four living in an inefficient home, practicing no water conservation, and heating water with an electric storage heater can use more than 102,000 gallons of water a year for these purposes and spend up to $2,659 annually for the luxury of so much hot and cold water. Even if your household isn't quite this wasteful, chances are members of your household are using much more water than is necessary to perform routine tasks.

The use of water conserving fixtures in the bathroom and at all your sinks, water-efficient appliances in the laundry room and kitchen, and better habits wherever water is used can control the flow of water by up to 73 percent. For the household that is badly in need of efficiency upgrades across the board, making changes and investments that will cut water use by more than two-thirds can translate to an annual savings of $1,942 in water charges and water heating expenses! A savings like that is ample enough to warrant spending—or even borrowing, if need be—the money to make those upgrades possible.

Americans use more than ten times the minimum daily per capita water consumption recommended by the World Health Organization (WHO) for drinking, cooking, and personal and domestic hygiene.[3]

Draining the Tank

Toilets account for the most water used inside the home, or about 27,000 gallons a year in a typical home with non-conserving toilets.[4] A non-conserving toilet is one that was manufactured prior to 1994, and it could use anywhere from 3.5 gallons per flush (GPF) up to 7 GPF. Any toilet manufactured since 1994 uses 1.6 GPF or less.

Determining What You Have

If you aren't the original owner of your toilets, there are a few ways to find out how much water they use. First, look for a mark either near the seat hinge or inside the tank that states the flush volume of the toilet—expressed as either GPF or GPL (gallons per liter). If you can't find a mark, look for a date stamped on the underside of the tank lid or on the tank wall, and use table 29 to determine approximate flush volume.

Table 29: Toilet Water Use Through the Years

Year Made	GPF
1981 or earlier	5 to 7
1982 to 1993	3.5
1994 or later	1.6 or less

If all else fails, you can calculate approximate flush volume using a tape measure or measuring stick. Take the following measurements in inches:

A. Inside length of the tank, left to right
B. Inside width, back to front, of the tank (at a median-width point)
C. High depth of water (when tank is full)
D. Low depth of water (after the toilet has been flushed)

Plug the measurements into the equation

$$\frac{A \times B \times (C-D)}{231} = GPF$$

For example:

$$\frac{15.25" \times 6.5" \times (7.5"-4")}{231} = 1.5 \ GPF*$$

Retrofitting a Tank

If you have a high-flush toilet, but not the current finances to replace it with a low-flush model, you may be considering installing a water-saving device to save water with each flush. Be careful. Traditional solutions such as water displacement bags and early-close flappers are cheap, but they reduce flush volume *every time* you flush. And since non-conserving toilets are not designed to work with less water, you could be unhappy with the performance of a toilet following a retrofit that uses less water.

The newest retrofit devices are volume controllers that allow you to choose between a full flush and a half flush, and some of these devices have received good reviews, but at a cost close to $100. If you have that amount in your bank account, it would probably be wise to put it toward a moderately-priced conserving toilet. The simple truth is that no retrofitted toilet will work as well or save as much as an ultra conserving toilet.

---

* Because many tanks are tapered and curved, and their components take up volume in the tank, it's impossible to measure the volume of water precisely using this method, so whatever figure you come up with is an estimate.

Do Now and Save

- If you have both low-flow and high-flow toilets in your home, try to use the low-flow toilet predominantly until you can replace the other(s).
- Consider flushing liquids less often.

Estimated Annual Savings: $21–$109

Reusing Water

All that water that exits homes each day from bathroom sinks, dishwashers, clothes washers, tubs and showers is called gray water, but before it leaves your home, what if you could claim some of that water and use it for flushing toilets? After all, it's a little crazy to use clean drinking water to flush waste, wouldn't you agree? Gray water systems for toilets basically work by collecting water from a bathroom sink and holding it until it's needed to refill a nearby toilet. And don't worry, a filter and disinfecting tablets ensure that the water isn't nasty by the time it enters your toilet bowl. A system like this costs about $300 and may require a plumber to install, so you'll see the quickest payback when installed in a bathroom that receives lots of use at both the sink and toilet.

Toilets: Versions 1.6, 1.28, and 1.0

The very first Ultra Low Flow Toilets (ULFT) that rolled off the assembly line in 1994, just after the new 1.6 gallon flush standard went into effect, were pretty poor performers. Many manufacturers didn't change their toilets' mechanics—only the amount of water in the tank. The results were pretty dissatisfying, and word traveled quickly that if you knew what was good for you, you'd hang on to your older high-flow toilets for as long as possible. That was then. Today, low-flow toilets use new technology, not just less water, to get the job done.

New advances in toilet technology now make it possible to flush with up to 50 percent less water than even the ULFTs use. High Efficiency Toilets (HETs) that earn the EPA's WaterSense label use only 1.28 GPF; but the lowest water users are dual flush toilets—averaging just 1 GPF. Dual flush toilets give the user a choice between a 0.8 gallon flush (for liquids) and a 1.6 gallon flush (for solids).

Table 30: Estimated Savings When Upgrading One Toilet in a Two-Person Bathroom

TYPICAL SCENARIO Avg. flush vol. 3.6 GPF	($96)						
GREENER SCENARIOS	Initial cost less rebate, DIY installation	↑Annual water and sewer costs↓	Annual water savings	First year ROI	Payback period (in years)	10-year net savings
Ultra low flush toilet (ULFT), 1.6 GPF	($124)	($43)	$53	43%	2.3	$408
High efficiency toilet (HET, Watersense), 1.28 GPF	($144)	($34)	$62	43%	2.3	$477
Dual flush toilet, 1 GPF (avg.)	($216)	($27)	$69	32%	3.1	$476
HET (1.28 GPF) hooked up to small self-contained under-sink gray water system	($439)	($21)*	$75	17%	5.9	$308

Assumes 5.2 flushes per capita per day.[5]

*Includes an additional $0.23 for electricity costs and $5 for chemical costs.[6]

Spotlight on Savings

When replacing an inefficient toilet, one dual-flush toilet, which costs marginally more than a standard ULFT toilet, can pay for itself in one year through reduced water and sewer charges.

Dirty Laundry

Washing machines are second only to toilets when it comes to the biggest water users in the home.[7] A family of four may use as much as 22,000 gallons a year for laundry if their machine uses 41 gallons per wash cycle, as most conventional washing machines do.

The amount of water used by a machine also affects how much energy it uses, most notably when the water is heated. The more water a machine uses during a warm wash cycle, the more energy it takes to heat the water. In fact, during a hot wash cycle, 90 percent of the energy used by a washing machine is used to heat the water.[8] If you have an older inefficient machine and are accustomed to using warm water wash cycles, you could be paying more than $267 a year for water and electricity before you've even dried your laundry. One way to bring the cost of clean laundry down is to wash fewer loads and wash them in cold water, but if your laundry habits are already good, only a machine that uses less water and energy can save you more.

Do Now and Save

- Run only full loads. Color-fast darks can be added safely to a load of whites as long as no bleaching agents are used.
- Use cold water to wash clothes. Newer machines and cold-water detergents get the job done.
- Adjust the water level to the size of each load if you have a top loader.
- Sounds simple, but don't wash clean clothes! Look, smell, *then* judge whether something needs to be laundered.

Estimated Annual Savings: $18–$60

Upgrading Your Machine

A new washing machine is expensive—especially the high efficiency types. But hanging on to an old machine that won't last much longer could be costing you an additional $167 to $202 every year compared to a water conserving machine due to high water and energy consumption. If your machine is more than ten years old, start shopping around for the machine and features that will be the best investment and save you the most money.

Front loading machines have several advantages over top loading machines: they use less water, don't agitate clothes, use less detergent, and remove more water from clothes leading to shorter dry times. All these advantages don't come cheap, however, so you may need to look at Energy Star top loading machines to balance price and efficiency.

Features that will save you money in the long run include a Delay Start setting so you can program a load to run during periods of lower utility rates (available from some electricity providers) and a Water Level Control (for top loaders) to save water when washing smaller loads. (Front loaders match the water level to the load size automatically.)

Think carefully about size. If your next machine is too small, you'll end up running more loads leading to higher energy and water use—and more wear and tear on the machine. If it's too big, you'll pay a premium for capacity you don't really need and waste energy and possibly water with every load. Table 31 can be used to approximate machine capacity for your household, but you really need to analyze the size of *your* typical load and determine future needs and use patterns. Will you be adding to your family or is a child moving out soon? Will you begin consolidating smaller loads so you run larger loads less frequently? And size will also depend upon how much space you have, so don't forget these measurements when ordering your new appliance!

Table 31: Washing Machine Capacity

No. in household	Pounds of laundry	Capacity in cu. ft.
1 to 2	4 to 8 lbs.	2.5 to 3.0
3 to 4	8 to 12 lbs.	3.0 to 3.5
5 to 6	12 to 16 lbs.	3.5 to 4.2

Look for the Energy Star label. Energy Star washers use less water and energy than standard machines saving the consumer about 42 percent in water and energy costs (see table 32). In addition, refer to the yellow EnergyGuide label on machines to compare kWh usage for different models. And finally, compare MEF (Modified Energy Factor) and WF (Water Factor) numbers among machines. The higher a machine's MEF, the less energy it uses. The machine's WF indicates the gallons of water consumed per cubic foot of capacity. A machine with a lower WF not only saves water but energy to heat water.

Table 32: Washing Machine Comparison

Machine	Initial cost less rebates and incentives	Annual operating cost	10-year lifecycle costs
2002 top load washer (3.5 cu. ft., 41 GPL)	existing	($267)	end of life
Conventional top loader (3.4 cu. ft., 31 GPL)	($500)	($174)	($2,240)
Energy Star top loader, (3.6 cu. ft., 21.48 GPL)	($549)	($100)	($1,549)
Energy Star front loader (3.5 cu. ft., 12.36 GPL)	($799)	($65)	($1,449)

Assumptions: 400 loads per year[9], gas storage water heating

Spotlight on Savings

An Energy Star-qualified washing machine can save its owner almost $800 over its useful life compared to an unqualified machine.

To recap, the best washing machine will . . .

- be a front loading machine if your budget is over $700,
- be Energy Star–qualified,
- have the highest MEF and the lowest WF among similarly-sized machines,
- have the lowest estimated yearly operating costs (noted on the yellow EnergyGuide label) compared to other similarly-sized machines,
- be carefully sized for your space and your current and future laundry needs and usage,
- come with a water level control if a top loader, and
- come with a delay start feature, if your utility company charges low-peak rates.

Up to 50 percent of a typical city's energy bill goes to supplying water and cleaning it after use.[10]

Falling Water

Faucets get turned on and off several times a day, dispensing 11 gallons of water per person per day on average.[11] A small amount of that is used to fill things like drinking glasses, watering cans, cook pots, and pet bowls, but in the typical home, most of the water that runs from taps runs off things and down the drain. When we wet and rinse dishes, hands, faces, sponges, toothbrushes, and razors, for example, only a fraction of the falling water is actually used, the rest is wasted. The longer the faucet runs and the higher its flow rate, the greater the waste.

We can't help that water goes down the drain as we perform many daily chores, but we can control how much of it goes down the drain—to an extent.

Dish Duty

Many households wash dishes by hand in lieu of a dishwasher. Whether due to space, finances or by choice, 41 percent of U.S. homes either don't own or don't use a dishwasher[12]—which may partly explain why water consumed nationally by faucets is 16 percent of total household use, compared to just 1.4 percent by dishwashers.[13] Although an extremely frugal dish washing person can use less than four gallons of water to hand wash a day's dishes, closely matching the efficiency of an Energy Star dishwasher, generally hand washing dishes uses up to 7 times more water than a water efficient automatic dishwasher.[14] And the more water we use to wash dishes, the more energy needed to heat it.

Go Automatic

A high-efficiency dishwasher uses 4.25 gallons of water per cycle or less, making the use of one up to 85 percent more efficient than hand washing. Switching from hand washing to an Energy Star dishwasher can save substantial water and energy to heat water, saving the typical family the most if they are heating with an electric storage heater, or $97 a year.

Look for a dishwasher that has a food disposer (also called a grinder or macerator). Food disposer-equipped dishwashers can grind up small food chunks in the rinse water, so dishes don't have to be rinsed clean before being loaded—saving potentially many gallons of hot and cold water. Another feature to consider is an "overnight" or "delay start" feature: if your utility rates rise and fall over a 24-hour period, this feature will save you money by allowing you to set the dishwasher to run during hours when energy costs are low.

Table 33: Dishwasher Comparison

Type and water usage	Initial cost less rebates	Annual utility costs	10-year lifecycle costs
Hand washing, 96 gallons per week	n/a	($161)	($1,610)
Hand washing, 24 gallons per week	n/a	($40)	($400)
Conventional dishwasher, 6 GPC*	($329)	($89)	($1,219)
Energy Star dishwasher, 4 GPC	($429)	($64)	($1,069)
Energy Star dishwasher, 2.85 GPC	($674)	($37)	($1,044)

Source: www.energystar.gov

Assumes electric storage water heater (.86 AFUE) and 6 loads per week.

* Gallons per cycle

Make sure your new dishwasher is Energy Star–approved: standard sizes use at least 17 percent less energy than non-qualifying dishwashers and up to 66 percent less water. The EF (Energy Factor) can also be used to compare the efficiency of similar models. The higher the EF number the less energy the appliance uses per cycle. EnergyGuide labels are also required on dishwashers, allowing you to compare estimated annual operating costs of different machines.

 Spotlight on Savings

An Energy Star washing machine costs, on average, $25 less every year to operate compared to a non-qualifying conventional dishwasher.

To recap, the best dishwasher will . . .

- be a hand washer if they use less than 4 gallons of water to clean a day's dishes and there is no budget for an automatic dishwasher,

- be an Energy Star model with the lowest water use (gallons per cycle) and highest EF among similarly sized models if there is a minimum budget of $379 for the appliance,
- grind food particles to eliminate the need to pre-wash dishes before they are loaded, and
- be a model that has an "overnight" or "delay start" setting, especially if your utility discounts electric rates at night.

Do Now and Save

- Check with your utility to find the optimum time to run appliances (i.e., during low-peak hours where available).
- Run only full loads. Washing a few things you need by hand is usually better than running a dishwasher that is only half full.
- If your dishwasher has a macerator, don't waste water rinsing dishes. Just scrape and load.
- Open the door after the rinse cycle and let your dishes air dry for greater energy savings.

Estimated Annual Savings: $11–$26

Give Your Water Some Air

A faucet aerator—a device that slows down the flow rate of a faucet and adds air to the water—can save several gallons of water every day and energy used to heat water. Faucet aerators easily screw onto the end of faucets with threaded spouts and they cost only between $2 and $10 each.

Do Now and Save

- If water is needed for wetting and rinsing only, make sure to turn off the water between uses.
- Running water at maximum volume is unnecessary for most tasks. Except when filling a vessel, faucets should be turned on only a quarter to halfway to avoid needless waste.
- Use hot water sparingly.

Estimated Annual Savings: $102–$230

To determine if you need an aerator for a faucet, turn the water on to full volume. If the water is clear—like water looks when poured from a pitcher—the spout has no aerator and is dispensing two to eight times the amount of water compared to a faucet with a low-flow aerator. If the water looks white under full pressure, there is an aerator in place, but depending on its gallons per minute (GPM) flow rate, you may want to swap it for a lower flow aerator to achieve greater savings. (The aerator's flow rate is engraved onto its rim.)

Follow these guidelines to help you choose the right aerator for the job:

Bathroom sink: 0.5 to 1.0 GPM

Kitchen sink: 1.5 to 2.0 GPM

Bar or prep sink: 1.0 to 1.5 GPM

Table 34: Estimated Savings When Installing Aerators to Three Heavily Used Faucets

TYPICAL SCENARIO 1.9 avg. GPM	($340)					
GREENER SCENARIOS	One-time cost	↑Annual utility costs↓	Annual utility savings	First year ROI	Payback period in years	10-year net savings
1.67 avg. GPM	($12)	($297)	$43	358%	0.3	$417
1.33 avg. GPM	($12)	($235)	$105	875%	0.1	$1,040
0.83 avg. GPM	($12)	($150)	$190	1583%	0.06	$1,889

Assumes three sinks, 4-member household, gas water heater, 8.1 minutes daily per capita faucet duration,[15] 73 percent hot water.

 Spotlight on Savings

Faucet aerators that cut water flow by half among three heavily used sinks can save the typical household $190 annually.

According to the World Bank, global demand for water is doubling every twenty-one years.

Getting Soaked

Most Americans prefer a shower to a bath by almost seven to one.[16] As a result, showerheads dispense the majority of water used for bathing in the average home, and this fact makes showers the third largest water user in the typical home behind toilets and the washing machine.

With the average shower in this country lasting just over eight minutes, and the average showerhead flowing at a generous 3 to 5 gallons per minute,[17] a single American can use more water during one shower than a person in Denmark uses in a whole day![18] And since much of the water we use for showering is heated, lots of energy is consumed during a good spray down as well.

Retrofitting showerheads, as necessary, to conserve water and also making sure showers don't become long drawn out rituals can greatly reduce monthly utilities—especially for large households heating water with electric storage heaters.

Shower Power

Older showerheads are anything but efficient—flowing at a rate of 3 to 8 GPM. Luckily, each year more and more of these high-flow showerheads are replaced, and new showerheads flow at 2.5 GPM or less. If you don't know a showerhead's flow rate, check it, because a showerhead that dispenses 5 GPM not only dumps more than twice the amount of water needed for a satisfactory shower down the drain, but also costs a typical family of four with an electric hot water storage tank an extra $548 annually in utility costs.

To test the flow rate of your showerheads, hold a one-gallon bucket under the showerhead and turn the water on. If you can fill the bucket in twenty seconds or less, your showerhead is high-flow and wasting precious water and money with every shower: time to replace it.

Reduce the Flow

Showerheads sold today cannot exceed a 2.5 GPM flow rate, making them up to three times as efficient as a showerhead that's been hanging around since the 1980s. Ultra efficient showerheads use even less water—as little at 1 GPM. The lower the flow rate you achieve, the bigger the savings.

Whatever you do, don't penny-pinch and buy a cheap low-flow showerhead that simply restricts water flow. Look for aerated types that mix air into the stream of water to enhance pressure and provide quick rinse action. Pay attention to the water pressure these showerheads are designed to work best with—pressure is expressed in PSI, or pounds per square inch. If you don't know what your water pressure is, just call your water supply company and ask them. They will probably give you a range like 40–60 PSI. If the pressure of water entering your house is in a range that matches the ideal range expressed for the low-flow showerhead, go for it!

A new low-flow showerhead is a small investment that can save you lots of money, especially if you or other people in the home tend to take frequent or long showers (see table 35).

Stop the Flow

Plenty of people take long showers if they have the time. A hot, steaming shower feels pretty good—so good that we can stretch a shower out for several minutes without really trying. Why rush a good thing, right? Well, while rushing in and out of the shower isn't absolutely necessary, using water more efficiently while you're in there is, because water is a precious resource; and it isn't free.

If you take long showers, sixteen minutes say, it's twice as long as the average shower and three times as long as it probably needs to be. If you can't make it out of the shower in five minutes, you can reduce water use while you're in there by turning the water off in the middle of the shower while you lather up and shampoo. This could save 50 percent of the water you would normally have used if the showerhead was continuously on. To stop and restart water flow during a shower, install a showerhead that comes with an on/off switch, or install a separate shut-off valve between your existing showerhead and the pipe exiting the wall (very easy to do). With the switch in the "off" position, water should still trickle to keep the hot and cold water mixed properly and avoid a sudden surge of hot or cold water when the flow is restored.

Table 35: Showerhead Comparison

Showerhead flow rate	Initial cost	Annual utility costs with gas storage water heater	10-year lifecycle cost with gas storage water heater	Annual utility costs with electric storage water heater	10-year lifecycle cost with electric storage water heater
3 GPM	existing	($355)	($3,550)	($612)	($6,120)
2.5 GPM	($30)	($296)	($2,990)	($509)	($5,120)
1.75 GPM + off switch engaged for 4 minutes	($30)	($105)	($1,080)	($181)	($1,840)
1.0 GPM	($20)	($115)	($1,170)	($198)	($2,000)

Assumes 4.7 showers per capita per week at an average 8 minutes each[19], 4-member household, storage tank water heater.

To recap, the best showerhead will . . .

- be an ultra low flow shower head with aeration technology,
- flow between 2.5 GPM and 1.75 GPM if you won't be happy with a lighter spray,
- flow between 1.5 GPM and 1.0 GPM if you will be happy with a lighter spray and can order online (the ultra efficient ones are harder to find at national home improvement centers), and
- cost enough (generally $30 and up) to include good quality parts.

 Spotlight on Savings

A four member household with average showering habits can save between $240 and $414 a year when replacing outdated 3.0 GPM showerheads with low flow showerheads. Over ten years, that can translate to a savings of $2,380 to $4,120!

Drip, Drip, Drip

This next statistic is going to shock a lot of people: On average, leaks inside the home account for almost as much water use as faucets or showerheads. Even small leaks can waste thousands of gallons in one year, and one steady leak in a toilet can waste 200 gallons of water every day, according to the EPA. If you're unfortunate enough to have such leaks—known or unknown to you now—you're not only paying for water you don't see, but you could be paying to repair property damaged by leaks down the line: In 2007, State Farm Insurance Company reported that damage to homes caused by leaks cost policyholders $7,500 on average to repair.[20]

Nationally, households lose an average 14 percent of water delivered to it through leaks.[21]

A faucet that drips twice every second wastes 6,307 gallons of water a year. If the faucet streams instead of drips, the waste can exceed 15,700 gallons annually.[22] One leaky faucet can add $44 to your annual water and sewer tab—that's if the leak is in a cold water line: if it is in a hot water line, the roughly 17 gallons of heated water lost each day will cost a typical homeowner $69 to $162 a year.

The good news is: faucet leaks are easy to spot. Toilet leaks on the other hand—the silent kind—can be harder to notice, and they waste a lot more water than the typical faucet leak. Toilet leaks waste between 30 and 500 gallons a day according to the California Urban Water Conservation Council. CUWCC also warns that a leak you can hear will waste much, much more. An audible running toilet that is leaking 500 or more gallons a day will cost the average household more than $1,200 a year in additional water fees.

Toilet and faucet leaks are the most common, but leaks can occur from supply connections to dishwashers, washing machines, and icemakers; and water heaters and swamp coolers can also leak. Detecting, locating, and repairing leaks should be an urgent priority (see sidebar, "Resources for Detecting and Fixing Leaks").

Resources for Detecting and Fixing Leaks

Drip calculator:
www.awwa.org/resources-tools/public-affairs/public-information/dripcalculator.aspx

Finding and fixing leaks:
www.epa.gov/watersense/our_water/howto.html

Leak detection specialists:
www.americanleakdetection.com

Spotlight on Savings

Repairing a leaky toilet can save, on average, 73,000 gallons and $517 a year, or about $360 the first year if you hire a plumber.

OUTDOORS AND OUT OF CONTROL

Water use—or rather misuse—in the summer amounts to a colossal waste. According to the EPA, during summer months, outdoor water use can exceed water use for all indoor uses combined by a ratio of three to one. Domestic and recreational uses of water around the home keep our outdoor spigots working overtime in the summer—especially in hot, dry regions of the country.

Hosing down driveways, sidewalks, and lawn furniture; washing domestic animals; de-griming our vehicles; filling swimming pools; irrigating gardens; and the big one—watering our lawns—consume an estimated 3.57 trillion gallons of fresh, usually drinking-quality water every year in the United States.[23] The average home uses more than 29,000 gallons of water outside the home in one year,[24] but water use varies considerably, and depending on the geographic area, landscaping choices, and patterns of use, outdoor water use can be off the charts.

The American Lawn

Private lawns are so popular with American homeowners that they now cover approximately 25 million acres in the United States.[25] It's easy to see why they are popular—they are inexpensive to install from seed, provide a soft play surface for our pets and kids; and they feel a lot better under our feet than rocks or bark. But when we extol the virtues of the lawn, we are overlooking some serious drawbacks: For starters, lawns con-

> ## Do Now and Save
>
> - Install a hose bib lock to stop unauthorized use of the hose.
> - Always operate a hose fitted with a water-conserving trigger nozzle or valve.
> - For water play, use a sprinkler or nozzle with a water-conserving mist setting.
> - Collect rainwater for use outdoors with easy to install rain barrels that catch rain from gutter downspouts.
> - Cover pools when they won't be used for extended periods to avoid evaporation.
> - Give your lawn one inch of water a week including precipitation (about 624 gallons per 1,000 sq. ft.).
> - Don't try to keep lawns lush green through droughts. Give a lawn just enough water to hang on until rain returns.
>
> **Estimated Annual Savings: $32–$589**

sume time and money to maintain. The typical homeowner spends forty hours[26] and $428[27] a year maintaining a lawn, and the environmental impacts from fertilizing, watering, and mowing (primarily with gas-powered machines) our collective lawns—several million acres and growing—is staggering.

According to the Audubon Society, every year 80 million pounds of pesticides and 100 million tons of fertilizer are applied to residential lawns. As much as 40 to 60 percent of chemicals applied to lawns end up in surface or groundwater, and impacted air and soil become toxic to many earthworms, insects, and birds.[28]

> Runoff from overfertilized urban lawns carries toxic levels of chemicals or excessive nutrients into lakes, streams, and groundwater, often contaminating drinking sources and harming and killing wildlife.

The EPA estimates Americans use upwards of 2.5 trillion gallons of water for landscaping each year—3.7 times the recommended amount. Not only do we waste water in the pursuit of a super-green lawn, we also waste fuel making sure it's impeccably trimmed. Gas-powered lawn mowers consume roughly 720 million gallons of gasoline each year[29], and according to EPA estimates, an additional 17 million gallons of fuel is spilled every summer in the process of refilling lawn mowers and garden equipment.

Do Now and Save

- If you have a small lawn, switch from a gas-powered mower to an electric or manual reel mower.
- Use fertilizers sparingly. Up to 25 percent of your fertilizing needs can be met by spreading an inch of home compost over your lawn each spring and leaving grass clippings on the lawn to decompose.
- Adjust sprinkler heads that are misdirecting water onto pavement.
- Buy an inexpensive lawn moisture meter that will tell you if you're overwatering.

Estimated Annual Savings: $77–$555

Those that say having a "perfect" lawn gives them a sense of pride surely don't realize the high costs associated with achieving something that is as unnatural as any living thing can be. Grass—which has a dormant season and natural defenses against pests and disease—that comes in the form of a poorly located and overtended lawn, begins to rely on being watered and fertilized to survive. The whole unnatural cycle is a misuse of water and puts chemicals in contact with us, our children, our pets, our homes, our food, and our water sources.

One two-stroke lawn mower emits as much smog-forming pollution every hour as a car driven fifty miles.[30]

Reduce Turf

Turf grass requires much more water, fertilizer, and maintenance than plants, groundcovers, and shrubs. This is generally
the case, but even more so when grasses used by homeowners
are not native to the area in which they are grown, thus requiring excessive water and fertilizer to grow.

Although a healthy, established lawn requires only about
one inch of water each week to survive, experts say that most
of us routinely overwater our lawns or otherwise waste water
through the lawn care process. Typical automatic irrigation
systems overwater by several hours a week, applying water to
lawns at five or six times the rate that the turf and soil can ab-
sorb,[31] they also misdirect lots of water onto hard surfaces. Re-
grettably, the EPA estimates that 50 percent of all the water
used for irrigation goes to waste due to runoff, evaporation,
wind or improper system design. This kind of water misuse not
only inflates the summer water bill, but it's becoming harder
and harder to excuse with water quality suffering and water
shortages on the rise for much of the United States. It's also
harder to get away with in the face of expanding and increasingly strict water restrictions being adopted by many cities.

It can be both less expensive and easier to do away with
lawns in regions that receive insufficient rainfall—or at least
greatly reduce the area devoted to them. Some communities
are offering lawn replacement rebates worth $0.50 to $1.00 for
each square foot of lawn replaced with either non-plant materials, water conserving plants or a combination of both.

Another benefit of replacing lawn area is doing so can increase your home value. A well-landscaped yard can add up to
15 percent to the selling value of a home, according to the
American Nursery and Landscaping Association; and while
beauty is in the eye of the beholder, a bland lawn doesn't enhance a home's appeal like attractive plants, patios for entertaining, and trees that provide both sound and privacy barriers.

Landscaping can be expensive—around $11/square foot if you have a landscape company do all the installation, so do as much of the work as possible to save money, and don't try to do it all at once: install landscaping and outdoor areas in stages, as money becomes available. You can also save money in the following ways:

- Amend your soil! Don't put expensive plants into poor soil.
- Check with your city for free giveaways (e.g., trees, mulch, and compost).
- Ask your neighbors if they have extra perennials to share.
- Look for plant sales in the classified ads.
- Choose less expensive, young plants from the nursery.
- Buy plants in the fall, when they are discounted.
- Source reclaimed pavers or bricks—even broken concrete slabs—for patio projects.

Resources for Creating and Maintaining Sustainable Landscapes

Conservation practices used on agricultural land adapted for the backyard:
www.tinyurl.com/84s596u

Native plant database:
www.wildflower.org/plants
www.plantnative.org/

Expert advice on creating an edible landscape:
www.garden.org/ediblelandscaping/

Drip irrigation basics:
www.youtube.com/watch?v=SSJeOT97Vws

All about mulch:
www.savvygardener.com/Features/mulch.html

If you decide to design your own landscape plan, a consultation with a professional, first, is a good investment toward avoiding mistakes; and when it comes to choosing vegetation, consult a local nursery—or a local university's extension office—to help you select the right plants, trees, and shrubs for your site. Once your low-water landscape is planted, irrigate with a drip system that can cut water use by 60 percent compared to a sprinkler system.

Table 36: Estimated Savings When Replacing Turf Grass with Low- and No-Water Alternatives

TYPICAL SCENARIO 3,000 sq. ft. lawn (turf): 3" water per week (wpw)						
		($621)				
GREENER SCENARIOS	Initial cost less rebate	↑Annual utilities, supplies↓	Annual savings	First year ROI	Payback period (in years)	30-year net savings
1,500 sq. ft. turf: 1" wpw 950 sq. ft. non-turf ornamentals and mulch, 150 sq. ft. edible beds + buffer 400 sq. ft. hardscape patio and paths	($3,280)	($357)	$264	8%	12	$4,752
1,000 sq. ft. turf: 0.8" wpw, 1,300 sq. ft. non-turf vegetation + mulch, 300 sq. ft. edible beds + buffer 400 sq. ft. hardscape patio and paths	($3,960)	($284)	$337	9%	12	$6,066

Assumes DIY installation and 14-week irrigation cycle.

In the American West and Southwest, the scarcity of water has led to the purchase of water rights away from farmers in order to supply needy cities and townships—turning once-irrigated, productive farmland into wasteland.[32]

Catch It If You Can

Municipal water supplies are comprised of clean drinking water, not the sort of water we should, ideally, use to keep our ornamental plants alive. The ideal situation is to plan our landscapes so they can be sustained by annual rainfall, but the reality is very few landscapes have been designed that way; and even as we move toward that goal, young plants will always need extra water in the beginning to become established.

We can ease up on municipal water supplies, however, and save some money on our water and sewer bill at the same time by accessing water sources that come from directly inside and outside our home—gray water (wastewater from inside the home from any source except the toilet) and rainwater, respectively. Systems that collect gray water or rainwater for reuse vary from simple and inexpensive to complex and expensive. The latter will have a very long payback period unless you live where water and sewer rates are among the highest in the country and the system's capacity is commensurate with irrigation requirements.

The simple and inexpensive systems are the way to go for most folks. They won't save households a huge amount of money—even where water and sewer rates are three times higher than the national average—but local rebates may pay for the system outright and any amount of gray water and rainwater collected reduces potable water use. Additionally, gray water recycling can be beneficial for regional sewage treatment facilities; and rainwater collection helps prevent rain from becoming polluted storm water.

Reusable Wastewater

Gray water can be diverted to a system outside the home and used for subsurface irrigation of non-edible landscape plants—*if* permitted by local regulations. Not every state allows gray water recycling at this time. States that do allow it require proper system design, installation and use to protect the water table, sewer flows and effluent levels.

It probably sounds complicated, and while there are highly complex and costly systems, there are simple, low-cost systems too. If your state's regulations mandate a complex system, gray water recycling will most likely not be economically feasible. If, however, you get the green light to install a simple laundry-to-landscape system, there are do-it-yourself kits that can keep costs down; some DIYers even improvise by using an old bathtub or industrial drum as the holding tank and inexpensive filtering mediums such as plants or sand. Whatever materials and design you use, local and environmental codes still need to be met every step of the way.

 Spotlight on Savings

For a typical urban lot, replacing grass primarily with plants can reduce maintenance and water costs by $337 a year.

When It Rains It Pours

A second source of water is the rain that falls from your roof, but collecting rain water isn't a no-brainer. Rain barrels, which collect rain running off the roof via gutters and downspouts, aren't much help in drought situations unless the capacity of

Table 37: Estimated Savings When Supplementing Outdoor Water Needs with Captured Water

TYPICAL SCENARIO 200 gal. municipal water used each week	($55)					
GREENER SCENARIOS	**Initial cost less rebate**	**↑Annual costs↓**	**Annual savings**	**First year ROI**	**Payback period (in years)**	**10-year net savings**
Laundry-only gray water system collecting 154 gal. of gray water each week.	($125)	($13)	$42	34%	3.0	$294
220 gal. rainwater catchment system recharged three times	($40)*	($40)	$15	38%	2.7	$109

Assumes DIY installation, 12 weeks of irrigation, $0.023/gallon combined water and sewer rates (about three times the national average)

*Cost based on existing rain gutters and downspouts

the system closely matches the water needs on your property. That's hard to do. A simple 4-barrel residential system with 220 gallons of capacity won't water many plants for very long once the rain ends. That makes a small system best in sections of the country that receive some rain during the growing season, with only short dry stretches. In this case, rain barrels can get refilled and provide irrigation water beyond their initial capacity.

If you already have gutters and downspouts to work with, rain barrels can be economically installed, so try a couple, and see how it goes; adding on is always easy. You can find good deals ($100 and less) on reconditioned food-grade plastic barrels that have been modified into rain barrels and assembled with a spigot and overflow fitting; or for about half that, you can pick up reclaimed barrels* and adapt them yourself with DIY kits.

 Spotlight on Savings

When a laundry gray water system supplies 77 percent of water needs to a small garden, the typical household can save about $42 a year.

---

* When you are choosing rain barrels, read the fine print; you want reclaimed barrels or those made from 100 percent recycled plastic. Avoid barrels that are newly manufactured with virgin plastic.

HEALTHY FOOD CAN BE AFFORDABLE

ealthy food is natural food that has been grown and raised
as close to the way nature intended as possible—plain
and simple. Food that has been tweaked and tampered with is
rarely better than food in a natural form.* But this simple truth
hasn't stopped much of the U.S. agriculture and food industry
from doing a number of things to create unnatural, and unnecessary, food choices for consumers worldwide. From unnatu-
rally "enhancing" livestock to genetically altering plants to
loading food products with artificial ingredients, tinkering with
food and agriculture to the extent we are is creating a dangerous situation: Food diversity is low, food quality has suffered,
natural resources have been exploited and diet-related diseases are responsible for three out of four American deaths each
year.[1] The Declaration of Healthy Food and Agriculture, a col-
laborative document framed by policy makers and healthy food

---

* "Natural" in the strictest sense of the word means letting seeds fall where they may and animals
roam the earth freely. It wouldn't necessarily include *any* food raised in a crop or animal raised in
captivity. For the purpose of this discussion, "natural" foods are those that come from nature.
Beyond that, if you want guarantees that what began as a natural food hasn't been overtly changed
and affected by human intervention, you need to consider how what began as natural food was
grown and processed. You're about to read all about that.

advocates, is calling for a radically different approach to food and agriculture. The consumer's role in this radical change includes selecting natural foods for their diet, including some organic foods, whenever possible. But can every American afford to "naturalize" their diet? Yes!

A 2012 study conducted by the U.S. Department of Agriculture's Economic Research Service looked at 4,000 foods and ranked them by price based on calories, weight and portion size. The report found that when using weight and portion size as the guide, healthy foods were not any more expensive than unhealthy foods. In fact, when it came to portion size, *unhealthy food was the most expensive*; and grains, fruits, and vegetables were among the least expensive.[2] This study validates what healthy food advocates have been saying for years, but the definition of healthy food has gotten more complicated. Sure a peach or bowl of spinach is better for you (and often cheaper) than a bag of potato chips, but in this age of chemically-intensive, industrial farming, we are being advised to buy some fruits and vegetables—and other foods—in organic form if we want to make truly healthy choices. ("Organic" in this book is short for USDA-certified organic. For an explanation of "organic" and "certified organic," see "Food 101" on page 180.)

Is a healthy diet that includes organic foods also less expensive than an unhealthy one? Well, as the co-author of the USDA report, Andrea Carlson, said in an interview with *USA Today*, "You can always find healthy foods that are cheap and healthy foods that are expensive. The same is true of less healthy foods." In other words, yes, maintaining a healthy diet—even one that includes foods produced organically—can be less expensive than maintaining an unhealthy diet, but you have to choose the right foods. The choice isn't just between organic and non-organic versions of things you already eat. You may need to make better choices about how and what you eat.

Those who have priced organic versions of foods and judged them to be too expensive are not powerless to make some changes. First, whatever the cost of organic foods, smart shopping, conscientious meal preparation, and good eating habits can bring the overall cost of your food bill ($4,016 per capita in 2010) down[3], thus making room in your budget for food that is healthier. Second, as good as organic food is, it's not the only option for earth- and health-conscious consumers: seasonal, sustainable foods that are sourced locally—or that you grow or make yourself—can be less expensive and equally if not more beneficial than the USDA-certified organic food you find at mass retailers.

This chapter will show consumers who can't always afford to eat organically grown foods how to afford them more often as well as how to become better at identifying other healthy foods and incorporating them into our diets. But first, let's look at why and when it's beneficial to replace conventional foods with organic, sustainable, and local foods wherever available.

FOOD 101

Fifty years ago there weren't huge differences in how food was raised from one farm operation to the next, but today it's a whole new ballgame. Now there are big differences between the dominant system of modern farming—what is called "conventional" farming—and the other three farming systems: organic, sustainable, and biodynamic. These differences produce different results for our food and the environment. Below is a summary of these four farming system models.

- *Conventional* farming today has a primary goal of getting the highest possible production and yield of a given commodity at the lowest possible expense of capital. This pursuit has led to the overuse of synthetic chemical herbicides, insecticides and fertilizers to assist plant growth—chemicals that taint soil; cling to food; pollute waterways and ground water; and kill beneficial insects, bees, and birds. Animal confinement and overcrowding is permitted and animals may receive antibiotics, synthetic growth hormones, and medications to prevent disease and promote abnormal growth.

- *Organic* farming employs methods that preserve environmental health and produce high-quality agricultural products. Certified organic farming is organic farming that is done according to standards and practices set by the U.S. Department of Agriculture's National Organic Program. USDA NOP standards mandate naturally occurring or naturally derived methods and materials to control weeds and pests and to fertilize. Some chemicals that are derived from natural sources—such as plants and minerals—are permitted, but are typically only used as a last resort. Animals are allowed access to the outdoors, never administered antibiotics or growth hormones and they receive organic feed or are grazed on natural grass.

- *Sustainable* farming emphasizes long-term environmental health of natural systems to ensure the indefinite production of a given crop or commodity. Sustainable farms often meet or even exceed the same quality and safety standards used by certified organic farms. However, in lieu or organic certification, some sustainable farms pursue other available certifications to assure customers of their natural growing practices and healthy and humane treatment of animals; among them Animal Welfare Approved, Certified Naturally Grown, Certified Humane or Food Alliance Certified.

- *Biodynamic* farming meets the organic standards including the prohibition of synthetic chemical fertilizers, pesticides, herbicides and fungicides, but then it goes much further. Biodynamic farms treat soil, plants and animals as one system and use nature's inherent properties and tendencies to foster self-nourishment and balance within the system. Certified biodynamic farms in the United States follow the guidelines set by Demeter USA.

As you may be able to tell from the above descriptions, the playing field is anything but level when it comes to producing foods the organic and sustainable way versus the conventional way. The chemical agents and drugs used in conventional farming are quick fixes, while growing food and raising animals the way nature intended takes more time, care and money. If farms pursue certification, it can be an expensive undertaking. Additionally, large agribusinesses are heavily subsidized by the government, while family farms are getting shortchanged in the subsidies department. These are some of the reasons why organic and sustainable food will probably never be as cheap as conventional food, nor should it be; but it can be affordable if you are willing to make necessary changes to the way you budget, shop, prepare food and eat.

WHY BUY ORGANIC
(OR CLOSE TO IT) AND WHEN

The method of raising food our grandparents can remember, based on farm pride and product purity, has been disappearing, giving way to profit and processing; the result is a broken food system. The vast majority of our food is produced by too few industrial scale agribusinesses, using obscene amounts of chemical fertilizer and pesticide; with a cruel easiness for animal suffering and with the intrusion of unwholesome scientific wizardry. The bottom line: our food on the whole is cheaper, but it's neither humane nor sustainable; and it has deteriorated in quality and nutrition.

Clearly, it is not the willful intent of compassionate and conscientious consumers to support cruel and polluting agricultural practices or consume food that could actually be hurting us, but when we don't know the facts about what we are eating, that's exactly what happens. Every food dollar we spend on food produced within an injurious system is a vote for more of the same; so we need to know where our food comes from. That little bit—or big bit—of knowledge will logically steer us away from what we find disagreeable; and just as logically prompt us to make food choices that favor more wholesome and humane alternatives available to us such as organic and sustainable foods.

When prioritizing which products to buy in one of these forms, it's pretty simple: meat, poultry, dairy and at-risk produce, as well as foods (and their derivatives) that have a propensity to be genetically modified, such as corn, soybeans, canola, cottonseed, sugar beets, U.S. zucchini and yellow squash, and Hawaiian papaya.

Animal Products (i.e., Meat and Dairy)

The Food and Agriculture Organization of the United Nations (FAO) has called livestock production one of the major causes of the world's most pressing environmental problems, including global warming, air and water pollution, land degradation and loss of biodiversity.

How have livestock animals become such a grave problem to a clean and sustainable environment? According to the documentary movie *Food, Inc.,* it began when the United States started overproducing corn. To get rid of the surplus, we turned it into cheap livestock feed. This made meat cheaper and more accessible to the masses. Suddenly meat was the cornerstone of fast food franchises and dinner plates across America. Unsustainable demand for cheap meat gave rise to industrial scale rearing operations, and here we are. Now, more than 50 percent of animals raised for food live their lives within the confines of intensive animal production systems known as Concentrated Animal Feeding Operations (CAFOs).[4] CAFOs aren't farms, they are factories, designed to output as many animals as possible as fast as possible for the least cost.

CAFOs create massive amounts of manure and the concentration of wastes in one location—not spread out over several hundred acres as in pasture farming—impacts air, water, and land quality. One CAFO can create as much sewage as a U.S. city, but the sewage isn't treated like human sewage is. Raw animal waste—along with present contaminants like pharmaceuticals, hormones, arsenic, and phosphorous—is dumped on the surrounding land; and since it is way more waste than the land can handle, most of it runs off into rivers and lakes which can lead to massive fish kills and toxic algal blooms. CAFOs also produce dangerous gases such as methane, ammonia, and hydrogen sulfide—as well as dust, or particulate matter, which can cause acute respiratory problems.

In addition to environmental impacts from raising animals for food in CAFOs, the standards for animal care and health create additional problems. Within these CAFOs animals are deprived of space to exercise—or even to move at times—putting them under great stress. If you think you can picture this, you don't have to try: go to www.farmsanctuary.org/photos and look into the eyes of an animal so constrained that it cannot get up when it falls. Not only is this cruel and inhumane, but animals raised like this are weak. Disease in these unhealthy, overcrowded systems can only be controlled by dosing animals with nontherapeutic (i.e., for disease prevention rather than treatment) antibiotics that end up in the environment and on our dinner plate.

Using antibiotics as a means of disease prevention, and growth enhancement, inside CAFOs is so common that it has created two problems: First, the overuse of antibiotics has resulted in new strains of antibiotic-resistant superbacteria; so despite the dosing of animals, what reaches the grocery store shelves can still be contaminated with these bacteria.* Second, eating meat tainted with antibiotics the animals received in their lifetime threatens the effectiveness of those antibiotics to fight bacteria that invade our own bodies.

Another common practice in livestock CAFOs is injecting animals with synthetic growth hormones. Eighty percent of beef cattle[5] and 17 percent of dairy cows[6] raised in the United States each year receive growth hormones. Beef cattle are injected to promote faster and larger growth than normal, while dairy cows receive the injections to stimulate higher than normal milk production. Like antibiotics, hormones administered to animals during their lifetime are released to the environment, and growth factors can be passed to humans via meat, milk, cheese, and yogurt consumption.

Farmers who administer growth hormones are fond of arguing that animals produce hormones naturally, so shooting them up with more hormones is no big deal—so they say. But here's the *real* deal: farm-administered hormones are a genetically engineered variant of the natural growth hormones produced by cows. According to the Center for Food Safety, two of the six hormones approved for use in beef cattle, estradiol and zeranol, are likely to have negative human health effects, including cancer and effects on child development. The growth hormone given to dairy cows, rBGH or rBST (trade name Posilac), is known to cause harm to cows—including mastitis, lameness, and reproductive complications—and may pose harm to

---

* In 2011, researchers who tested random samples of chicken, turkey, pork, and ground beef purchased at twenty-six grocery stores in five cities around the country, found 47 percent contained antibiotic-resistant *Staphylococcus aureus*, a common cause of infection in people. The study, published in the journal *Clinical Infectious Diseases* (4/15/11), concluded that the livestock themselves—rather than contamination during processing and packaging—were the source of the bacteria.

humans as well—most likely due to increased IGF-1 levels in milk which have been linked to an increased relative risk of breast and prostate cancer.[7]

Now that you know all this, let's discuss how you can find meat and dairy products produced by suppliers who don't break all the rules of nature and have more compassion for living things. Then later in the chapter we have some advice for reprioritizing meat and dairy so that you can afford a diverse and well-balanced diet of über-healthy foods.

Agriculture is the leading source of pollution for 76 percent of assessed rivers and 56 percent of assessed lakes in the United States.[8] Water is impacted primarily through runoff pollution from bacteria, antibiotics, and hormones present in animal waste, along with fertilizers and pesticides used to spray feed crops.

The Real Grade-A Alternatives

The alternative to industrially raised animals (and their derivative products) is sustainably raised animals, meaning animals that are raised on enough land to naturally process their waste and under conditions that accommodate their health and natural behavior, including time spent outdoors with shade, shelter, exercise areas, fresh air and direct sunlight. Certified sustainable products will have met all these conditions. Unfortunately, organic products may not, because current organic standards permit semiconfinement of animals with only *access* to the outdoors being provided. Whether the animal spent any time outdoors or not, they can still be certified organic. Until organic standards are revised to correct this, animal welfare on sustainable farms can be superior to that on some large organic farms.

The organic label is much more reliable on the matters of nontherapeutic antibiotics and hormones. Neither of the above are permitted on organic farms. Ditto that on biodynamic and sustainable farms. Lest you think sick animals will be left to suffer, organic and sustainable standards allow antibiotics to treat a specific problem; it's just their use as a prophylactic that is prohibited.

In the final analysis, organic meat, poultry and dairy is typically more expensive and often no better than sustainable counterparts. So think outside the organic box: There are lots of other labels to explore.

Once again, trustworthy certifications besides the USDA Organic label include Animal Welfare Approved, Certified Naturally Grown, Certified Humane, Food Alliance Certified and Certified Biodynamic. While these certifications make it easy to determine the integrity of a product, they are an expense for the producer being certified, and some of that cost gets passed on to the consumer. You will almost always pay a premium for certified products. This is why it is important to look at the small, local producers in your area that often offer comparable products but without certification—and without the markup (see "The Benefits of Local Food," page 194). The sidebar, "Resources for Finding Local Food Growers and Producers," on page 196 will help you connect with the farmers in your area— either directly or via a local grocer—who raise food naturally.

Doable Dairy

The sheer amount of cow's milk that kids consume has many parents especially wary of hormones in milk. Marks that guarantee dairy products *do not* come from hormone-treated animals include the following certification marks: USDA Organic, Certified Naturally Grown, Certified Biodynamic, Certified Humane, Animal Welfare Approved and Food Alliance Certified. But, as mentioned above, you'll pay a premium for certified milk. An alternative is to find noncertified milk (and other dairy products) from a producer that tells you, flat out (in person or via a product's package), that their cows were not given synthetic hormones. A claim with no certification behind it, however, hasn't been verified by a third party, and you are taking the producer at their word.

To complicate matters further, the absence of a hormone-free claim doesn't necessarily mean a product is not hormone free, especially if the dairy the product comes from is small (fewer than 100 cows). Only 10 percent of small dairies use the rSBT/rBGH growth hormone, according to Food and Water Watch, yet for whatever reasons some dairies choose not to fuss with a hormone-free label. Between nonverified claims and no claims at all, it can be hard to accurately access any product without a certified mark. To solve this problem, some organizations have compiled lists of rSBT/ rBGH-free dairies and products. With these lists (see "Resources for Lists of Non-rBGH Dairies"), you can identify hormone-free brands and products beyond those that are certified or labeled as such.

Resources for Lists of Non-rBGH Dairies

www.organicconsumers.org/rBGH/rbghlist.cfm
www.eatwellguide.org/i.php?id=dairymap

Produce + Pesticides: A Toxic Marriage

With billions of pounds of chemical pesticides (insecticides, herbicides, and fungicides) permitted for use in agriculture, it's inevitable that some of them will make it onto our plate. What goes onto, and into, our food as it is being raised becomes a part of it and gets passed on to the consumer. Levels should be low and tolerable,* but chemicals build up over time in the body. Therefore, the real risk of consuming pesticide residues is that harmful effects will develop in the longer term.

Conventional foods that are grown in fields sprayed with synthetic pesticides are much more likely to contain chemical residues than organic produce. Pesticide testing by the USDA from 1994 to 1999, on washed produce samples, showed that 73 percent of conventional produce had residue from at least one pesticide compared to just 23 percent for organic produce. Conventional foods are also six times more likely to have multiple pesticide residues than organic samples.[9] The fact that organic produce contains synthetic pesticide residues† at all has been attributed to the presence of persistent pesticides in the environment, like DDT‡ (a legacy of past conventional farming), and to what's known as pesticide drift, the movement of pesticides through the air away from the original point of application.

Avoiding produce that has been treated with synthetic pesticides is important to minimize ingestion and avoid possible health issues ranging from the mild, including dizziness and nausea, to the serious, including long-term neurological, developmental and reproductive disorders. Choosing the least contaminated food possible is most important when we are feeding children. Children are most at risk due to their smaller and developing bodies, and unborn fetuses are very at risk, even though problems resulting from pesticide exposure may not show up until much later in life. [10]

---

* The EPA sets limits, called tolerances, for pesticide residues in food. As long as the amount of pesticide remaining in and on a food commodity is below the tolerance, the EPA considers the risk of ingestion acceptable, or "safe." The EPA does not set tolerances for all pesticides used in agriculture: some pesticides are exempted from the requirement to have a tolerance. The FDA and USDA share responsibility for enforcing pesticide tolerances in food.

† Pesticides are permitted in organic production, but they are naturally-derived (not synthetic) and are categorized as "least toxic" among pesticide solutions that range from least toxic to highly toxic.

‡ DDT, a highly toxic pesticide, was banned from use in the United States in 1972; however, it is still found in soil and water samples today.

Ninety percent of the 939 million pounds of pesticides used in agriculture never reach their target, but rather are released into the air and water.[11]

Fleshing Out Better Choices

We do not have to buy organic produce exclusively to reduce our exposure to pesticides. The Environmental Working Group's *Shoppers Guide to Pesticides in Produce* ranks forty-five of the most popular fruits and vegetables according to the presence of pesticides. According to the report, the fifteen least contaminated (cleanest) fruits and veggies can be consumed in nonorganic form without concern, while the twelve most contaminated (dirtiest) fruits and veggies should always be bought in organic form when possible (see table 38). Avoiding the "dirty dozen" and instead eating the least contaminated produce can lower pesticide consumption by 92 percent, according to EWG calculations.

This list doesn't just help us avoid pesticides, it helps us save money. Choosing fruits and vegetables in nonorganic form, when it is safe to do so, can save us the typical 10 to 40 percent markup on organic produce.

Genetically Modified Organisms (GMOs) in Our Food

Back in the 1970s scientists discovered they could create plants with specific desired traits much faster than by way of the traditional breeding process by forcibly transferring genes from the DNA of one plant to another, and—here's the kicker—from nonplant organisms to a plant. This was the dawn of the modern biotechnology era, and ever since, biotech companies have been experimenting with our food, injecting bacteria, viruses and other organisms into plant genomes to create novel

Table 38: Pesticides in Produce

Cleanest (most to least)	Dirtiest (most to least)
1. Onions	1. Apples
2. Sweet corn	2. Celery
3. Pineapple	3. Sweet bell peppers
4. Avocado	4. Peaches
5. Cabbage	5. Strawberries
6. Sweet peas	6. Nectarines (imported)
7. Asparagus	7. Grapes
8. Mangos	8. Spinach
9. Eggplant	9. Lettuce
10. Kiwi	10. Cucumbers
11. Cantaloupe (domestic)	11. Blueberries (domestic)
12. Sweet potatoes	12. Potatoes
13. Grapefruit	Plus
14. Watermelon	* Green beans
15. Mushrooms	* Kale/Greens

Source: www.ewg.org/foodnews, 2012

*May contain pesticide of special concern.

traits that do not occur naturally. For example, according to the USDA, 94 percent of soybeans and 72 percent of corn grown in the United States in 2011 were genetically modified for herbicide tolerance (HT); and 73 percent of all corn has been modified to produce bacterial Bt toxin, which is poisonous to insect pests. The hype on these GM foods goes something like this: HT crops will reduce the amount of herbicides needed and promote minimum-till farming; and Bt plants that produce their own insecticide will reduce the need for chemical sprays. But there's more to the story.

HT crops have actually led to an overwhelming *increase* in the use of the herbicide glyphosate (a.k.a. Roundup), according to a report by the Organic Food Center and based on information from the USDA.[12] Perhaps due to the fact that no amount of herbicide will harm the HT crops, farmers began comfortably overspraying crops to kill weeds, impacting the air, water and soil around farms and accelerating the weeds' resistance to the herbicide. Now, farmers are battling Round-up-resistant superweeds that require more potent herbicides and frequent plowing.

The toxin inserted into Bt corn kills many species of insect larvae indiscriminately—including beneficial insects, not only crop-damaging pests. Bt crops are overplanted too, which is kind of like overusing a pesticide—it's just inside the plant instead of outside the plant. Scientists expect pests to develop resistance to the Bt toxin due to its overuse and again, new, more potent pesticides will be needed to fight the superpests that evolve.

The biotech industry that promised a less pesticide-dependent agricultural system could actually be creating one that is more pesticide-dependent.

There is great concern over the potential impacts of biotech products in the environment, not just from resistant weeds and pests, but from unintended harm to other organisms and gene transfer to nontarget species. There is also growing concern that GM plants are unstable and that manipulating DNA can introduce carcinogens, anti-nutrients and toxins into previously safe foods. Simply said, genetic engineering is an infant technology, and it could take years before associated human health and environmental problems emerge. Perhaps we should have given the whole genome project thing more time and study before planting 165 million acres of the stuff and allowing GMOs into the food supply.

You can vent your frustration at the three different government agencies that have jurisdiction over GM foods in the United States: the EPA, USDA and FDA. They have been harshly, and justifiably, criticized for failing to require independent studies or exercise adequate regulatory oversight of GMOs. While consumer interest groups, physicians groups and scientists put pressure on the above agencies to get a clue, we can stop supporting GMOs by not eating them.

In the United States, there has been a 38-fold increase in acreage devoted to GM crops since 1995, from approximately 4.3 million acres to 165 million acres in 2010, according to a report by International Service for the Acquisition of Agri-biotech Applications. Worldwide, one billion hectares have now been planted with genetically modified crops.

Keeping It Real

The prevalence of GMOs in U.S. grocery stores is widespread. While very few whole fruits and vegetables available are genetically modified, the majority of corn, soybeans, canola and cottonseed are genetically modified, and this means that any products derived from them—and highly processed foods containing those products—likely contain GMOs. By some estimates, as much as 80 percent of items in the typical supermarket contain GMOs.

Perhaps the worst part about so many GMOs being put into our food is that there is no labeling. Despite a huge public outcry for labeling of GMOs, so far, the FDA has sided with the biotech industry and refused to require any. You can avoid GMOs, however, when buying foods with the USDA Organic label or the Non-GMO Project Verified label. There are also a couple online shopping guides to help you identify and avoid products and brands that contain GMOs, www.truefoodnow.org/shoppers-guide and www.nongmoshoppingguide.com.

If you switch away from a product with GMOs, let the manufacturer know you have withdrawn your support of their product until they remove GMOs. Consumer rejection of ingredients derived from genetically modified crops can be very effective at convincing giant food companies to remove them from their products. Jeffrey Smith, author of several books on GMOs, including *Seeds of Deception: Exposing Industry and Government Lies About the Safety of the Genetically Engineered Foods You're Eating*, wrote about such a case in England where, following strong public opinion against GMOs, all the major food manufacturers committed to remove GM ingredients in the same week.

THE BENEFITS OF LOCAL FOOD

Perhaps the simplest way to avoid overindustrialized food, without getting a doctorate in label reading, is to shop for locally produced foods. The majority of Americans live quite far from the industrial feedlots and farms that produce so much of our food. For most of us, *local* agriculture is synonymous with small family farms; and small-scale farms have a different outlook on raising food than the industrial-scale producers that are degrading and polluting impacted land and water through energy and chemical intensive practices.

Farmers that live where they work and want to preserve their land for future generations typically use sustainable principles that protect farm workers, soil health, nearby water and ultimately food quality. Small, sustainable farms provide myriad benefits to the communities in which they are located, the customers who consume their products and the larger environment by refusing to sacrifice principles for profit.

Local food is also closer to home and that means less energy will be consumed getting it from farm to table. A peach that travels from a small local farm to your city's Farmers' Market consumes much less energy, and packaging, than one grown on a distant farm and transported across several state lines by way of a refrigerated storage facility and an 18-wheeler.

> Due to the growth in the global transport of food, by air and sea, transportation-related emissions from the food sector have risen dramatically in the past decade.[13]

Shopping as a Locavore

The term "locavore," according to the Oxford University Press blog, was coined in 2005 by a group of San Franciscans to describe individuals that prefer to source and eat foods that are produced locally—preferably within a 100-mile radius of where they live. Locavores make it a habit to buy from the best sources for locally produced food including natural grocers, food cooperatives, farmers' markets and Community Supported Agriculture programs (CSAs).* But, don't count out your neighborhood supermarket entirely: the local food movement has caught the attention of some supermarket giants and regional chains alike that are devoting a small but growing share of shelf space to locally produced foods. These sources can be used, alone or in combination, to obtain highly nutritious, flavorful and locally produced food. To find your closest sources for organic produce and pasture raised animals do a quick search by zip code or City/State using one of the websites listed in the sidebar, "Resources for Finding Local Food Growers and Producers," on page 196.

Local fruits, vegetables and herbs won't necessarily feed you all year long, but making an effort to seek out locally raised

---

* Community Supported Agriculture programs sign up members who pay an annual fee in exchange for weekly shares in the farm's bounty throughout the growing season.

products when they are readily available will boost local economies, reduce environmental impacts from long-haul food transport and improve the freshness and nutritional value of your diet. Stock up during the growing season if you have the will and means to preserve some of the bounty for winter consumption (see "Preserve the Season," page 210).

If you're a meat eater, consider purchasing a whole side of beef or pork with several other people. According to Deck Family Farm in Junction City, Oregon, purchasing sides from a farm that sacrifices and butchers its animals onsite is the least expensive, most environmentally sound and most humane way of purchasing meat. The animal spends its entire life on the farm without ever being shipped and the cost for processing in this manner is significantly less, so the savings is passed on to you, the customer.

You might also look to see if you can find a local buying club for sustainable foods. A buying club allows members to cooperatively buy in bulk to get the best value. Using the website www.eatwild.com, click on your state or country, then click the "Beyond the Farm" link in the right margin to find buying clubs. If you find nothing there, try searching Google or consider starting your own buying club; www.startabuyingclub.com can help you with the process.

Resources for Finding Local Food Growers and Producers

www.localharvest.org

www.eatwellguide.com

www.eatwild.com

www.ams.usda.gov/AMSv1.0/farmersmarkets

www.organicstorelocator.com

American farmland is being lost to development at the rate of 2,880 acres a day.[14]

FOOD FROM THE SEA

The oceans and seas are not exempt from the effects of the industrialization of our food system. According to the FAO, industrial fishing fleets have overfished 82 percent of fish stocks, resulting in the decline of fisheries on a worldwide scale: 50 percent of the world's fish stocks are fully exploited, meaning they are in imminent danger of collapse; and 32 percent of stocks range from overexploited to depleted to recovering. Only 15 percent of fish stocks are estimated to be underexploited (3 percent) or moderately exploited (12 percent) and, therefore, able to produce more than their current catches.[15]

Not only are large fishing fleets taking more fish from an area than the ecosystem can recover from, but many methods used to catch targeted fish also remove other marine species and life that aren't targeted (called bycatch). As a result, we are losing species as well as entire ecosystems.

Consumers of fish and seafood can help by consuming these products in moderation and using buying guides, such as the *Seafood Watch Guide* produced by the Monterey Bay Aquarium (www.montereybayaquarium.org/cr/seafoodwatch.aspx). The guide indicates which seafood items are "Best Choices," "Good Alternatives," and which ones you should "Avoid," and it is available online, in printable pocket guides, or on your mobile device (the latter is available only to iPhone and Android users at this time).

THE ECONOMICS OF REAL FOOD

Now that you generally know what better food choices look like, it's time to look at the true costs of food and the affordability of better food through smart shopping, conscientious meal preparation, and good eating habits.

You will very likely pay more for organic and sustainable foods, because the true costs aren't hidden as they are with so-called cheap food. Whether coming from an industrial farm, feedlot or processing plant, "cheap" food is anything but cheap. First, it costs a small fortune in subsidies ($167.3 billion from 1995–2010[16]) from the U.S. government to keep food at an artificially low price point. And cheap labor provided by undocumented immigrants (an estimated half of all crop farm workers are undocumented[17]) isn't cheap at all: numerous studies have documented that providing services to undocumented immigrants is a significant fiscal burden.[18] American taxpayers, by and large, pay for these services of course. Second, the environmental costs of industrial agriculture must be factored in as well: extremely high water, energy, and chemical inputs are degrading and polluting the environment. And third, processed food derived from cheap commodity crops is eroding public health: consumed in excess, sugar, salt, and trans fats—common in processed foods—lead to increased risk of cancer, type 2 diabetes, obesity, and heart disease.[19] According to Michael Pollan, author of *In Defense of Food*, being stricken with type 2 diabetes will lead to $13,000 a year in added healthcare costs.

The hidden costs of "cheap" food expose it for what it really is: *expensive food*—we pay a nominal price at the supermarket then make up the difference through higher taxes and healthcare costs. In contrast, natural, unprocessed foods may have a higher shelf price, but what you pay out of pocket is the true cost: ostensibly, there's nothing hidden.

Until more people choose sustainable foods over conventional foods, the population will share a heavy tax burden for artificially cheap food that continues to find support. But anyone choosing to invest in more sustainable foods today is like-

ly to see a noticeable reduction in their healthcare costs because of the power of natural, healthy foods—particularly
when replacing unnatural and unhealthy foods—to improve
health.

Making Room in Your Budget for Healthy Food

The environmental, social and economic savings associated
with consuming a diet rich in sustainable, fresh, local foods are
very real, but we can easily get sidetracked and discouraged
when confronted, for example, with the choice of spending
$4.29 a pound for organic bell peppers versus $2.99 a pound for
the conventional variety. It can be hard to pay 43 percent more
for anything, understandable, but the price spread between
conventional and organic versions of grains, legumes, fruits,
and vegetables is typically closer to 20 percent on average, and
can be as low as 7 percent. If only you were saving money on
something else and were prepared to increase your food budget enough to afford more sustainable foods. Wait! Aren't you
saving money, or about to? If you're reading this book from
start to finish, you've just read five chapters describing, in detail, how you can save hundreds, perhaps thousands, of dollars
a year as a result of adopting a greener lifestyle. There should
be no doubt that you can save money in other areas, and if you
are willing to take some of that money and put it toward food,
it can make affording better food much easier.

But not so fast, even though preceding chapters have provided ample suggestions for saving money—more than enough
to allow for an increase in your food budget—the focus of this
chapter is not to convince you to spend what you are saving
elsewhere on food. That's a choice this book can empower you
to make, but this chapter, from here out, assumes you'd like to
find ways to afford better food with the food budget you already have, or at least something very close to it.

The average American spends $11 a day on food according to the USDA's 2010 Food Expenditure Tables, which is more than enough to afford a diet of nutritious, energy-sustaining foods. In fact, it's possible to pull off a healthy diet on just $7 a day. For most folks this will be ambitious because it requires making more than just meals from scratch, including easy to make food products you may consume regularly, like yogurt, salad dressings, stir fry sauces, and bread, for example.

Your success in affording mostly sustainable food on a budget that is somewhere between $7 and $11 a day will depend upon your caloric needs (not wants) and your willingness to make disciplined food decisions and to make food a priority.

So, if you're ready to change the way you eat and what you eat so that you can afford real food that is good for you and the planet, read on!

U.S. agriculture uses 10 calories of fossil-fuel energy to produce a single food calorie.[20]

Watch Your Portions (and Those Snacks)

It's no secret that America is an overweight nation. On the whole, we make very bad food choices. Part of our mistake is eating too many foods that are high in fat and added sugar, but we also overeat—either at each meal, between meals or both. Today Americans eat 570 more calories per day than they did just thirty-four years ago, and it takes only 50 extra calories per day to gain five pounds a year if you're not burning those extra calories.[21]

Portion sizes have increased—by a lot. This is especially evident in the food service industry. Consider Starbuck's Trenta—a 31-ounce cup for iced beverages—the equivalent of nearly three cans of soda; or 7-11's Double Big Gulp that holds about 64 ounces of soda or Slurpee—*twice* the amount of liquid the average adult human stomach can comfortably hold!

According to David Zinczecko, author of *Eat This, Not That*, the proper serving size of a bagel is 2 ounces, but try finding a bagel that weighs less than 4 ounces at your favorite bagel shop. A sandwich should weigh only about 5 ounces, but at most delis sandwiches weigh three times that! By serving larger portions, restaurant owners hope to convince us that we are getting more food for our dollar, but if we don't need those extra calories, we're just get fooled into paying higher prices and eating more. Even at home, we are eating larger portions, perhaps because our perception of a normal portion size has been skewed by the prevalence of large portion sizes almost everywhere we go.

Portion control isn't just a way to watch calories, it's a way to conserve food and save money. Try sharing a meal with someone if eating out; and at home, if you can reduce current portion sizes by 25 percent you'll save an equal amount on food, or $523 a year for the average person.

As big as portion sizes have become, the bigger culprit to increased calorie intake may be all those in between meal snacks. The percent of the American population eating three or more snacks a day increased from 11 percent in 1977 to 42 percent in 2002, and that trend hasn't changed in the last decade.[22] In fact, it may have gotten worse. From snack-filled vending machines in schools to snack-supplied business meetings to snack-flanked check-out registers, highly processed snacks are omnipresent, and quite unsuccessful at filling us up. Junk food can actually make us hungrier. That's because much of the nutrient density is depleted in processing and junk food usually contains simple sugars: it's a recipe for a quick energy boost and temporary satiation, but in no time you'll come crashing down much hungrier than you were before. Snacking that ends up stimulating your appetite leads to oversnacking, overeating during your next meal and over-spending on food in general.

If you need to snack between meals, that's fine—don't torture yourself! Just choose whole, nutrient dense foods: They will satisfy you and actually help you avoid going into your next meal overly hunger.

Reducing oversized portions at each meal and cutting out sugary and fatty snacks will have an immediate slimming effect on your food bill and a slimmer figure won't be far behind!

 ## Spotlight on Savings

Supersized portions result in overeating and food waste. Trimming portion size by 25 percent could save the average person $523 a year.

Eat Less Meat

Per capita, Americans eat 8.4 ounces of meat per day or 3.7 pounds each week[23]—more than twice the global average[24] and 42 percent more than the maximum daily allowance recommended by the USDA, up until 2011.*

Raising enough animals to satisfy western tastes for diets rich in meat is damaging our environment on almost every level. Livestock production consumes massive amounts of water, energy, and land (to raise the feed as well as the animals); it is the leading non-point source of water pollution in the United States; and it contributes significantly to climate change—producing nearly one fifth of global greenhouse gas emissions.[25] The United Nations Environment Program's International Panel of Sustainable Resource Management warns that as the world population surges toward a predicted 9.1 billion people by 2050, a global shift toward a diet that

---

* In 2011, USDA unveiled its new and improved dietary guidelines in which they no longer set limits for meat consumption. The new recommendations simply state to keep meat portions "small and lean."

doesn't include animal products is vital to save the world from hunger, fuel poverty, and the worst effects of climate change.[26]

According to the USDA, animal protein is the most expensive food by portion size.[27] Beef, pork and poultry costs an average $3.53 per pound, and prices are rising.[28] Keep in mind, also, that the cost per servable pound of meat and poultry can be much higher because we often pay for bones, fat, and skin that get discarded.

Now let's look at the price per pound of low-cost proteins like legumes. Table 39 shows the average price of foods within different food groups and among nonorganic and organic options. Legumes as well as some whole grains are excellent low-cost sources of protein, costing 56 percent less than meat on average in conventional form and 48 percent less than meat on average in organic form. Nuts and seeds are good sources of protein as well, but you'll want to consume those in moderation due to their high price point (and in the case of nuts, high fat content).

For meat-lovers, cutting back on meat consumption will be an adjustment, so start by controlling portion size at each meal where meat is present, followed by gradually replacing meat with vegetarian sources of protein until you're eating just sixteen ounces of meat per week or less.

You'll need to make sure your new meat-light diet meets the recommendations for protein intake, but you may not have to

A 2006 report authored by FAO scientists found that globally livestock production accounts for more greenhouse gas emissions than transportation.[29] This includes energy-related emissions from feed crop production, processing, and transportation as well as emissions from animal waste including nitrous oxide and methane—greenhouse gases that are 296 and 23 times as warming as carbon dioxide, respectively.[30]

Table 39: Average Retail Price of Food Per Pound
(Unless Otherwise Noted)

Food group	Conventional	Sustainable	Combination*
8 different types of bulk dried legumes	$1.54	$2.03	
14 different types of bulk grains and pasta	$1.57	$2.08	
Whole milk and yogurt	$2.11/qt	$2.47/qt.	
51 different types of fresh vegetables	$2.07	$2.79	$2.31
24 different types of fresh fruits	$2.72	$3.18	$2.91
Eggs	$1.49/doz.	$3.59/doz.	
9 different beef, pork and chicken products	$3.62	$6.07	
Butter and cheese	$4.39	$6.49	
7 different types of seeds	$5.46	$9.04	
5 different types of nuts	$7.65	$11.33	

Sources: www.ers.usda.gov/data-products/meat-price-spreads.aspx, Whole Foods, Safeway (Q2 2012)

*Only "dirty dozen" in organic form, all else conventional (see table 38).

match the protein content, gram for gram, of the meat you are giving up. That's because many people who eat a lot of meat get too much protein. Most adults only need about 0.36 grams of protein per pound of body weight each day. That's about fifty-four grams for a 150-pound active adult. Since some people need more or less than the national guidelines suggest, it's always a good idea to check with a doc before making any big changes to your diet.

Once you know how much protein your body needs, use the links within the "Resources for Vegetarians" sidebar to match plant protein sources with your dietary tastes and needs. The American Dietetic Association states that protein needs can easily be met by consuming a variety of plant protein sources over an entire day; and choosing more plant proteins over animal proteins can save you money too (see table 39 and table 40).

Resources for Vegetarians (Present and Future)

First-rate nutrition guides:

www.veggieglobal.com

www.veganhealth.org

www.highproteinfoods.net

News and analysis on health, ethics, and environment:

www.thevegetariansite.com

Extensive database of vegetarian recipes:

www.vegetariantimes.com/recipe

Table 40: Meat Consumption Comparison (Household of Four)

Meat as a portion of dinner relative to plant-based foods (in ounces per capita*)	Per serving cost†	Weekly cost for 4 similar meals (4 servings per meal)	Annual cost
1 to 1 (8 oz. meat, 3 oz. veggies, 5 oz. grains)	($2.69)	($43.04)	($2,238)
1 to 2 (4 oz. meat, 5 oz. organic veggies, 5 oz. organic grains)	($2.43)	($38.88)	($2,022)
1 to 3 (3 oz. certified sustainable meat, 6 oz. combination veggies, 5 oz. organic grains)	($2.65)	($42.40)	($2,205)
Meatless (8 oz. organic legumes, 8 oz. organic veggies)	($2.42)	($38.72)	($2,013)

Assumes average cost of referenced food groups noted in table 39.

* Generally and proportionally, meat weighs more than plant-based foods, so a one-to-one ratio in portion size of meat to plant foods does not always translate to a one-to-one ratio in weight.

† Includes only meat, vegetables, grains and legumes: does not include other ingredients.

Spotlight on Savings

A family of four that consumes conventional meat at the majority of their meals can save up to $1.08 per meal when replacing some or all of that meat with healthier foods. Assuming a family shares 780 home-prepared meals together over a year, if 30 percent of those meals were meatless, the annual savings would be around $256.

Buy "On Sale" and Save With Coupons

Research shows that shopping with a list saves money, and while this is true, reserve flexibility for supervalues that await you wherever you shop. Remain flexible, but don't give way to abandon! Before buying something on sale, you need to have a plan to use it up quickly if it is perishable. This may mean knocking one or many things off your carefully prepared shopping list in order to incorporate the sale item into this week's menu plan. Keep your menu plan for the week and the shelf life of food products in mind at all times.

For nonperishables, or things with a very long shelf life, if the sale is good and it's something you use regularly, buy it! You can save up to 30 percent when buying things on sale, and this is a critical markdown when it comes to being able to afford some organic brands. Buying more than was on your list will cause the total check to go up, and it may feel like you are overspending, but things will balance out on your next shopping trip. Just don't wait too long to incorporate your sale items into a week's menu plan, so you can quickly see the savings.

Coupon proponents claim you can cut your grocery bill in half—or more—by using coupons. This kind of savings, however, may be reserved for the shopper who isn't choosey about what brands they buy, because coupons for organic brands aren't falling from the sky. That doesn't mean they aren't out there, and with average per capita spending for food prepared at home amounting to $2,093 in 2010,[31] even a 5 percent savings from the use of coupons could save a family of four $419 a year. That should be worth clipping a few coupons! Coupons are easier to find now with the Internet: visit manufacturer websites; your grocery store's website; and coupon-finder websites that allow you to search by product category, store, or brand.

When using coupon-finder websites, steer clear of those that trade coupons for your personal information—don't provide anything more than an email; and it wouldn't be a bad idea to set up a dedicated email account, using Google or Yahoo!, for this purpose to keep offers from clogging up your main email inbox; this way, if the offers become unmanageable, you can just delete the account. Most coupon-finder sites favor conventional brands, but www.mambosprouts.com and www.organicdeals.com are coupon sites devoted to healthy brands.

Another tactic is to email or call your favorite organic or natural food manufacturer directly to request coupons be sent to you by email or physical mail. Also, check product packaging before recycling it for coupons printed anywhere on the packaging, including inside boxes and under labels. Also, keep a lookout for instant coupons, including stickers and tear sheets attached to the product itself or the shelf below, respectively.

> The mechanized, monoculture model of industrial agriculture has been steadily destroying topsoil which is disappearing at a rate seventeen times faster than nature can create it.[32]

Grow Some of Your Own

You may not have the space or time to cultivate a large garden, but even a simple 4' × 8' raised planter bed in a sunny corner of your lot, or containers on a patio, can produce the makings for fresh salsa, salad greens, herbs, or whatever you have a taste for and will grow in your climate. Whether you have a short or long growing season, you can almost always save money by producing some of what you eat yourself. There are no guarantees in gardening, though; a late frost, pests, disease, a broken irrigation system. Lots *could* go wrong, but if you are conscientious and willing to learn, there is little risk in sinking some money into a starter garden and seeing how it goes. For the cost of some compost, seeds, and irrigation water, you can provide nutritious, fresh fruits and vegetables for your family for up to several months a year.

If you're a beginner gardener, read everything you can get your hands on about the vegetables you plan to grow: for example, when to plant them, how to care for them and what preventive steps to take to protect them against common diseases and pests.

Resources for Edible Gardens

Cooperative Extension System look-up:
www.csrees.usda.gov/Extension

Regional gardening reports and blogs:
www.garden.org/regional/report

Raised planting systems:
www.eartheasy.com/yard-garden/raised-garden-beds-kits-planters

Urban organic gardening blog:
www.urbanorganicgardener.com/blog

Gardening tools and supplies plus "learn and share"
section with how-to guides and planning tools:
www.gardeners.com

For the landless looking for land to share or rent:
www.acga.localharvest.org
www.sharingbackyards.com
www.urbangardenshare.org (limited cities)

Table 41: Estimated Savings When Growing Some of Your Own Vegetables

TYPICAL SCENARIO Organic and non-organic blend, store-bought produce	($220)					
GREENER SCENARIOS	**Startup costs***	**↑Seasonal cost↓**	**Seasonal savings**	**First year ROI**	**Payback period (in years)**	**10-year net savings**
Homegrown (raised bed garden†)	($587)	($26)	$194	33%	3	$1,358
Homegrown (in-ground garden)	($130)	($26)	$194	149%	0.7	$1,804

Assumes a seasonal yield of 14 lbs. leaf lettuce, 6 lbs. spinach, 3 lbs. green beans, 5 lbs. carrots, 16 lbs. zucchini, 40 lbs. tomatoes, 16 lbs. cucumbers, 5 lbs. bell peppers, 1 lb. basil, 8 lbs. onions, 4 lbs. Brussels sprouts, 6 lbs. cabbage

* Supplies (excluding fencing), seeds, dirt, compost, and recycled plastic lumber (greener option) for two 4' × 8' organic garden plots.

† Raised beds are built on top of existing soil allowing for closer and earlier plantings, good drainage, and more root development. Good choices for raised bed systems include nontoxic plastic lumber made from recycled milk jugs, concrete blocks, and reclaimed metal and untreated cedar, locust, or cypress wood which are naturally rot resistant. Treated (or preserved) wood is a cheap option, but small amounts of the preservative compounds will leach into the soil that feeds your plants.

If you're a seasoned gardener, and could benefit from some higher yields, think about taking your garden to the next level. That could mean expansion of an existing garden plot, or gradually transforming your entire landscape around the house into a mostly edible one that provides as much bounty as possible. Fruit trees, berry-producing bushes and vines, herbs, vegetables, and even edible flowers can grow alongside ornamental plants to create a beautiful landscape that produces cheap food for your family and then some—there's nothing like sharing the bounty of your garden with others.

No space whatsoever? Don't throw in the trowel just yet: there's a good chance you can find a neighbor with unused yard and garden space and trade your gardening skills and some of your yield in exchange for use of that space. You can strike out and make an arrangement on your own or take advantage of online yard-sharing networks set up to connect gardeners lacking space with land owners willing to loan theirs (see "Resources for Edible Gardens," page 209).

 Spotlight on Savings

A vegetable garden that produces 124 pounds of fresh produce each season can save the average shopper $194 in food costs annually.

Preserve the Season

Take advantage of foods when they are cheaper, such as fresh produce when it is in season. Seasonal foods from your region are cheaper because they aren't grown in heated greenhouses or shipped great distances. Stock up on foods when they are plentiful and cheap and then preserve them to enjoy all year long. Canning, pickling, drying and freezing are all methods of preservation (see sidebar, "Resources for Food Preservation Basics, Instruction and Equipment," on page 211).

Can It

Canning requires some special equipment and attention to instructions to avoid spoilage after canning, but it is not difficult in the least, and canned foods have a long shelf life.

Pickle It

Pickling is one of the oldest methods of preserving foods; it involves preserving food with an acid solution such as vinegar.

Dehydrate It

Dehydration is an easy and cheap way of preserving food, and once food has been dehydrated, or dried, it is very resilient and long-lasting. In addition to a food dehydrator, all you really need is a sharp knife to start drying food.

Freeze It

Freezing is the simplest form of food preservation, and according to the USDA, freezing keeps foods safe indefinitely when stored at 0° F—the temperature needed for prolonged storage of frozen foods. Food flavors and texture will deteriorate with time, however, so date food packages with the date they go into the freezer and follow recommended storage times posted on the FDA's gateway website on food safety at www.foodsafety.gov.

Resources for Food Preservation Basics, Instruction and Equipment

Recipes, How-to Guides, product links and a community of other preservers sharing tips and advice:
www.freshpreserving.com

The National Center for Home Food Preservation:
www.uga.edu/nchfp/

Shop for the Lower Price-Per-Unit

Few things are a bigger waste of money—and resources—than food and beverages that come packaged in inefficient small-serve packaging. When you choose brands that use extra packaging to contain smaller portions of food, you are paying a premium for the additional packaging the manufacturer had to use and making more trash than is necessary. To save money on groceries and reduce packaging waste, always look for products packaged in large or bulk quantities. You'll save around an average 46 percent on an item's price per unit when it is packaged in a much larger quantity and weight.

Let's be clear about the definition of *bulk* for this purpose: we're talking about bulk quantities that use the lowest packaging-to-food ratio possible. Eight individual 15-ounce cans of chili packed in a box that's then shrink-wrapped with plastic (commonly seen at wholesale "clubs") is not the kind of bulk purchase that leads to less packaging, but a single 6.75 pound can definitely qualifies! With any bulk purchase, make sure you don't get carried away and buy more than you need or can use within the product's shelf life.

If your market has a bulk bin section, compare the price per pound for bin items you consume compared to packaged economy sizes of those items. Buying from bins is usually less expensive, but not always.

Of U.S. fossil fuel consumption devoted to the production and consumption of food, as much as one-third is used for processing and packaging.[33]

Buying from bins is also a way to reduce packaging waste, but again, not always. Bulk bins in the supermarket offer a chance to help ourselves to as much or as little food as we want. When we help ourselves to large quantities, these bins are remarkably helpful in reducing packaging waste, but bulk food bins aren't just used to purchase large quantities. They can be just as appealing when we want very small quantities of something; and those bulk food stations get wasteful pretty quickly when customers use generously-sized paper or plastic bags for a mere handful of raisins or a cup of rice. Help reduce waste by bringing bags or containers from home that can be washed and reused indefinitely. If using your own rigid container, use a sticker (usually provided at bulk stations) to note its tare (the weight when it is empty) before filling. Sometimes scales are provided, but you may have to enlist the help of available store personnel.

Unlike many packaged foods, bulk foods obviously don't come in premeasured servings or with cooking instructions. The best guide ever written on cooking bulk foods is *World Taste: Wild Oats' Guide to Buying & Preparing Bulk Foods*. It's only available used, so if you can, get your hands on one! If you can't, the Moscow Community Coop in Moscow, Idaho, publishes basic bulk food cooking instruction on their website, www.moscowfood.coop/content/view/49/76/.

Three hundred pounds of packaging waste are generated each year for each person in the United States.[34]

Pass Up Convenience Foods

As much as possible, stay away from expensive convenience foods like ready-made meals: You pay a premium for prepackaged meals compared to multiple ingredients in their whole form that you put together yourself at home. And it's not just meals-to-go that steal our money. Anything made for us is usually more expensive than if we made it at home ourselves. Yogurt, cottage cheese, granola, salad dressing, bread, pesto, hummus, marinades, and sauces are easy to make and cost a fraction compared to store-bought varieties.

For example, vegan, organic split pea soup in a can costs around $0.17/ounce, but made from scratch it will only cost $0.08/ounce—53 percent less! Incidentally, $0.08/ounce is also about *half* what a nonorganic brand of canned split pea soup costs. And while organic bread can cost $5 a loaf at the grocery store, you can make a loaf of organic bread from scratch for around $0.69!

Bringing home fewer premade meals and food items and more *ingredients* that have to be combined will lead to more time in the kitchen, but if a sizable share of your diet currently includes prepackaged, processed foods, selecting fresh, whole ingredients more often will not only save you money—lots of money—it will also greatly improve the quality of your diet. Those are darn good reasons to find some time to cook.

Lack of time is the number one excuse people give for why they don't cook. Here are some ideas.

Making time for cooking:
- Trade some TV time for time in the kitchen. If you are "average," you're watching close to five hours of TV a day! If you absolutely can't give up your shows, bring the TV into the kitchen.
- Put your home office close to the kitchen. In between sending emails you can accomplish a lot and keep a close eye on the stove.
- Redistribute household chores within the family. If you're going to start cooking, let go of something else.
- Stop shuttling your kids around to places they can safely bike or walk. If you're nervous about letting your kids out of your sight, teach them what they need to know to be safe and implement a buddy system so they can't go anywhere without a friend. (There's safety in numbers!)
- Cook in stages. On days when you have some extra time to spend in the kitchen use it to get a jump start on meals that are planned later in the week. Make a sauce, wash and chop vegetables, or measure out spices that are required for a future recipe and store until needed. You can

cut cooking time dramatically for recipes that benefit from components prepared in advance.

- Use time productively. Try to cook large batches so your effort produces enough for two to three extra meals, which you can put aside and reheat another night.

Speeding up cooking:

- Choose simple recipes. If you doubt your ability to prepare a meal from scratch in less than thirty minutes, maybe you haven't been using the right recipes. Simple, healthy, quick meals are the subject of many cookbooks—and TV shows.
- Read a recipe from start to finish before beginning. Flubbing a recipe can do more than delay dinner and waste your time: if it renders a dish unpalatable, it wastes money too. Protect your investment in the ingredients you've purchased and familiarize yourself with each step of a recipe before you begin.
- Get organized. Preparing and organizing recipe ingredients should always be done before assembly and cooking starts. This enables us to seamlessly move from one step in the recipe to the next without risk of getting behind and overcooking something while we try to play catch up.
- Use a slow cooker to take the cooking element out of meal preparation. You'll still need to prepare ingredients, but everything goes in raw and will be ready by the time you come home from work.
- Don't do it alone—unless you want to. Get everyone involved—especially the kids. Our youth receive terrible messages about food from food companies that disproportionately target them in marketing high-calorie, low-nutrient-dense foods; and the quality of school lunch programs has suffered under budget cuts and pressure from industry lobbyists to undermine nutrition

Table 42: Prepackaged Meal Versus Scratch Meal Comparison (Two Servings)

Meal description	Cost of meal	Cost of 100 similar meals	10-year costs
Frozen skillet meal in a bag	($9.50)	($950)	($9,500)
Scratch stir fry made with organic veggies, sustainable chicken, sauce from jar + organic white rice	($6.95)	($695)	($6,950)
Scratch stir fry made with organic veggies, organic tofu, homemade sauce + organic brown rice	($5.26)	($526)	($5,260)

Assumes 6 oz. protein, 12 oz. vegetables, 4 oz. sauce, and 3 oz. dry rice (cooked).

standards.* Invite your kids into the kitchen and allow them to learn good food lessons at an early age.

- Get equipped. Having the right equipment at your fingertips can make the difference between having fun in the kitchen or getting slowed down and frustrated. For a list of what every kitchen needs—at a minimum—visit www. greenmatters.com/blog/kitchen-equipment. Beg, borrow, or barter and get as much on this list as you can!

People who live to be 100, and live out their later years in good health, have certain lifestyle traits in common: among them, the use of natural foods and traditional cooking methods.[35]

---

* When it comes to national school lunch nutritional guidelines, a slice of pizza (due to the small smear of tomato paste) and a serving of French fries both count as a vegetable. We have the frozen pizza and potato lobbies—and of course the U.S. Congress who went along with this—to thank. While this ruling is not in imminent danger of being reversed, the USDA has issued new guidelines aimed at improving school lunch nutrition. The changes will be phased in—and no doubt challenged by industry lobbyists—over time.

Spotlight on Savings

When simple scratch meals replace prepackaged, heat-and-serve versions, the home cook can save around $1.28 to $2.12 per serving even when including some organic ingredients.

Eat In

In 1955 we spent a third of our food budget on meals away from home. In 2010, nearly half of what we spent on food for the entire year was for meals away from home, or $1,923 per capita on average;[36] and it doesn't really matter where you're spending that money, be it at a sit-down restaurant or a drive-in burger joint, you will almost always pay more for food—any food—that you didn't cook for yourself at home.

It's not just high-income earners that dine out; according to a 2009 CBS news poll, 41 percent of households earning between $30,000 and $50,000 dine out at least once a week.[37] Since restaurant meals tend to be much more expensive than home-cooked ones, you'll have more money to spend on healthier food if you cut back on eating out. One trip to a moderately priced sit-down restaurant could cost a family of four between $50 and $70 after leaving the tip. But a similar amount—$67—can provide four people three, mostly organic, meals a day for two days! (See table 43.)

Even if you reserve sit-down-style restaurant dining for only very special occasions, the ubiquitous fast food establishment is harder to avoid—especially if you are male or have young kids, according to the CBS poll. For many of us, grabbing a burrito and soda for lunch and picking up a pizza or a round of Happy Meals for the kids' dinner is part of our daily routine. But as discussed in chapter 1, fast food is no bargain; the average meal from a fast food establishment costs over $10. You don't have to spend $10 on fast food to lose money, however: A $5 fast food meal is still more expensive than a balanced and more healthful meal you could make at home (see table 43).

Table 43: Three Mostly Organic Meals,
All for Under $9 Per Person Per Day (Household of Four)*

Breakfast: Egg and sausage on toast	Lunch: Mediterranean salad	Dinner: White fish with lemon butter sauce, veggie and brown rice
4 certified humane eggs, $1.10	Large sized head of organic leaf lettuce $1.69	1 lb. sustainable white fish, $8.99
4 slices multigrain toast, $1.07	½ small red onion, $0.75	1 lb. organic broccoli, $1.69
8 oz. organic vegetarian breakfast sausage, $4.99†	7.5 oz. garbanzo beans, $0.45	1.5 c. organic brown rice, $1.72
1 pound seasonal organic fruit, $2.29	2 oz. organic feta cheese $2.00	1 lemon, $0.69
Serves 4	2 oz. pitted Kalmata olives, $1.83	3 T. organic butter, $0.87
	One dozen organic grape or cherry tomatoes $1.14	Serves 4
	half a medium cucumber, $0.39	
	¼ cup each olive oil and red wine vinegar, $1.87	
	Serves 4	
Total: $9.45	Total: $10.12	Total: $13.96
Total per serving: $2.36	Total per serving: $2.53	Total per serving: $3.49

*Based on Whole Foods prices, Q2 2012

†This price is for premade sausage patties. A yummy vegetarian sausage crumble or lentil hash is easy to make from scratch and costs a fraction as much! Search for recipes online, make ahead of time, then brown and serve for quick breakfasts.

 Spotlight on Savings

Mostly organic meals can cost the same or less than cheap fast food. A cheeseburger, side salad, and medium fries from a major fast food restaurant costs $6.37, or $2.88 more than a simple home-cooked meal of fish, organic vegetables, and organic rice.

Of course, avoiding dining out and fast food means more grocery shopping, cooking, and cleaning up. There's really no way to get around that fact. Those who use fast food as a crutch because they lack time to cook or who seek it out for pleasure to satisfy the neuroaddictive response that is triggered by overconsumption of junk food,[38] well, those folks have some legitimate obstacles to work through. This chapter—this book in fact—cannot show all the ways to make time for what's important or how to break addictions (be them to junk food, shopping, or something else), but it will show that when it comes to choosing a greener lifestyle and healthy foods, money is often the least of all hurdles.

Buy Only What You Will Eat and Let Nothing Go to Waste

Of all the ways to get more from your food dollars, eliminating or severely reducing food waste is possibly the easiest and most profitable of them all. The average American family throws out five hundred pounds of food, worth $1,200, each year because they buy more than they can eat before food spoils.[39] Throwing uneaten food away is not only one and the same with throwing money away, but it also wastes all the freshwater and fossil fuels it took to grow or manufacture the food, transport raw ingredients, process and package it, ship the end product and finally haul and process it as waste.

Plan meals and make shopping lists carefully to avoid food waste and to ensure that the freshest foods get eaten first follow these tips:

- Prepare meals incorporating fresh ingredients first, saving meals that use dry, canned or frozen products for later in the week.
- Don't keep hyperprocessed—and potentially addictive— meals in the house that will tempt you when you should be using fresh ingredients at meal time.
- Likewise, don't keep processed snack food around. When there's nothing to snack on but a raw carrot or piece of fruit, it will disappear very quickly.

- Give food away to a neighbor if you know you can't use it. In all likelihood, you won't lose money from your generosity—just gain good Karma, putting you on the receiving end the next time that neighbor must part with a flat of fresh u-picked strawberries!

When perishable foods have passed peak freshness, but aren't ready for the composter, grab them and turn them into something wonderful:

- Make a quick slaw of grated vegetables and salad dressing.
- Puree fruit to make a smoothie.
- Make soup! Download soup recipes from the Internet that contain whatever you have on hand and must be used fast.
- Turn over-ripe bananas into banana bread.
- Stew nearly passed berries for an ice cream or yogurt topper.
- Make croutons, bread pudding or stuffing out of stale bread.

As hard as we may try, there will inevitably be some food waste. Don't put food scraps into the garbage pail if it can be helped: when food decays in landfills, it creates methane—a greenhouse gas that is—as mentioned earlier—twenty-three times more potent than CO_2! The best way to deal with food scraps is to compost them at home or sign up for curbside composting if offered by your sanitation company. Use a garbage disposal only if you lack composting options: Food waste present in wastewater from homes and businesses takes considerable energy to remove.

Give Up Kitchen Disposables

What we spend on disposable "convenience products" doesn't add up to nearly as much as what we spend on meat, food that's never eaten or food we don't cook ourselves, but we don't spend nothing on it either; and a daily reliance on disposable kitchen products like plastic film, plastic bags, paper napkins and paper towels is a sad waste of resources. All this stuff we couldn't imagine living without, well, we don't need any of it. We might as well be throwing dollar bills away—bills that can add up to hundreds of dollars each year. And there is considerable harm caused by the never ending production and disposal of throwaway products.

Production, in the case of virgin plastic, requires petroleum and toxic chemicals and creates highly hazardous waste. Unsustainable paper production has resulted in half the world's forests being cleared or burned, and 80 percent of what's left has been seriously degraded, according to the Environmental Paper Network. Like the factories that make plastics, pulp and paper mills are one of the most polluting industries.

The disposable plastic and paper so many of us use in the kitchen may only account for a fraction of the 55 million tons of all nondurable paper and plastic thrown into U.S. landfills each year[40], but it's pretty disappointing that throwaway products—that are easily and economically replaced with durable ones—are contributing to the overall impact of two very polluting industries and aggravating waste management problems. And what are they costing us, out of pocket? In the process of preparing, eating, storing, and packing food as well as cleaning up our food messes the typical four-person household spends $563 annually on disposable paper and plastic kitchen products (see table 44).

Tough Trumps Trash

Instead of covering food with plastic film (and aluminum foil for that matter) or placing it in a plastic bag, transfer food into reusable containers. Disposable plastic is a major environmental problem; only about one in ten plastic bags, sacks, and wrap end up recovered for recycling.[41]

Table 44: Estimated Annual Consumption of Disposable Kitchen Products and Their Cost (Household of Four)

Product	Cost
78 rolls of paper towels	$130
4,672 paper napkins	$75
944 plastic food storage bags	$286
730 feet of plastic cling wrap	$11
648 paper lunch sacks	$14
300 paper plates	$12
146 plastic cups	$9
260 plastic straws	$6
104 plastic tall kitchen garbage bags	$20
TOTAL	**$563**

Try to match the size and shape of the food you need to store to the container. One cause of food spoilage is air and oxygen, so you want as little air trapped inside the container with your food as possible. For this reason, it's important to have differently sized storage containers: tall and skinny, wide and flat, and stout and round. If something doesn't fit perfectly, that's okay, just eat it up as soon as you can.

The best reusable containers for food are made of durable heat- and cold-resistant glassware—hands down. You can freeze and reheat in them (follow manufacturer guidelines) and even serve in them. Another bonus to glass is that you can see inside, so less food gets forgotten and spoils. With proper use, glassware can last forever!

For packing kids' lunches, glass storage containers however are not ideal—too heavy and breakable. If you have lunches to pack, check out www.reuseit.com, a website with just about anything you could need for this purpose, including insulated and noninsulated bags, plastic-lined fabric pouches and wraps with Velcro closures for sandwiches or snacks, thermal and nonthermal food jars, bento boxes, BPA-free* bottles, utensil sets, nontoxic ice packs, even reusable straws.

Prepare yourself: One reusable sandwich bag can cost between $6 and $9, but there is good reason: you don't have to worry about it leaching toxins into your food, it is dishwasher or washing machine safe, and made in America. And each bag has the potential to replace thousands of disposable baggies in its lifetime, so there is a great savings overall to switching to reusable products.

 ## Spotlight on Savings

It will cost one-sixth to one-tenth as much to assemble an eighteen-piece set (thirty-cup equivalent storage capacity) of high quality-reusable containers as the typical household spends on plastic bags and film in one year.

Go Paperless

And then there are paper products. Most people can't imagine life without paper towels and napkins, until they try living without them, and then they discover how easy it is. A collection of reusable rags can handle most jobs that we've come to rely on paper towels to do. The trick is to have enough on hand and keep them within easy reach. Assemble a set of rags that are different sizes, thicknesses, textures, and absorbencies, so you'll have a rag for any chore that previously required a paper towel.

---

* BPA (bisphenol A) is a chemical used primarily in polycarbonate plastic bottles, can linings, and epoxy resins. There is concern that exposure to BPA from food that comes in contact with it may pose risks to human reproduction and development. Based on its review of two industry-backed studies, the U.S. Food and Drug Administration recognizes BPA exposure from food contact materials as safe, however, a number of independent studies highlight the links between BPA exposure and adverse health effects.

According to 1-800-RECYCLING.com, as many as 51,000 trees per day are required to replace the number of paper towels that are discarded every day in the United States.

If you must use paper towels for "special" messes (a few things come to mind), purchase a brand that is recycled and unbleached, which requires less energy and also produces less particulate emissions, less wastewater, and less solid waste during manufacturing. Unbleached towels don't have to go into the trash either: they can go into a compost bin as long as they weren't used for anything hazardous.

As far as giving up paper napkins goes, stuff a drawer with cloth napkins and don't look back. Give everyone in the house their own color so you can keep track of whose is whose. This

---

Resources for Reusable Kitchen Products

Glass storage containers:
www.pyrexware.com
www.freemarketorganics.com

Plastic containers made from 100 percent recycled plastic:
www.preserveproducts.com

Innovative, reusable sandwich wraps and snack bags:
www.reuseit.com

Reusable towels:
www.naturallinensboutique.com/unpapertowels
www.willowpads.com
www.peopletowels.com

Organic napkins:
www.greenhome.com
www.pristineplanet.com

is important because you won't always want or need to wash a napkin after each meal. But do have plenty of extra napkins on hand in case you need to take soiled ones out of the rotation before laundry day.

Don't even question whether washing cloth towels and napkins—water and energy it takes to do so and all—is better for the environment than replenishing disposables over and over and over. Increasing our laundry loads by 6 to 13 percent has minimal environmental impacts compared to manufacturing, transporting, and discarding paper. You may not even need to do extra laundry loads, but rather each time you run a load of clothes or linens, just toss a few soiled towels and napkins into the machine along with them.

Table 45: Estimated Savings When Kicking the Paper Towel and Napkin Habit (Household of Four)

TYPICAL SCENARIO 78 rolls of paper towels and 4,672 paper napkins		($205)				
GREENER SCENARIOS*	Initial cost	↑Annual cost↓	First-year savings	Five-year net savings	Ten-year net savings†
Conventional cloth napkins and towels	($84)	$0	$121	$941	$1,954
Organic cotton napkins and towels	($220)	$0	($15)	$805	$1,797
Homemade organic napkins and towels	($36)	$0	$169	$989	$2,012
Assembled napkins and towels from thrift stores	($18)	$0	$187	$1,007	$2,028

*Set of 12 napkins and 24 towels

†Assumes 30 percent of towels will need replacing after five years.

Spotlight on Savings

Kicking the paper towel and napkin habit can save a typical household a minimum of $121 the first year and over $200 each year thereafter.

AN ORGANIC APPLE A DAY KEEPS THE DOCTOR AWAY

Before moving on to another topic, it's worth emphasizing the relationship between diet and health and health and financial well-being. Poor nutrition has been linked to heart disease, high blood pressure, stroke, some types of cancer, diabetes, and obesity; and diet-related diseases cost afflicted families thousands of dollars a year in out-of-pocket medical costs and lost productivity. So better nutritional choices can not only make you healthier, but wealthier too!

According to the National Institute of Cancer, one of the easiest ways to lower your chances for all the diet-related diseases is to eat five to nine servings of fruits and vegetables every day. The most beneficial fruits and vegetables are those that are grown in nutrient-rich soil, haven't been sprayed with harmful chemicals and have spent the least amount of time sitting around between harvest and consumption. In other words, fruits and vegetables that are organic, sustainable and local— if not all three, shoot for as many as possible.

Predicting how much money there is to be saved by adopting a healthier diet is impossible—that depends on how your body reacts to chemicals, additives, and nutritional deficits to which you're exposed through your food choices; and lots of things can make you feel bad or make you sick—not just what you eat—so fixing your diet is just part of the solution to improving long-term health. But for almost anyone who starts eating cleaner, natural foods the first change they'll notice is that they feel better. Maybe the big change for you will be more energy. Maybe you will avoid a major illness down the road. Everyone is different, but any improvement in the way you feel and your clinical health is a sound plan for avoiding extraordinary healthcare costs.

> In 1960, we spent 18 percent of our take home pay on food and 5 percent on health care. Now we spend 9 percent of our take home pay on food and upwards of 17 percent on health care.[42]

ANYTHING YOU CAN BUY
NEW IS CHEAPER USED

The level at which we consume today has escalated in a relatively short amount of time. Fifty years ago small, independent local businesses supplied most families and businesses. Today, we buy so much stuff that the most successful retailers are literally warehouses of consumer goods; consumers can't seem to resist helping themselves to just about anything they could want when they want it—even if it means going into debt to have it. According to the Sierra Club, since 1950 alone, the world's people have consumed more goods and services than the combined total of all humans who ever walked the planet before us. Shopping is now as much a part of our lives as sleeping and eating. Most of us buy something besides food daily and are always thinking about our next purchase.

All this consumption is putting strains on the environment like never before: we are using up resources at an unsustainable rate, polluting the planet through toxic manufacturing and long haul transport of goods, and creating mountains of unmanageable, toxic waste from discarded consumer products. Unfortunately, at the moment most of us prepare ourselves to buy something the last thing on our mind is where it came from and where it will end up when we're done with it. The typical consumer is more concerned with whether the product satisfies a need or desire and if they can afford it; also important considerations, but not the only ones, especially not in today's world.

If we want to live in a sustainable world, we need to be much more careful regarding what we buy, how much we buy, and be willing to look for alternatives to newly manufactured things. This chapter is primarily about the latter, because buying used versions of things is not only an opportunity to be an earth conscious consumer, but an opportunity to spend less while still meeting our material needs.

In chapter 1 we talked about how reducing the scale and quantity of our consumption can reduce pressure on the environment and increase our wealth. In that same vein, below we discuss briefly how to acquire some of the things we need without buying them at all (and no, it doesn't involve stealing!). But mostly, this chapter explores a category of earth-friendly goods often overlooked except by the most frugal Americans: previously-owned, gently used things. Despite a few exceptions, whenever the purchase of a brand new something-or-other can be avoided—and a secondhand alternative found—money is saved, resources are preserved, pollution is avoided, and perfectly useful stuff is kept out of the waste stream.

Buying used will not always be your best option (see "When Used Is Not OK," page 242), but there are many occasions when used merchandise makes good sense, and depending on your shopping list and your success, you could save hundreds or even thousands of dollars a year through reuse.

U.S. industrial facilities reported releasing 4.1 billion pounds of 650 identified toxic chemicals into the environment in 2007.[1] This amount represents only a small fraction of actual chemicals released to the environment.[2]

RENT, BARTER, BORROW

The first rule of saving money is not to spend so much of it! And the first rule of doing less environmental harm is to reduce the amount of resources we consume. So, buy less and you'll at once become a better saver and a better earth steward.

But how can we spend less and reduce consumption while still making sure we get the things we need or want? Well, there are lots of ways. Before two cars per household, warehouses of cheap consumer goods, and easy credit provided us with a greater ability to get what we want immediately, people were more resourceful. When we needed a ladder to clean the gutters, we borrowed our neighbor's. If the vacuum stopped working, we'd take it to the local repair shop. When we needed baby clothes, we could rely on friends and family for a stash of clothes their kids had outgrown. You get the picture. Saving money and resources wasn't something people really had to consider doing; it was an automatic reaction. Today, however, most people's automatic reaction is to buy—or charge—whatever they think they need—even if that need is temporary, rare, or could be avoided through repairing, mending, or updating something we already own.

You can save great sums of money by extending the useful life of things you own; and for the things you don't own, seek out what others are offering—on either a temporary or permanent basis—by renting, bartering and borrowing when it makes sense to do so. (See sidebar, "Resources to Avoid or Put Off Expensive Purchases.")

In addition to the resources in the side bar, make sure to do a Google search for a tool library that might be available to you. They are a great inexpensive—often free—resource for hand tools and power tools, as well as some free advice on your next project! Most tool libraries charge a yearly membership fee, but checking tools out is free. For typical rarely needed yard equipment and home tools, borrowing from a local tool library instead of purchasing can save the typical homeowner around $623 (see table 46).

Resources to Avoid or Put Off Expensive Purchases

How-to video sites teach novices how to repair things:
www.instructables.com
www.monkeysee.com

Swap something you have for something you need:
www.listia.com
www.u-exchange.com
www.swapmamas.com

Rent things you own or things you need:
www.loanables.com
www.snapgoods.com

Share with and borrow from willing and trusted friends, family and neighbors:
www.isharestuff.org
www.neighborrow.com

Find and offer things for free:
www.freecycle.org

Table 46: Estimated Savings When Avoiding Ownership of Seldom Used Home and Garden Equipment

TYPICAL SCENARIO Seldom used home tools and yard equipment	$623		
GREENER SCENARIOS	↑Cost↓	Yearly cost	5-year costs
Rented as needed from tool library	$0–$30 membership fee	$0 to $30	$0 to $150
Borrow as needed from friends and neighbors	$0	$0	$0

Assumes a hole digger, pull saw, electric hedge trimmer, handheld brush cutter, wheelbarrow, 20' aluminum extension ladder and power drill.

Spotlight on Savings

For typical rarely used yard equipment and home tools, borrowing instead of purchasing can save the typical homeowner around $623.

OWN JOINTLY

Pooling your money with another individual or family to buy certain things is like getting what you want at a 50 percent discount—or a 66 percent discount if you're splitting the cost among three parties. If you live right next door to family or longtime friends, the amount of items you could own together and share is limited only by your activities, usage patterns and the amount of trust you are willing to put in each other.

If you aren't living next door to a perfect joint-ownership candidate, but live within, say, fifteen miles of such a candidate, sharing expensive equipment can still work out nicely as long as the need for whatever you intend to share is infrequent. Camping gear makes a whole lot of sense to share for families that visit a campground only once or twice a year. For another group, it might make sense to share beer making supplies, a meat smoker, a sewing machine, a steam carpet cleaner, or a color photo printer.

In the past three decades alone, one-third of the planet's natural resource base has been consumed.[3]

As sensible as sharing is, it's not always easy. Sharing means you have to plan ahead to avoid squabbles and misunderstandings. In fact, it's a good idea to put some ground rules, and maybe even a tentative schedule, down on paper, even when (or especially when) the arrangement is between family members and good friends. As formal and unnecessary as that sounds, do it. The printed word rules, and it's hard to bicker and accuse when a previously agreed-to document is there to settle the debate over anything from usage to maintenance to depreciation.

 ## Spotlight on Savings

A basic camping setup for a family of four including tent, air mattresses, sleeping bags, stove, cooler, camp furniture, and lanterns will cost around $1,449, but if purchased with another family and shared 50/50, the cost would drop by 50 percent to $725.

REDEFINE YOUR MARKETPLACE

Most of us define our marketplace as the brick-and-mortar and Internet retailers that sell new products and materials. But in the case of durable goods, purchasing brand new products when earth-friendlier, used versions are available causes unnecessary resource depletion, environmental disturbance, and waste.

This chapter isn't about scavenging thrift store bins and yard sales for obscure items that can be repurposed for uses around the house—although don't rule out this fun activity! Rather, this chapter is about using the ever expanding reuse marketplace that has grown far beyond thrift stores, yard sales, and newspaper classifieds, and now includes infinitely more than used cars, used books, vintage clothing, and collectibles. Today, a growing network of online and brick-and-mortar businesses provide a wide variety of gently-used items—in good condition and with many years of useful life left in them.

The public interest in reuse, as evidenced by the success of online classified websites like www.craigslist.org and the auction website www.ebay.com, is fueling the start-up of more businesses seeking to connect buyers and sellers of pre-owned goods. From buy/sell websites that specialize in a single class of goods—like wedding dresses or textbooks—to those offering everything *and* the kitchen sink to reuse brick-and-mortars that trade in goods ranging from budget to upscale, there's never been a better time to find pre-owned things at deep discounts that will provide value and can meet or exceed your expectations.

Built-In Bargains

A preference for brand new, just-off-the-assembly-line products and materials may be status quo for most Americans, but so is the desire to save money. It's safe to say that Americans' drive to shop is roughly equal to our drive to find a bargain. We are largely a nation of sale hunting and discount seeking consumers; our motivation to save money evident by our choice of where we shop. After all, Wal-Mart is not the number one retailer because of the quality of their merchandise or their customer service. And it's not just the middle class going out of their way to pay less. There are lots of well-off folks who get giddy over the money they save at stores like Wal-Mart, Costco, and other deep-discount retailers.

And if "everyday discounts" don't lure us out of the house, a "big sale" surely will. We are a nation of spenders, but even more so when something is on sale. We are obsessed with the deal, and though great sales on new stuff do come along every now and then, most sales are just markdowns on overpriced stuff or tricks—set up in such a way as to get us to spend more money and buy more than we need.

If you *really* want to save money—the *most* money—when buying durable goods, it's hard to beat the genuine bargains on previously owned goods, sold through both businesses and private sellers. With the exception of collectibles and antiques that have appreciated in value, secondhand goods cost a fraction of what comparable items would cost new, and you don't necessarily have to give up quality. The reuse marketplace is as diverse as the new-product marketplace, offering everything from fair to excellent quality goods for sale: it's your choice what quality you settle on.

> The average cardholder holds 3.7 credit cards and is carrying $4,244 in revolving debt.[4]

Time Is on Your Side

If anything you learn in this chapter is going to work, you may as well surrender any expectations about instant gratification following every impulse to buy. We have become a nation of consumers that solve our material needs by jumping in the car, running down to the store, and charging, if need be, whatever it is we want. Without much, or any, forethought or discretion, we can go from wanting something to having it in mere minutes. However, with a few exceptions, there is very little we need right away; so what's the rush?!

Conventional shopping is largely about putting ourselves in a place and position where copious amounts of merchandise, enticing sales, and instant credit approval lead to hasty decisions we may later regret. On the other hand, reuse shopping is a chance to slow down and allow ourselves time for critical thinking about why and what we should or shouldn't buy. Often, given some time in between when we believe we need something and when we actually intend to buy it, we will change our mind, realizing we don't need it after all. Nothing saves money like time—time to really consider our purchasing decisions.

> In 2010, 40 million tons of durable goods were discarded.[5]

HELPFUL HINTS FOR SUCCESSFUL REUSE SHOPPING

Reuse shopping is a bit different than what many of us are used to. For one thing, there's no one-stop outlet where you will find a basketball, a shop vac, and wine glasses—unless you get lucky. For another, shopping the reuse marketplace is a process—not a quick fix. Finally, there can be minor defects in used goods that will need attending to—unless you prefer them that way or can overlook the flaws. But for all its short-

Table 47: Alpine Ski Package (Skis, Poles, Boots) Comparison

Source	Condition	Typical cost
National outdoor retailer	New	($1,007)
Ski swap	Used—excellent	($585)
Consignment store	Used—very good	($495)
Craigslist.org	Used—good	($250)

Table 48: Kitchen Cabinets Comparison

Source	Condition	Typical cost
Home improvement center— stock cabinets	New	($5,000)–($7,000)
Craigslist.org	Used—very good	($800)–($1,900)
Building salvage store	Used—good	($600)–($800)

Assumption: 10' × 12' kitchen

Table 49: Portable DVD player Comparison

Source	Condition	Typical purchase price
Big box store	New	($120)
Online auction	Used—very good	($47)–($72)
Amazon.com	Used—very good	($55)–($89)
Local pawn shop	Used—very good	($60)

comings, there's plenty of promise too. The chance to save considerable money and do something really good for the environment is just too good to pass up!

Know Where to Look

It's easy to get discouraged when looking for something secondhand if you are shopping in the wrong places. Knowing what reuse enterprises are typically best for certain items will increase your success.

- Clothing for all ages and all occasions: thrift stores, consignment/reuse stores, online exchanges
- Upscale or special occasion clothing: clothing consignment/reuse boutiques, online exchanges, classifieds*
- Computers, electronics and small appliances: pawn shops, refurbishers, classifieds, online auction sites
- Sporting goods and musical instruments: sporting goods and musical instrument consignment/reuse stores, swap meets, classifieds, pawn shops, online auction sites
- Upscale furniture and home decor: estate sales, antiques stores, local auctions, home consignment stores, classifieds
- Retro furniture and miscellaneous home decor: used furniture stores, estate sales, thrift stores, classifieds
- Miscellaneous household items: estate sales, thrift stores
- Tools: pawn shops, tool consignment/reuse stores, estate sales, classifieds, online auction sites
- Kitchen wares and cooking utensils: cooking consignment stores, estate sales, thrift stores
- Large appliances: classifieds, used appliance stores

---

* "Classifieds" include newspaper advertisements as well as posts on "listing service" websites like www.craigslist.org and www.oodle.com as well as a whole host of websites that cater to a particular market niche (e.g., wedding dresses, optical equipment, auto parts, etc.)

- Children's toys, games and clothing: thrift stores, swap meets, classifieds, online auction sites, online exchanges
- Nursery furniture and baby accessories: baby consignment/reuse stores, thrift stores, swap meets, classifieds, online auction sites, online exchanges
- Office and school supplies: estate sales, thrift stores, school-sponsored swap meets
- Office furniture: office furniture consignment/reuse stores, estate sales, classifieds, going out of business sales
- Building and renovation products and materials: building salvage lots, Habitat for Humanity stores (where available), classifieds, demolition sites*
- Books: used book stores, thrift stores, swap meets, online booksellers, library sales
- Music and movies: music consignment/reuse stores, pawn shops, online media sites
- Photography and video equipment: classifieds, pawn shops, online auction sites

 ## Spotlight on Savings

Used merchandise can cost from 40 to 90 percent less than a newer version of a similar item.

> Plastic doesn't biodegrade. Over time—500 to 1,000 years according to estimates—plastic will photodegrade into many tiny pieces, but once made plastic will never disappear.

---

* Demolition sites are dangerous and off limits to the public unless escorted onto the site by an authorized worker; and very often what is salvageable will already be spoken for by the time you happen along. So, never go poking around a demolition site by yourself. If you see something you may like, call the demolition company and make an inquiry.

Be Patient

Perhaps the biggest secret to finding what you require from the used marketplace is to have patience. That means anticipating purchases far enough ahead of when you may need them to give yourself adequate time to find them.

There's no such thing as instant gratification when shopping for previously owned goods—unless you get lucky. Typically it will take more time to find what you are searching for amongst such diverse sellers and an uncertain selection. Even if what you seek is available right now, on a website like www.ebay.com or www.ubid.com, you may have to wait for the auction to end to find out if you are the winning bidder. And when responding to a classified ad, it may take a couple days for someone to get back to you. Shopping for previously owned goods can take a bit more time, but it can be well worth it.

Be a Smart Buyer

We have to be just a bit more on our toes when buying from the used marketplace: after all, used items will likely have some visible wear ranging from very minor to moderate, and things with moving parts may or may not work perfectly. Also, older models of any product may not have the exact features you are looking for. Therefore do your research and take your time considering a used item before purchasing it.

Furthermore, private sellers are just average people trying to make some extra cash. On the one hand, novice sellers may be a bit unsophisticated, but the flip side of that is people selling their own stuff have personal knowledge about it, which they can share with you. But are they honest? Well, the vast majority of sellers are honest people, but it's still up to you to exercise appropriate carefulness to protect yourself from disappointment or fraud.

Shopping Locally

Before buying something from a local merchant, inspect all merchandise and be reasonably sure you can accept the item in its current condition or refurbish it to your satisfaction. Make sure you know the store's return or exchange policy and that it's one you can live with.* Mechanical and electrical items should come with a 30-day, money-back guarantee. You won't get this kind of guarantee from a thrift store that sells items "as is," but even they will usually allow you to exchange an item you've changed your mind about for store credit, so you won't get stuck with a dud. The bottom line is this: reputable merchants should have no problem offering you a reasonable period to test merchandise at home.

When it comes to buying from private sellers, get as much information about the item as you can over the phone. This will give you a chance to learn more about the seller and their motives as well as the item itself. If you want to be safe and cautious (a good idea), insist on meeting at a public place to preview the item. If the item is too large to move, take a friend along with you when you go to see it and tell a third person where you are going.

Private sellers typically won't come right out and offer a money-back guarantee, so if you'd like one, ask for it. A seller on the up and up shouldn't have a problem allowing you a brief but reasonable period to return something if your dissatisfaction is justified: in other words, unless what you purchased doesn't work as described, transactions between a buyer and private seller are usually final. There's no changing your mind for changing your mind's sake!

---

* Regardless of a store's policy, the FTC's Cooling off Rule permits you three days to return something purchased for over $25 for any reason; however there are some exclusions. Read more about the rule at www.ftc.gov/bcp/edu/pubs/consumer/products/pro03.shtm.

Online Transactions

The best way to protect yourself when buying (or selling) something over the Internet is to follow these guidelines:

- Read the Federal Trade Commission's consumer protection literature regarding online shopping and e-payments, available at www.ftc.gov/bcp/menus/consumer/tech/online.shtm.
- Use only trusted sites that have earned the confidence of users.
- Look for evidence that the website is utilizing security software that protects the information it collects from you during a transaction. (e.g., VeriSign or Entrust)
- Read every word of a seller's advertisement from the item's description and condition to shipping charges and the refund policy.

Can't Return? Resell!

The great thing about used items is they have already depreciated, so if you do decide you are unhappy with something weeks after a purchase, you can often turn around and sell it for about what you paid for it. To help your item sell quickly, follow these tips:

- Do a quick search on the classified site you want to advertise on and see what other sellers are asking for the same item. You want to be priced competitively, but consider condition. If your item is a more recent model or in better condition, don't give it away!
- Provide as much detail as possible in *both* the title and description. Most buyers won't click through on a title that doesn't immediately communicate important details, and they won't waste their time chasing down information that should have been included in the ad in the first place (e.g., measurements, specifications, age, etc.).

- Include several good quality pictures. If the listing website you've chosen to advertise on limits the number of photos you can upload, you can upload additional photos to another website, like www.photobucket.com, and include a link to the website in your ad.
- Include your phone number in the ad. If a buyer is in a hurry for more information or wants to make a quick purchase, you don't want email to be their only way of contacting you. If you're not online to get their email, he or she may just move on to another seller. Make it easy for a buyer to reach you when their motivation is high.

WHEN USED IS *NOT* OK

Reuse keeps one person's unwanted things out of the waste stream and satisfies another person's need while causing none of the environmental impacts that would come with new production. Things get a bit trickier if the item consumes significant energy, such as with a heating appliance or refrigerator, for instance. Compared to a newer, updated model, an older appliance will likely burn fuel less efficiently or use significantly more power to run. So, don't be tempted to buy an old wood burning fireplace insert that is not EPA-certified and is therefore unable to meet minimum efficiency standards. Likewise, pass up energy hogs like old refrigerators and clothes dryers.

Stay far away from hazardous substances that aren't in their original containers. If you can't positively identify things like fertilizers, pesticides, household cleaners, and solvents—and check expiration dates—the bargain isn't worth the risk.

There are also used items that can put us or loved ones at risk. The category of baby products, for example, is one you want to be particularly careful with. Cribs, car seats, booster seats, and jumper seats—from one manufacturer or another—frequently find themselves on national recall lists.

The best policy when buying a used product (aside from obviously risk-free products) is to check the U.S. Consumer Product Safety Commission's website (www.cpsc.gov/cpscpub/prerel/prerel.html) for recalls and product safety rules. Anything from a ladder to a door lock to a fondue set can be recalled for a safety reason, so screen with care. Regardless of the age of an item you are considering for purchase, it should perform both to your expectations and meet applicable local or national environmental and safety standards that exist for your protection. If you do discover a recalled item for sale online, don't ignore it. Do a solid and report the ad (i.e., email the link) to websafety@cpsc.gov.

REUSE, THE ENVIRONMENT AND THE ECONOMY

Of course the current reuse marketplace can't keep up with all our needs, nor should it. The creation and sale of new goods will never cease entirely because products and materials eventually wear out; new products offer improved features (e.g., better efficiency, convenience, and safety); and the manufacturing of new goods provides economic benefits we would sorely miss and could hardly do without.

Nevertheless, we live in a finite world, and the predominantly linear system we use to support our materials economy is not sustainable. Right now we, principally, extract new raw materials that are manufactured into finished goods: these then go into distribution, then into use by consumers, and eventually into the waste stream (i.e., they get trashed). On the extraction end of this linear system we're using up natural resources too fast; in the middle, we're polluting the environment with toxic industrial byproducts; and on the disposal end, we're creating too much trash that is *also* polluting the environment.

We need solutions that conserve natural resources and put off disposal for as long as possible. Reuse accomplishes this: instead of trashing a still-useful product or material and making a new one to fill the void, reuse moderates the need for extraction, production, and disposal.

Furthermore, supporting reuse helps create jobs here in America. Unlike new consumer goods, of which 60 percent are produced overseas,[6] consumer *services* are 96 percent "made in the USA."[7] When consumers en masse look for used goods and seek markets for their own used things, all kinds of opportunities arise for existing and new businesses eager to meet the increased demand for advertising, collecting, cleaning, sorting, reconditioning, refurbishing, remanufacturing, updating, refinishing, reupholstering, repurposing, repairing, mending, distributing, and selling used products, parts, and materials. Whew! The economic possibilities are only limited by our creativity.

So give a hand to the environment, the economy, and yourself—become a reuser!

ADDING IT ALL UP

I f you've read all previous chapters and started making greener choices within all the areas explored, then you are probably already saving more money today than you were before you
started reading Going Green. If you're still digesting all the information presented in previous chapters, this final chapter
will help get you motivated to go back, dig into the chapters
one by one, and start making some progress toward a greener
way of life, confident in the fact that by pursuing change your
bank account can grow as a result.

The amount one individual or one typical family can save
when implementing some of the money-saving strategies pre-
scribed in this book will vary depending on current habits and
expenses, where and how you live, the size of your home and
family, the ages of all those living in the home, and so much
more. The savings can be significant when you add it all up, and
that's the purpose of this chapter—to show what is possible.

The figures in this chapter are the aggregation of approximate savings already detailed in previous chapters. The numbers show overwhelmingly that a commitment to living more
consciously can be worth thousands of dollars, which you
could use to pay off your credit card debt, pay for a semester's
tuition, pay for a down payment on a home, or start a retirement or college savings plan.

If you can invest some of what you save, your gains can be even greater. However, only consider investing if you have a stable and secure source of income and have put enough money aside to cover financial emergencies. With investing comes risk—the potential to lose some of your assets always exists, so learn as much as you can about investing before deciding to commit any amount of money.

To estimate a financial picture of the future if one were willing and able to invest some or all of the money they saved as a result of this book, we assumed annual contributions equal to the first-year contribution over ten years and compounded annually on various investments with a 2 percent average rate of return (typically called an increasing annuity). This rate of return is extremely conservative and reflects the state of our current economy. A more aggressive investment strategy, the return of a healthier economy, or both, could double or triple the return we've used as an example.

No matter how much you are able to save or earn through investing, the point is that when it comes to greener living, money is not the obstacle, it is the *reward*. The real obstacle is ourselves. We have to be willing to live our values, change habits of convenience and take the long view when assessing purchasing decisions. It takes practice and determination to stay on track, but it gets easier with every week. If you can make green living your "new normal," you *can* achieve greater wealth!

EASY MONEY

Opportunities to green up our daily routine and home are all around us, and along with them, the opportunity to save substantial money. Chapter 2 taught us that we shouldn't underestimate the financial rewards that come from making simple, small changes. Some of our most common earth-*un*friendly behaviors are easily correctible and can save us the most.

Table 50: Savings Outlook Estimate from Chapter 2

		10-year outlook	
Savings potential	One-year outlook	Not invested	Invested earning 2% compounded annually
Low-end	$6,407	$64,070	$79,368
High-end	$10,016	$100,160	$124,075

Assumes typical household savings from all twenty correctible actions proposed in chapter 2.

HOME ENERGY SAVINGS PLAN

Chapter 3 gave us a lot to think about and do in the area of home energy management. It may seem like an overwhelming task to make a home truly energy efficient, but the upside is that the more practices and areas of our homes we can improve the more money we can save. Correcting wasteful habits and systematically fixing or replacing energy-sucking appliances, systems, and electronics in the home with more energy-efficient ones will always result in lower operating expenses. As long as the difference in operating costs offsets the cost of the equipment over its expected life, energy-efficiency upgrades are a viable way to achieve long-term, and in some cases short-term, savings.

Table 51: Savings Outlook Estimate from Chapter 3

		10-year outlook	
Savings potential	One-year outlook	Not invested	Invested earning 2% compounded annually
Low-end	$736	$7,360	$9,117
High-end	$3,597	$35,970	$44,559

Assumes typical household savings from non-competing correctible scenarios proposed in chapter 3.

TRANSPORTATION SAVINGS PLAN

Very few people are prisoners to the vehicle they've chosen to drive and *all* the miles they drive when in it. In one year you could dramatically change your driving habits, possibly the vehicle you currently drive, and your overall transportation costs as a result. Chapter 4 gave us the information to evaluate transportation decisions in a financial context, and boy is driving expensive! Just owning a car is expensive, and using it—a lot—as most of us do, costs the average driver $1,984 annually in fuel alone, but additional costs put the true cost to own a standard passenger car at an average $7,048 annually, according to Edmunds.com's *True Cost to Own* online calculator.

Chapter 4 provided lots of suggestions for reclaiming some of the money our vehicles have been burning up. Doubling fuel economy and adopting conservative driving habits can save the typical driver around $827 in fuel costs annually. But, the driver willing to go further will be *much* richer in both the short and long term. If you have to own some kind of vehicle, and many of us do, car ownership expenses will plummet when ownership or trips are shared, fuel economy is doubled or tripled, and alternatives to driving become habits for getting us where we need to go.

Table 52: Savings Outlook Estimate from Chapter 4

| | | 10-year outlook | |
Savings potential	One-year outlook	Not invested	Invested earning 2% compounded annually
Low-end	$773	$7,730	$9,576
High-end	$7,048	$70,048	$87,309

Assumes typical driver's savings from non-competing scenarios proposed in chapter 4.

WATER WISER SAVINGS PLAN

For most of the country, water is cheap. As a result, it is one of the most wasted resources. The inexpensive cost of water has also led many Americans to discount water conservation as a viable way to save money. Big mistake! The reality is we absolutely can save money through water conservation for a couple reasons: First, on average, 73 percent of indoor water is heated, so high water use leads to higher energy costs; and second, during the summer months household water use can *quadruple* causing water costs to spike.

The sum of all water-uses in and outside the home provides many areas in which to reduce the flow and save money. The examples presented in chapter 5 showed us how much water is wasted through daily activities and how much we can save when we get water wiser; and conserving a resource as vital as fresh water is enormously important as well.

Table 53: Savings Outlook Estimate from Chapter 5

| Savings potential | One-year outlook | 10-year outlook | |
		Not invested	Invested earning 2% compounded annually
Low-end	$585	$5,850	$7,247
High-end	$2,168	$21,680	$26,857

Assumes typical household savings from non-competing correctible scenarios proposed in chapter 5.

THE BETTER FOOD SAVINGS PLAN

The majority of our food is now produced more for profit than for people—at least not for people in the sense that it does not offer potent nutrients, flavor without artificial additives, variety, nor foster good health, all of which are critical traits for simultaneously enjoying and benefiting from food as nature intended.

Reclaiming nutrients, natural flavor, and healthful benefits from our food doesn't cost a fortune as chapter 6 thoroughly explained. Whatever the cost of healthier foods—smart shopping, conscientious meal preparation, and good eating habits can bring the overall cost of our food bill down, thus making room in our budget for food that is better for people and planet.

In addition, if your new whole food, sustainable diet helps you achieve vitality and amazing health, you can protect yourself from developing a poor diet-related illness or disease that could cost thousands of dollars to diagnose and treat—not to mention the wearisome experience of suffering through it. This potential savings isn't factored into table 54, but poor diet is a leading cause of heart disease, high blood pressure, stroke, diabetes, and obesity. Improving your diet is a sound plan for avoiding an illness that could result in a large financial loss for you and your family.

Table 54: Savings Outlook Estimate from Chapter 6

Savings potential	One-year outlook	10-year outlook	
		Not invested	Invested earning 2% compounded annually
Low-end	$934	$9,340	$11,570
High-end	$3,738	$37,380	$46,305

Assumes average household savings between 10 and 36 percent.

REUSE SAVINGS PLAN

Chapter 7's title suggested that "everything is cheaper used." Well, it might not be a hard and fast rule, but it is generally true. Things depreciate in value as they age, and only if and when something old becomes somewhat of a collector's item could it possibly appreciate to a value that exceeds a newer version of the same thing. The depreciation of new things, in most cases the instant it is purchased, makes buying things used an extremely money-wise strategy. Certain categories of goods are obviously excluded, but durable goods that are current enough to provide all or most of the benefits of their newer counterparts can cost a mere fraction of something that just rolled off an assembly line somewhere else in the world.

Not everything we buy has to be semi-current and in "like-new" condition, though. The biggest bargains come from items that need some TLC, and the savings can be worth replacing a few parts or cleaning it up.

Table 55: Savings Outlook Estimate from Chapter 7

| Savings potential | One-year outlook | 10-year outlook | |
		Not invested	Invested earning 2% compounded annually
Low-end	$1,019	$10,190	$12,623
High-end	$3,058	$30,580	$37,882

Assumes average overall household savings of 25 to 75 percent on average expenditures for various durable goods.

THE BETTER LIFE SAVINGS PLAN

If you want to green up several areas of your life, there will be rich rewards for your efforts. The potential to save tens of thousands of dollars in a relatively short amount of time is possible, especially if your household is an ideal candidate to implement many of the suggestions in this book (see table 56).

Increasing your financial situation and lowering your ecological footprint won't be the only benefits to following the advice in this book. You can look forward to a more comfortable home in a more natural, low maintenance setting, a connection to the seasons and place, improved social

Table 56: Savings Outlook Estimate, All Chapters

		10-year outlook	
Savings potential	One-year outlook	Not invested	Invested earning 2% compounded annually
Low-end	$10,454	$104,540	$129,501
High-end	$29,625	$296,250	$366,986

connections, and better health. These are ancillary benefits of making greener choices in life that add up to a *better* life for you and your family.

NOTES

Introduction and Chapter 1

1. Richard Morin, "Feeling Guilty: Americans Say They Aren't Saving Enough," www.pewresearch.org, May 14, 2008

2. Pew Social and Demographic Trends, "The Great Recession" Series, www.pewsocialtrends.org, 2010–2012.

3. New American Dream Survey Report, newdream.s3.amazonaws.com/19/e3/b/2268/ND2004Finalpoll-report.pdf, September 2004.

4. U.S. Census Bureau for the Bureau of Labor Statistics, *Consumer Expenditures 2010*, Current Expenditures by Income Before Taxes, Table 2.

5. "Study Says Fast Food Remains Popular," June 20, 2008, qsrmagazine.com (accessed March 21, 2012).

6. Ibid.

7. U.S. Chairman of the Council of Economic Advisers, *Economic Report of the President 2012*, Table B-30, www.gpo.gov/fdsys (accessed March 27, 2012).

8. Edmond's True Cost to Own Calculator, edmunds.com/tco.html (accessed March 2012).

9. U.S. Green Building Council, "Green Building by the Numbers," March 2009, www.usgbc.org.

10. Julia Wilkinson, "Amazon Breaks eBay's Record for Unique Visitors," January 27, 2010, AuctionBytes Blog, blog.auctionbytes.com/cgi-bin/blog/blog.pl?/pl/2010/1/1263752913.html (accessed March 2012)

11. "Put Your Cash Away: Bartering Is Back," *The Independent* (London, England), June 17, 2006, www.independent.co.uk/money/invest-save/ (accessed January 19, 2009).

12. U.S. Environmental Protection Agency, Municipal Solid Waste Generation, Recycling, and Disposal in the United States: Table and Figures for 2010, December 2011, Tables 4, 7.

13. Lou Carlozo, "Are You Throwing Away Cash with Disposable Cleaning Products?" February 17, 2010, DealNews.com (accessed March 20, 2012).

14. Real Diaper Association, "Diaper Facts," realdiaperassociation.org/diaperfacts.php (accessed March 20, 2012)

15. U.S. Environmental Protection Agency, Municipal Solid Waste Generation, Recycling, and Disposal in the United States: Table and Figures for 2010, December 2011, Tables 12, 13.

16. Energy Information Administration, Short Term Energy Outlook, Table 2: U.S. Energy Prices (2002 thru 2009), www.eia.doe.gov/emeu/steo/pub/contents.html (accessed April 6, 2009).

17. Eugene M. Trisko, *The Rising Burden of Energy Costs on American Families* (Americans for Balanced Energy Choices), December 2007, 8.

18. Energy Information Administration, "Emissions of Greenhouse Gases Report," December 3, 2008, www.eia.doe.gov/oiaf/1605/ggrpt/carbon.html (accessed December 20, 2008).

19. Ibid, Table 6.

20. World Watch Institute, "Making Better Energy Choices," www.worldwatch.org/node/808 (accessed March 2012).

21. Centers for Disease Control and Prevention, "Overweight Prevalence," www.cdc.gov/nchs/fastats/overwt.htm (accessed November 2008).

22. Janice Loyd, "Report Links Rise In Cancer to Inactivity, Obesity," *USA Today*, March, 29, 2012.

23. Research and Innovative Technology Administration, Bureau of Transportation and Labor Statistics, "National Household Travel Survey: Daily Travel Quick Facts," www.bts.gov/programs/national_household_travel_survey/ (accessed October 2008).

24. *Sierra*, January/February 2009, 10.

25. Mayo Clinic, "Walking for fitness: How to trim your waistline, improve your health," www.mayoclinic.com/health/walking/HQ01612 (accessed November 2008).

26 U.S. Environmental Protection Agency, Human Health Effects of Chemicals, www.epa.gov/NHEERL/research/human_health.html (accessed November 2008).

27 Kristin S. Schafer, "Biomonitoring: A Tool Whose Time Has Come: Finding Pesticides in Our Bodies," Pesticide Action Network North America, www.panna.org/legacy/gpc/gpc_200404.14.1.02.dv.html (accessed December 2008).

28 Michael Pollan, *In Defense of Food*, (The Penguin Press, 2008), 115.

Chapter 2

1   Natural Resources Defense Council, *Bottled Water: Pure Drink or Pure Hype?* www.nrdc.org/water/drinking/bw/exesum.asp (accessed October 2008).

2   Edward Humes, "Earth Day Analysis: How Waste Hurts the Economy," April 22, 2010, *The Wall Street Journal*.

3   *The Story of Bottled Water*, Free Range Studios, www.storyofstuff.org/movies-all/story-of-bottled-water/ (accessed May 2012).

4   National Coffee Drinking Trends 2010, National Coffee Association.

5   Ibid.

6   "McDonald's Premium Roast Coffee Serves 500 Million Cups of Coffee," franchise-hit.com, March 15, 2006.

7   U.S. Environmental Protection Agency & U.S. Department of Energy, Energy Star program, http://www.energystar.gov (accessed October 2011).

8   U.S. Environmental Protection Agency, Municipal Solid Waste in the United States: 2010 Data and Tables, tables 15,16, 17, 20

9   U.S. Environmental Protection Agency, National Center for Environmental Economics, *Savings from Using Economic Incentives*, 3.4.1 Marginal Cost Pricing for Household Waste, yosemite.epa.gov/ee/epa/eed.nsf/webpages/SavingsFromEconomicIncentives.html (accessed January 2009).

10 National Research Council of the National Academies, *Health Risks from Dioxin and Related Compounds: Evaluation of the EPA Reassessment* (Washington D.C., National Academies Press, 2006), 26.

11 Matt Kures, "Serving Downtown Office Workers," *Downtown Economics* (University of Wisconsin-Extension), no. 125 (2007): 2.

12 American Institute for Cancer Research (AICR), *Awareness and Action: AICR Surveys on Portion Size, Nutrition and Cancer Risk*, July 17, 2003, www.icrsurvey.com/Study.aspx?f=AICR_0703.html (accessed September 2008).

13 United States Department of Agriculture, Economic Research Service, *Amber Waves: The Economics of Food, Farming, Natural Resources and Rural America* (November 2005), "US Food Consumption Up 16 Percent Since 1970," www.ers.usda.gov/AmberWaves/November05/ (accessed November 2008).

14 Californians Against Waste, "Fast Food Waste Threatens our Marine Environment, Drags Down Diversion Rates," www.cawrecycles.org/issues/fast_food (accessed January 2009)

15 Consumer Expenditure Survey, U.S. Bureau of Labor Statistics, September, 2011

16 Mark Whitehouse, "Number of the Week: Americans Buy More Stuff They Don't Need," *The Wall Street Journal*, April 23, 2011.

17 See endnote 16.

18 Pew Research Center, "Luxury or Necessity? Things We Can't Live Without: The List Has Grown in the Past Decade," December 14, 2006, pewresearch.org/pubs/323/luxury-or-necessity (accessed January 2009).

19 "Comparing Energy Costs Per Mile For Electric and Gasoline-Fueled Vehicles, U.S. Department of Energy, avt.inel.gov/pdf/fsev/costs.pdf (accessed May 2012).

20 Paul A.T. Higgins, "Exercise-based transportation reduces oil dependence, carbon emissions and obesity," *Environmental Conservation*, no. 32 (2005), 197–202.

21 Stacy C. Davis, Susan W. Diegel, Robert G. Boundy, Transportation Energy Data Book: 30th Edition, June 2011, Tables 8.6, 8.8

22 See endnote 16.

23 U.S. Environmental Protection Agency, "Household Hazardous Wastes," www.epa.gov/epawaste/conserve/materials/hhw.htm#home (accessed January 2009).

24 "The Household Diary Study: Mail Use and Attributes in FY 2010," U.S. Postal Service.

25 Ibid.

26 Business Wire, "Average U.S. Household Has Over 50 Unused Items Worth $3100 According to eBay/Nielsen Survey," April 26, 2007, www.businesswire.com (accessed February 2009).

27 Greeting Card Association, "About Greeting Cards: General Facts," www.greetingcard.org (accessed September 2008).

28 World Watch Institute, "Paper," *Good Stuff? A Behind-the-Scenes Guide to the Things We Buy*, www.worldwatch.org (accessed December 2008)

29 National Retail Federation, www.nrf.com (accessed May 2012).

30 U.S. Environmental Protection Agency, "What's your EnviroQ? Answer Page," www.epa.gov/epahome/enviroq (accessed February 2009).

Chapter 3

1   American Coalition For Clean Coal Technology, "Energy Cost Impacts on American Families," 2001–2012.

2   Energy Information Administration, "Emissions of Greenhouse Gases Report," December 3, 2008, www.eia.doe.gov/oiaf/1605/ggrpt/carbon.html (accessed December 20, 2008).

3   Energy Information Administration, Residential Sector Energy Consumption, 1949–2007 (Table 2.1b), www.eia.doe.gov/aer/txt/ptb0201b.html (accessed December 2008).

4   U.S. Environmental Protection Agency & U.S. Department of Energy, Energy Star program, "Ducts That Don't Leak," www.energystar.gov (accessed October 2008).

5   Sustainable Energy Authority, Victoria, AU, *Insulation Benefits Fact Sheet*, www.sustainability.vic.gov.au/resources/documents/Insulation_benefits.pdf (accessed May 2012)

6   Ibid.

7   U.S. Department of Energy, *Energy Savers: Tips on Saving Energy and Money at Home*, 11–12.

8   Environmental Energy Technologies Division at Lawrence Berkeley National Laboratory, The Home Energy Saver Answer Desk, hes.lbl.gov/hes/answerdesk_dat.html#w1 (accessed December 2008).

9   World Watch Institute, "Making Better Energy Choices," www.worldwatch.org/node/808 (accessed November 2008).

10 Steel Recycling Institute, *Recycling Steel Appliances* (Brochure).

11 Environmental Energy Technologies Division at Lawrence Berkeley National Laboratory, "About the Appliance Module," hes.lbl.gov/hes/aboutapps.html (accessed December 2008).

12 Energy Information Administration, *Electric Power Annual*, www.eia.doe.gov/fuelelectric.html (accessed October 2008).

13 Underwriters Laboratories, www.ul.com/global/eng/pages/offerings/perspectives/consumer/ (accessed September 2008).

14 Energy Crossroads: A Burning Need to Change Our Course (Tiroir A Films Productions, 2007).

15 Gary Klein, "Hot Water Distribution Systems: Part 1," *Plumbing Systems and Design*, March/April 2004.

16 Paul Rauber, "Carbon Confessional," *Sierra*, September/October 2008, 73.

17 U.S. Department of Energy, "Air Conditioning," www.energysavers.gov (accessed September 2008).

18 Denny Schrock, "Beat the Heat with Landscape Plants," www.colostate.edu/Dept/CoopExt/4DMG/Trees/beatheat.htm (accessed December 2008).

19 Gary Reysa, "Window Shading for Cooling," May 2008, www.builditsolar.com/Projects/Cooling/Shading/Shading.htm (accessed January 2009).

20 California Energy Commission's Consumer Energy Center, "Shades and Awnings," www.consumerenergycenter.org/home/windows (accessed December 2008).

21 Solar Control Films, Inc., www.solarcontrolfilmsinc.com/id1.html (accessed December 2008).

22 National Association of Home Builders Research Center, "Radiant Barriers," www.toolbase.org/
    Technology-Inventory/Roofs/radiant-barriers (accessed January 2009).

23 Energy Information Administration, "US Household electricity consumption in 2001," July 2005, www.eia.
    doe.gov/emeu/reps/enduse/er01_us.html (accessed October 2008) and U.S. Environmental Protection
    Agency & U.S. Department of Energy, Energy Star program, "Information on Compact Fluorescent Light
    Bulbs and Mercury," July 2008.

24 U.S. Environmental Protection Agency & U.S. Department of Energy, Energy Star program, *Energy Star
    Qualified Light Bulbs: 2006 Partner Resource Guide,* 2.

25 Energy Information Administration, *Residential Lighting Use and Potential Savings,* September 1996,
    Chapter 2, www.eia.doe.gov/emeu/lighting (accessed October 2008).

26 Noah Horowitz, *"The Light Bulb As We Know It Is Changing,"* National Resource Defense Council's blog,
    October 18, 2010.

27 Julianne Pepitone, "Compact Fluorescent Bulbs and Mercury: Reality Check, Popular Mechanics
    magazine, June 11, 2007.

28 Philips Solid State Lighting Solutions, *LED Lighting Explained,* www.ledlightingexplained.com (accessed
    May 2012).

29 Consumer Electronics Association's energy calculator, greengadgets.org (accessed May 2012).

30 Brian Urban, Verena Tiefenbeck, and Kurt Roth, *Energy Consumption of Consumer Electronics in U.S.
    Homes: Final Report to the Consumer Electronics Association,* Fraunhofer Center for Sustainable Energy
    Systems, December 2011, 11.

31 "The Wasteland," 60 Minutes, CBS News, November 10, 2008.

32 Consumer Electronics Association, *10th Annual Consumer Electronics Ownership Study,* April 2008.

33 United Nations Department of Economic and Social Affairs, Sustainable Consumption and Production:
    Promoting Climate-Friendly Household Consumption Patterns, April 30, 2007, 29.

34 Danice K. Eaton, PhD, Laura Kann, PhD, Steve Kinchen, Shari Shanklin, MS, James Ross, MS, Joseph
    Hawkins, MA, William A. Harris, MM, Richard Lowry, MD, Tim McManus, MS, David Chyen, MS, Connie
    Lim, MPA, Nancy D. Brener, PhD and Howell Wechsler, EdD, Youth Risk Behavior Surveillance: United
    States, 2007, *Morbidity and Mortality Weekly Report,* June 6, 2008, www.cdc.gov/mmwr (accessed
    December 2008).

35 Nielson Media Research, "Cross-Platform Report: How We Watch From Screen to Screen," May 3, 2012,
    blog.nielson.com (accessed May 2012).

36 Anne Harding, "Too Much TV Time May Hurt Your Heart, January 10, 2011, www.cnn.com via www.
    health.com.

37 Donald F. Roberts and Ulla G. Foehr, "Trends in Media Use," Children and Electronic Media 18, no. 1
    (Spring 2008): 15.

Chapter 4

1   U.S. Bureau of Labor Statistics, "Consumer Expenditures 2010," Sept. 2011.

2   Institute for Energy Research, "Petroleum (Oil)," www.instituteforenergyresearch.org (accessed March 2010).

3   U.S. Environmental Protection Agency, "Inventory of U.S. Greenhouse Gas Emissions and Sinks
    1990–2010," Table 3-6, February 2012, http://www.epa.gov/climatechange/emissions/downloads12/
    Complete%20Report%20%28Main%20Text%29.pdf (accessed March 2012).

4   U.S. Bureau of Transportation Statistics, *National Transportation Statistics,* Chapter 1, Section D, Table
    1-35: U.S. Vehicle Miles, http://www.bts.gov/publications/national_transportation_statistics/ (accessed
    March 2012).

5   World Watch Institute, "Making Better Energy Choices," www.worldwatch.org/node/808 (accessed
    March 2012).

6   American Association of People with Disabilities, "New Census Disability Statistics Released: One in Five Americans have a Disability," January 2009, jfactivist.typepad.com/jfactivist/2009/01/new-census-disability-statistics-released-one-in-five-americans-have-a-disability.html (accessed March 2012).

7   2009 National Household Travel Survey, Federal Highway Administration.

8   Martin S. Lipsky, M.D., and Lisa K. Sharp, PhD, "Preventive Therapy for Diabetes: Lifestyle Changes and the Primary Care Physician," *American Family Physician*, January 15, 2004.

9   U.S. Census Bureau, Commuting in the United States: 2009, p. 2–3, September 2011

10   Eugene M. Trisko, *The Rising Burden of Energy Costs on American Families* (Americans for Balanced Energy Choices), December 2007, 7.

11   Les Christie, "New Yorkers are top transit users," CNNMoney.com, June 29, 2007, money.cnn.com (January 2009).

12   American Public Transit Association, "Public Transportation Benefits," http://www.apta.com (accessed March 2012).

13   Ravi S. Gajendran and David A. Harrison, "The Good, the Bad, and the Unknown About Telecommuting: Meta-Analysis of Psychological Mediators and Individual Consequences," *Journal of Applied Psychology* 92, No. 6 (2007):1524–1541.

14   Texas Transportation Institute, "What Does Congestion Cost Us?" *2011 Urban Mobility Report*, http://mobility.tamu.edu/ums/ (accessed March 2012).

15   Stacy C. Davis, Susan W. Diegel, Robert G. Boundy, Transportation Energy Data Book: 30th Edition, June 2011, Tables 8.6, 8.8.

16   American Automobile Association, *Your Driving Costs*, 2011.

17   Audatex Directions, Vol. 4, "What Drives Hybrid Repair Costs," 5, www.newsletter.audatex.com/AudatexDirections_Feb2009.pdf (accessed March 2012).

18   National Renewable Energy Laboratory, Costs and Emissions Associated with Plug-In Hybrid Electric Vehicles in the Xcel Energy Colorado Service Territory, prepared by K. Parks, P. Denholm, and T. Market, May 2007, page 12.

19   Plug In America, "What Are Plug-ins?" http://www.pluginamerica.org (accessed October 2008).

20   The International Council on Clean Transportation, Passenger Vehicle Greenhouse Gas and Fuel Economy Standards: A Global Update, 2007, 24.

21   Electric Power Research Institute and National Resouces Defense Council, "Environmental Assessment of Plug-In Hybrid Electric Vehicles: Volume 1: Nationwide Greenhouse Gas Emissions, Final Report, July 2007, 7.

22   California Energy Commission, "Myths About Energy, Energy Fallacies and Weird Energy Facts," www.consumerenergycenter.org/myths (accessed December 2008).

23   U.S. Department of Energy, Office of Energy Efficiency and Renewable Energy, www.fueleconomy.gov/feg/climate.shtml (accessed March 2012).

24   U.S. Department of Energy, Office of Energy Efficiency and Renewable Energy, *Just the Basics: Vehicles Emissions*, 2003, 1.

25   Ibid.

Chapter 5

1   California Urban Water Conservation Council, "Faucet Energy Savings," http://www.h2ouse.org (accessed November 2008).

2   U.S. EPA WaterSense, Indoor Water Use in the United States, June 2008.

3   Centers for Disease Control and Prevention, "Health on Tap: The Value of Tap Water," www.cdc.gov/ncidod/dpd/healthywater/features/drinking_water_week_07.htm#18 (accessed November 2008).

4   California Urban Water Conservation Council, "Toilet Water Savings," http://www.h2ouse.org (accessed November 2008).

5   Ibid.

6   Scott Glick, Angela Acree Guggemos, A.M. ASCE and Santosh Prakash, "Economic And Environmental Analysis Of Residential Greywater Systems For Toilet Use," www.urbanwater.colostate.edu/Final_GW_Toilet_Use_CRC.pdf (accessed April 2012).

7   California Urban Water Conservation Council, "Clothes Washer Water Use," http://www.h2ouse.org (accessed November 2008).

8   California Urban Water Conservation Council, "Clothes Washer Energy Savings," http://www.h2ouse.org (accessed November 2008).

9   U.S. Environmental Protection Agency and U.S. Department of Energy, Energy Star Consumer Information, www.energystar.gov/index.cfm?c=clotheswash.pr_clothes_washers (accessed June 2008).

10 California Energy Commission, Consumer Energy Center, www.consumerenergycenter.org (accessed June 2008).

11 California Urban Water Conservation Council, "Faucet Water Use," http://www.h2ouse.org (accessed November 2008).

12 Energy Information Administration, 2009 Residential Energy Consumption Survey, Survey Data Tables, Appliances.

13 See endnote 11.

14 U.S. Environmental Protection Agency and U.S. Department of Energy, *Dishwashers: 2007 Partner Resource Guide*, 2.

15 See endnote 11.

16 California Urban Water Conservation Council, http://www.h2ouse.org (accessed November 2008).

17 U.S. Department of Housing and Urban Development, Energy Conservation Measures: Domestic Water Heating Systems, nhl.gov/offices/pih/programs/ph/phecc/strat_w1.cfm (accessed June 2009).

18 European Environment Agency, State of the Environment Report, No 1, 2007, Water Pricing and Household Water Use in Denmark, dataservice.eea.europa.eu/atlas/viewdata/viewpub.asp?id=2687 (accessed June 2008).

19 California Urban Water Conservation Council, "Showerhead Water Use," http://www.h2ouse.org (accessed November 2008).

20 Dawn Fones for State Farm, "April Showers Not Leading Cause of Household Water Leaks," Reuters, May 19, 2008.

21 U.S. EPA WaterSense, Indoor Water Use in the United States, June 2008.

22 American Water Works Association, WaterWiser Drip Calculator, www.awwa.org/awwa/waterwiser/dripcalc.cfm (accessed January 2009).

23 U.S. EPA WaterSense, *Outdoor Water Use in the United States*, August 2008.

24 Ibid.

25 The Lawn Institute, "Interesting Facts About Turfgrass," www.thelawninstitute.org/faqs/?c=183313 (accessed January 2009).

26 Herber Bormann, Diana Balmori & Gorden Geballe, *Redesigning the American Lawn*, Yale University Press, 1993.

27 Bruce Butterfield, "Lawn and garden sales up 3 percent to more than $35 billion in 2007," www.garden.org/articles/articles.php?q=show&id=2989 (accessed January 2009).

28 Kate Gardner, "The Grass is Greener . . . and Safer!" www.organiclawncare101.com/ (accessed February 2009).

29 Sierra magazine, Summer 2008, 17.

30 PeoplePoweredMachines.com, "Cleaner Air : Gas Mower Pollution Facts," (accessed January 2009).

31 Lisa Iwata, "Xeriscape: Winning the Turf War Over Water," *Home Energy Magazine*, July/August 1994. www.homeenergy.org/archive/hem.dis.anl.gov/eehem/94/940711.html

32 Lester R. Brown, *Plan B 3.0: Mobilizing to Save Civilization* (Earth Policy Institute, 2008), 78–80.

Chapter 6

1   National Cancer Institute, NCI Health Information Tip Sheet for Writers: Diet and Diseases, www.cancer. gov/newscenter/tip-sheet-diet-related-diseases (accessed June 2009).

2   Nanci Hellmich, "Healthy Food No More Costly Than Junk Food, Government Finds," *USA Today*, May 17, 2012.

3   U.S. Department of Agriculture Economic Research Services, *Food CPI, Prices and Expenditures: Per Capita Food Expenditures*, Table 13, http://www.ers.usda.gov/briefing/cpifoodandexpenditures/ (accessed April 2012).

4   Doug Gurian-Sherman, CAFOs Uncovered, The Untold Costs of Confined Animal Feeding Operations (Union of Concerned Scientists, 2008), p. 9.

5   Center for Food Safety, "rBGH/Hormones," www.centerforfoodsafety.org/campaign/rbgh-hormones (accessed April 2012).

6   Food and Water Watch, "rBGH: Anything But Green," www.foodandwaterwatch.org/food/factoryfarms/ foodsafety-factoryfarms (accessed April 2012).

7   The European Commission, Scientific Committee on Veterinary Measures relating to Public Health, *Report on Public Health Aspects of the Use of Bovine Somatotrophin*, March 1999.

8   Edwin D. Ongley, Control of Water Pollution from Agriculture (Food and Agriculture Organization of the United Nations, Rome, 1996), www.fao.org/docrep/W2598E/w2598e00.HTM (accessed November 2008).

9   Marian Burros, "Study Finds Far Less Pesticide Residue on Organic Produce," *New York Times*, 8 May 2002.

10 U.S. Environmental Protection Agency, Protecting Children from Pesticides, January 2002, www.epa.gov/ pesticides/factsheets/kidpesticide.htm (accessed November 2008).

11 Oxfam America, www.oxfamamerica.org/whatwedo/where_we_work/united_states/news_publications/ food_farm/art2565.html (accessed July 2008).

12 Brett Cherry, GM Crops Increase Herbicide Use in the United States, Institute of Science in Society, January 18, 2010.

13 Els Wynen and David Vanzett, *No Through Road: The Limitations of Food Miles,* Asian Development Bank Institute Working Paper No. 118, October, 2008, p. 2.

14 Michael Pollan, "Farmer in Chief," *New York Magazine*, October 9, 2008.

15 Food and Agricultural Organization of the United Nations, The State of the World Fisheries and Aquaculture, 2010, 35.

16 Environmental Working Group, 2011 Farm Subsidy Database, http://farm.ewg.org/ (accessed April 2010).

17 Eric A Ruark and Aniqa Moinuddin, "Illegal Immigration and Agribusiness: The Effect on the Agriculture Industry of Converting to a Legal Workforce," www.fairus.org/DocServer/agribusiness_rev.pdf (accessed April 2012)

18 Federation for American Immigration Reform, "The Costs to Local Taxpayers for Illegal or 'Guest' Workers," www.fairus.org/site/PageServer?pagename=research_localcosts (accessed February 2009).

19 National Alliance for Nutrition and Activity, "National Health Priorities: Reducing Obesity, Heart Disease, Cancer, Diabetes, and Other Diet- and Inactivity-Related Diseases, Costs, and Disabilities," p. 6.

20 Michael Pollan, "Farmer in Chief," New York Magazine, October 9, 2008.

21 Kiyah Duffy, PhD, Barry M. Popkin, "Energy Density, Portion Size, and Eating Occasions: Contributions to Increased Energy Intake in the United States, 1977–2006," PLoS Medicine, June 28, 2011.

22 Jennifer Steinhauer, "Snack Time Never Ends," *The New York Times*, January 19, 2010.

23 Steve Meyer and Len Steiner, "Daily Livestock Report," February 2, 2011.

24 Mark Bittman, "Rethinking the Meat-Guzzler," *The New York Times*, January 27, 2008.

25 Henning Steinfeld, Pierre Gerber, Tom Wassenaar, Vincent Castel, Mauricio Rosales and Cees de Haan, *Livestock's Long Shadow: Environmental Issues and Options*, Food and Agriculture Organization of United Nations, Rome, 2006, 112.

26 Felicty Carcas, "UN Urges global move to meat and dairy-free diet," *The Guardian*, June, 2 2010.

27 See endnote 2.

28 U.S. Department of Agriculture, Economic Research Service, Summary of Retail Prices, ers.usda.gov/Data/meatpricespreads (accessed April 2012).

29 Henning Steinfeld, Pierre Gerber, Tom Wassenaar, Vincent Castel, Mauricio Rosales and Cees de Haan, *Livestock's Long Shadow: Environmental Issues and Options*, Food and Agriculture Organization of United Nations, Rome, 2006, 112.

30 FOA Newsroom, "Livestock a Major Threat to the Environment," November 29, 2006.

31 U.S. Department of Agriculture Economic Research Services, *Food CPI, Prices and Expenditures: Per Capita Food Expenditures*, Table 13, http://www.ers.usda.gov/briefing/cpifoodandexpenditures/ (accessed April 2012).

32 Center for Food Safety, Corporate Lies: Busting the Myths of Industrial Agriculture, p. 4.

33 Worldwatch Institute, "Making Better Energy Choices," www.worldwatch.org/node/808 (accessed November 2008).

34 Dogwood Alliance, Inc., 2008 Fast Food Industry Packaging Report.

35 Dan Buettner, The Blue Zone: Lessons for Living Longer From the People Who've Lived the Longest (The National Geographic Society).

36 U.S. Department of Agriculture Economic Research Services, *Food CPI, Prices and Expenditures: Per Capita Food Expenditures*, Table 13, http://www.ers.usda.gov/briefing/cpifoodandexpenditures/ (accessed April 2012).

37 Sean Alfani, "How and Where America Eats," CBS News, February 11, 2009.

38 Mark Bittman, "Is Junk Food Really Cheaper?" *The New York Times*, September 24, 2011.

39 Susan Koeppen, "Wasting the Food That Feeds You," CBS News, www.cbsnews.com/stories/2008/07/23/earlyshow/contributors/susankoeppen/main4285083.shtml (accessed July 2008).

40 U.S. Environmental Protection Agency, *Municipal Solid Waste in the United States: 2010*, December 2011, Tables 4 and 7.

41 Ibid, Table 7.

42 Mark Bittman, "A Letter That All Chefs (And Anyone Who Eats) Need to Read," markbittman.com, October 25, 2011.

Chapter 7

1 U.S. EPA Toxics Release Inventory Reporting Year 2007 Public Data Release, "Summary Key Findings," 1.

2 U.S. Public Interest Research Group, *Analysis of 2002 Toxic Release Inventory Data*, June 24, 2004, 1.

3 Ibid.

4 Kevin Foster, Erik Meijer, Scott Schuh, and Michael A. Zabek, *The 2009 Survey of Consumer Payment Choice*, Federal Reserve Bank of Boston, Public Policy Discussion Papers, p. 13, 79.

5 U.S. Environmental Protection Agency, *Municipal Solid Waste in the United States:2010*, DataTables,Table 11.

6 ABC World News series, "Made in America."

7 Galina Hale and Bart Hobijn, The U.S. Content of "Made in China," Federal Reserve Bank of San Francisco Economic Letter, August 8, 2011, Table 1.

INDEX

AC. *See* air conditioning

aerator. *See* faucet aerator

AFUE. *See* Annual Fuel
Utilization Efficiency

Annual Fuel Utilization Efficiency, 56, 79

air conditioners. *See* air conditioning

air conditioning, 17, 43, 55, 56, 61, 84, 85, 92, 93–98

antibiotics, 181, 184–185, 186–187

attic(s), 45, 50, 89, 90–91

automobile. *See* vehicle

awning(s), 87–88
adjustable, 87
fixed, 87

barter, 11–12, 230

bartering. *See* barter

bath. *See* bathroom

bathroom, 150, 154, 163
faucet, 74
sink(s), 71, 153, 162

bathtub. *See* bathroom

batteries, 32, 102, 142–143

biking, 30, 124–127

biodynamic farming, 181–182

biotech. *See* biotechnology

biotechnology, 190, 192, 193

Bisphenol A, 223

borrow, 28, 230–231

borrowing. *See* borrow

BPA, 223

build, 8, 73, 238

building. *See* build

bulk foods, 212–213

buying club, 196

CAFOs. *See* Concentrated Animal Feeding Operations

cancer, 18, 185–186, 226

car. *See* vehicle

car sharing, 137–139

carbon dioxide, 2, 16, 30, 65, 82, 85, 104, 146

car-free, 136–137

carpooling, 128, 129–130

caulk, 42, 43

CFLs. *See* compact fluorescent lamps

cheap food, 198, 209

chemicals, 17–18, 19, 31, 51, 169, 180–182, 189, 221, 229

chimney, 44

climate change, 146–147, 202–203

clothes dryer, 56, 65, 67

clothesline, 65, 66, 92

CO2. *See* carbon dioxide

coffee, 23–24

Community Supported Agriculture, 195

commuters. *See* commuting

commuting, 127, 128–129, 132

compact fluorescent lamps, 39, 101–108

computer(s)
desktop, 115–116
laptop, 99, 115–116
power management, 114
refurbished, 113–114, 116
tablet, 116
take-back program, 116

Concentrated Animal Feeding Operations, 184–185

conventional farming, 180–182

cooking, 213, 214–215, 218

coupons, 59, 206–207

CRT. *See* television(s), cathode-ray tube

dairy, 183–188
cows, 185
products, 186

diabetes, 18, 198, 250

diapering. *See* diapers

diapers, 13

diet-related diseases, 178–179, 226, 250

dining out, 217, 218

dishwasher, 54, 55, 65, 74, 159–161

disposable products, 12, 35–36

DOE. *See* U.S. Department of Energy

doors, 43–44

downspouts, 175–176

dryer. *See* clothes dryer

ducts, 45, 46

edible landscape, 172

EER. *See* Energy Efficiency Ratio

EF. *See* Energy Factor

Energy Efficiency Ratio, 56, 82, 94

Energy Factor, 56, 67, 69, 70, 72, 160

electric resistance, 78, 81

electric vehicle(s), 143

electronics, 58, 108–118
electronic waste, 117

energy audit(s), 41–42, 57

Energy Star, 47, 55–56, 63, 67, 72, 79, 82, 93, 94, 97, 115, 157, 158, 160

Energy Star-qualified. *See* Energy Star

EnergyGuide, 63, 67, 157, 160

EPA. *See* U.S. Environmental Protection Agency

EV(s). *See* electric vehicle(s)

evaporation, 92, 95, 169

evaporative cooler, 95–96

evapotranspiration, 92

fans, 92, 93, 94

farmers' market(s), 194–195

fast food, 4, 28, 217, 218–219

faucet aerator, 161–162

faucet(s), 158–159, 167

FDA. *See* Food and Drug Administration

feedlot(s), 194, 198

fertilizer(s), 169, 170, 182

FHR. *See* first-hour rating

first-hour rating, 70

flow rates, 73, 74, 158, 164

flush volume, 151–152

food

  animal products, 183–188

  fruits and vegetables, 188–194

  growing some of your own, 207–210

  portion sizes, 200–202

  storage, 210–211

Food and Drug Administration, 189, 192, 193, 211

food preservation, 211

food waste, 202, 219–220

fossil fuels, 65, 66, 68–69, 79

front loaders. *See* front loading machines

front loading machines, 156

fuel economy, 140, 144, 145, 146, 248

furnishings. *See* furniture

furniture, 9–15, 237–238

gallons per flush, 151–152, 154

gallons per minute, 71, 73, 74, 162–163, 165

garden, 207–210, 231

gardening. *See* garden

genetic engineering, 192

genetically modified organisms, 190–194

GHG(s). *See* greenhouse gases

GMOs. *See* genetically modified organisms

GPF. *See* gallons per flush

GPM. *See* gallons per minute

grass, 170, 171, 173

gray water, 153, 174–175

greenhouse gases, 15–16, 78, 146, 203

greeting cards, 34

ground water, 181

hand washing, 159–160

heart disease, 17, 18, 198, 226, 250

heat gain, 42–43, 45, 50, 85–87, 90, 92

heat pump(s), 69–70, 81–82, 84, 96–98

heating oil, 15

Heating Seasonal Performance Factor, 56, 82, 97

heating systems, 77–84

  baseboard(s), 78

  boiler(s), 79–81

  furnace(s), 78, 79–81

  wall heaters, 78

heat-shrink film, 49

HEVs. *See* hybrid electric vehicles

home office, 131–132

hormone(s), 181, 185, 187–188

hormone-free, 188

hose(s), 169

hot water systems

  direct combustion, 66

  electric point-of-use heaters, 74–75

  heat pump water heaters, 69–70

  solar, 75–76

  tank/storage, 55, 68–69

  tankless/on demand, 73–75

  whole house tankless, 72–73

household cleaners, 19, 242

HPWH. *See* hot water systems, heat pump water heaters

HSPF. *See* Heating Seasonal Performance Factor

hybrid electric vehicles, 141–142

insulating. *See* insulation

insulation, 41–42, 45–47, 50, 89

interior shades, 49–50

investing, 3, 246

irrigation, 171, 175–176

kitchen

  disposables, 220–221

  products, 222, 224

  sink, 71, 74, 162

landscaping, 172

laundry, 62, 155

lawn mowers, 170

lawn(s), 168–171

LCD. *See* television(s), liquid crystal display

leak(s), 41–42, 47, 50, 166–167

LED(s). *See* light bulbs, light emitting diode

light bulbs

compact fluorescent
  lamps, 39, 101–108
halogen, 102, 103, 106
incandescent/standard,
  39, 101, 103, 104, 106
Kelvin, 104-105
light emitting diode, 102,
  106–107
lumens, 102, 105, 107
lighting, 99–108
lighting controls
  motion sensors, 100
  occupancy sensors,
    100–101
  photo sensors, 100
  timers, 100, 102
livestock, 183, 185, 202
local agriculture, 194, 195
locally produced. See local
  agriculture
Manual J Residential Load
  Calculation, 83
meals
  from scratch, 200
  premade/prepackaged,
    213–214
meat
  consumption, 203, 205
  eat(ing) less, 5, 202–204
MEF. See Modified Energy
  Factor
Modified Energy Factor, 56,
  157
mercury, 104, 105–106
methane, 184, 203, 220
miles per gallon, 146
mpg. See miles per gallon
native plants, 171, 172
natural gas, 15, 66, 78, 79, 80
obesity, 17, 18, 198, 226, 250
organic farming, 181
packaging waste, 212–213
paper

napkins, 221, 222, 224
production, 221
towels, 221, 222, 223–224
passive cooling, 85
peak demand, 27, 70, 71
pesticide(s), 182, 189, 190,
  192
PHEV. See plug-in hybrid
pilot light, 81
planting. See plants
plants, 86, 92, 171, 172, 175,
  190–192
plastic
  bag(s), 25, 221
  bottles, 5, 21
  containers, 224
  film/food wrap, 13, 221
  lumber, 209
plug-in hybrid, 142
pollutants, 19, 51, 105,
  146–147
population, 18, 23, 198, 201,
  202
portion size(s), 179, 201, 203
POU(s). See hot water systems, electric point-of-
  use heaters
power
  generators/generation, 16,
    27, 105
  management, 114
  plant(s), 66, 74, 80, 105,
    144
  strip, 114, 118–119
  vampires, 117–118
previously-owned goods,
  234, 239
produce, 20, 183, 188–191,
  195, 210
protein, 203–204
public transportation,
  128–130
radiant barrier(s), 89–90, 91

rain barrels, 169, 175–177
rainwater, 169, 174–175
rebate(s), 59–60, 70, 87, 171,
  174
reclaimed, 172, 177
recycled
  cellulose, 46
  cotton, 46
  newsprint, 46
  plastic, 177, 209, 224
  steel, 62
recycling, 26, 60–61, 106,
  115, 174, 175, 221
reflecting, 89–91
refrigerator, 55, 57, 61, 62–64
renewable energy, 53, 76,
  102, 142
rent, 7–8, 137, 145, 230–231
renting. See rent
reusable
  bags, 25
  containers, 13, 221–222
reuse
  marketplace/stores, 10,
    233, 235, 236, 243
  shopping, 10, 235,
    236–237
ride sharing, 129–130
roof(s), 41, 45, 47, 90, 175
room air conditioners, 56, 61,
  94, 98
route(s), 126, 130, 134
runoff, 169, 186
R-value, 46–50
seafood, 197
sealed combustion, 80
Seasonal Energy Efficiency
  Ratio, 56, 82, 93, 97
SEF. See Solar Energy Factor
SEER. See Seasonal Energy
  Efficiency Ratio
SF. See Solar Factor

SHW. *See* hot water sys-
tems: solar
Solar Energy Factor, 56
serving ware, 28
Solar Factor, 56
shade. *See* shading
shading, 85–86, 93, 94
share, 37, 57, 109, 117,
129–130, 137–139, 232
sharing. *See* share
Shoppers Guide to Pesti-
cides in Produce, 190
shopping
as a locavore, 195–196
list, 206, 229
trips, 133
shower(s), 163–165
showerhead(s), 74, 163–165
sizing a heating system, 83
snacks, 200–202
solar
gain (*see* heat gain)
lights, 102–103
photovoltaic, 53, 102
shades/screens, 86, 87
water heaters/water heat-
ing, 56, 75–76
sprinkler(s), 5, 169, 173
standby power, 117–119
sustainable farming, 181
SUV(s), 139, 145
swamp cooler. *See* evaporative cooler
tax, 26, 33–34, 53, 59, 76,
132, 198
taxes. *See* tax
telecommute, 130–132

telecommuting. *See* tel-
ecommute
television(s)
cathode-ray tube, 37,
109–112, 119–120
liquid crystal display,
110–112, 114
plasma, 110–111, 114
viewing distance, 111
thermostat, 24–25, 62, 94
toilet(s), 151–155, 167
top loaders. *See* top loading
machines
top loading machines, 156
transformers, 109, 117–118
trees, 34, 36, 85–86, 88, 92,
224
trips, 18, 30, 124, 127,
128–129, 132–135
TV(s). *See* television(s)
U.S. Department of Agriculture, 20, 179–181, 189,
191, 200
U.S. Department of Energy,
38, 41, 73, 74, 117
USDA. *See* U.S. Department
of Agriculture
USDA-certified organic, 179,
180
U.S. Environmental Protection Agency, 19, 89,
147, 166, 168, 169
vegetarian, 203, 205, 218
vehicle
electric, 143
emissions, 128, 147
fuel economy/fuel ef-
ficiency, 140, 144, 145,
146, 248

gas-powered, 140, 169,
170
maintenance, 131
single occupancy, 128, 129
ventilating. *See* ventilation
ventilation, 51, 92–93
walking, 19, 30, 124, 126
washer. *See* washing ma-
chine
washing machine, 59, 61, 65
74. 155–157
water
bottled, 22–23
bottles, 23
conservation, 149–150,
249
gray, 153, 174–175
ground, 181
pollution, 183, 202
tap/drinking, 5, 22–23,
174
Water Factor, 157
weather stripping, 43–44
weatherizing, 41–42, 50
WF. *See* Water Factor
Wind, 53, 65–67, 87
window film(s), 90
windows
exterior storm, 48–49
exterior window treat-
ments, 87–88
interior storm, 49
replacement, 48